Princes of the Trenches

ANN P. LINDER

PRINCES
OF THE TRENCHES

NARRATING
THE GERMAN EXPERIENCE
OF THE
FIRST WORLD WAR

CAMDEN HOUSE

Copyright © 1996 by
CAMDEN HOUSE, INC.

Published by Camden House, Inc.
Drawer 2025
Columbia, SC 29202 USA

Printed on acid-free paper.
Binding materials are chosen for strength and
durability.

ISBN:1–57113–075–6

Library of Congress Cataloging-in-Publication Data

Linder, Ann P., 1947–
    Princes of the trenches: narrating the German experience of the
First World War / Ann P. Linder. -- 1st ed.
        p.   cm.
    Includes bibliographical references and index.
    ISBN 1–57113–075–6
    1. German fiction — 20th century — History and criticism. 2. World
War, 1914–1918 — Literature and the war. 3. War in literature.
I. Title.
PT772.L53   1996
833'.91209358 — dc20   96–14349
                                                                CIP

For my parents,
who educated me,
and my husband,
who puts up with the results

Contents

Introduction   1

1: The Spirit of August   5

2: The Children's Crusade   19

3: The Experience of War   45

4: Narrating the War Experience   115

5: Imagining War   128

6: Weimar and the War Narrative   151

Conclusion   181

Works Consulted   185

Index   199

List of Illustrations

*"The offering of our enemies for the salvation of European culture."
A German response to Allied accusations of barbarism. Postcard,
1914. Published in Weigel et al.,* Jeder Schuß ein Russ.   17

*"Weekly menu, 1914."The dishes are enemy soldiers served up in
national gastronomic styles. From Weigel et al.,* Jeder Schuß ein
Russ.   18

The French view of German Kultur. *Drawing by Georges Scott,*
L'Illustration, *29 August 1914 (165).*   44

*Poster for German war bonds. Fritz Ehrler, 1917. Courtesy of
Hoover Institute.*   114

Ekl Eber, Der Meldegänger *(The Message Runner, 1942).
Courtesy of Hoover Institute.*   179

A German cemetery in territory retaken by the French.
L'Illustration, *9 October 1918 (262-263). Bibliothègue
National Française.*   180

Acknowledgments

At the end of a long research project that involved several relocations, a number of people and institutions deserve thanks for the help they extended to a (mostly) independent scholar with little or no institutional support. In the early stages of the research the librarian and staff of the Faculty of Modern and Medieval Languages at Cambridge generously granted me borrowing privileges and access to their fine collection of German texts. A little later, the Cambridge University Library allowed me to use their splendid collections and facilities. I am also grateful to the library staffs of the University of North Dakota, of LSU-Shreveport, and of UCLA for their support.

To friends and colleagues who have listened to my monomaniacal monologues over the years, and who have criticized, read manuscripts and made suggestions, special thanks are due, especially to Linda Lane, Laura Morrow and Janet Lungstrom. I am also grateful to my colleagues at a 1994 NEH Seminar at the University of Iowa, and to its directors, Dudley Andrew and Steven Ungar, for their insights and encouragement. I am deeply indebted to my husband, who fostered the project from the beginning, and without whose emotional and financial support it would never have been completed. I am likewise grateful to my parents, whose encouragement was unfaltering, although my father, unfortunately, did not live to see the work completed.

Early drafts of certain portions of this book have been presented at conferences of the MLA, SAMLA, SCMLA and the Linguistic Circle of North Dakota and Manitoba. Parts of chapter 5 have previously appeared in a different form in *Comparative Literature Studies* 31:4 (1995). Some of the ideas in chapter 4 originated in my book review of Cobley's *Representing War* in *Sub Stance* (November 1995).

A. L.
October, 1996

Introduction

*". . . a not very high class of literature that
cannot be ignored by the historian."*
J. Knight Bostock, 1931

Another world war and changing fashions in criticism have intervened since
Bostock wrote those lines, but his judgment, both dismissive and astute, remains singularly valid, signaling both the importance of the First World War
narratives as historical documents, and their relegation to subcanonical literary
status. The remark is even more pertinent to the German war narratives than to
those of Britain and France, due primarily to the obscuring and distorting effect
of National Socialism on the history of the early twentieth century. As is the
case with most aspects of cultural and political life in the Weimar Republic, the
war narratives tend to be viewed in terms of their relationship to the Third
Reich, that is, either as leftist antiwar novels, or alternatively as proto-fascist
propaganda. The difficulty is exacerbated by the realization that most of the
German narratives differ radically in point of view from the received Anglo-
American version of the Great War.

Unlike the memoirs of generals and staff officers, which most readers easily
perceive as transparently self-interested, the combat narratives of young soldiers
and combat officers tend, dangerously, to be regarded as truth, primarily because
they provide a direct, usually first-person account of the experiences of representative front line combat soldiers. Often dedicated to comrades living and
dead, such accounts carry with them an air of unimpeachable authenticity. In
short, the author presents both the experience and the meaning of that experience as representative truth. The question of authenticity lies at the core of the
bitter debates that raged in the late twenties and early thirties over the literary
depiction of the war, because nothing less than the meaning of the war, not only
on a personal, but more importantly on a national scale, was at stake. Contradictory authentic experiences were unthinkable; there could be only one national
type of authentic experience — only one version of the war and its significance
inflated to the level of national myth.

Such myths of the war are, of course, fictions — recreations of experience
shaped by national cultural paradigms and the overwhelming need to validate
personal experience while creating a meaningful representative national myth of
the war.

The British "myth of the war" — the phrase is Samuel Hynes's — focuses
on meaningless suffering, loss and death, not only of men but of institutions and
even of the cultural and historical past. The British myth, built on Graves,

Blunden, Owen, Sassoon and Ford (to mention only the most important writ-ers) depicts a "damaged nation of damaged men, damaged institutions, and damaged hopes and faiths . . . . "[1] This is the world of the "lost generation," cut off from the past by the actual and psychological devastation of the war, searching fruitlessly for the hopeful future that was snatched from them in the trenches.

So pervasive is the myth that readers are tempted to see it in the other Western literatures as well. *All Quiet on the Western Front* clearly partakes of the same mythology, as does Barbusse's *Le Feu* and even Céline's *Voyage au bout de la nuit*. In her recent study of narrative structure in First World War narratives, Evelyn Cobley bases her conclusions on the presumed universality of the British myth of the war experience.[2]

The British myth embodies what Eric Leed calls the "liberal experience" of the war, which he juxtaposes to a different experience that he calls conservative.[3] In contrast to the liberal experience, the conservative experience focuses on the warmth of comradeship and community, and significantly, on survival and even regeneration.[4] This study will attempt to show that although the liberal experi-ence is present as a minority voice in Germany, it is the conservative experience of the war that dominates the German war narrative, and forms the German myth of the war — a myth of spiritual survival through comradeship, and of in-dividual and national renewal through a community of comrades. While the British war experience focuses on the damaged individual, the German conser-vative experience centers on a group of comrades strengthened by the test of combat, Ernst Jünger's "princes of the trenches, with their hard set faces, brave to madness . . . whom no dispatch ever mentions."[5] Jünger's glorification of the storm-troops he commanded is consistent with the conservative ethos of the hardened, disciplined soldier, devoted only to his comrades and his nation.

These significant differences in the German war myth have produced the re-markable misunderstanding and even more remarkable avoidance of the German narratives among Anglo-American critics. Imbued with the British vision of the

[1]Samuel Hynes, *A War Imagined: The First World War and English Culture* (New York: Athe-naeum, 1991), 353.

[2]Evelyn Cobley, *Representing War: Form and Ideology in First World War Narratives* (Toronto: U of Toronto P, 1993).

[3]Eric J. Leed, *No Man's Land: Combat and Identity in World War I* (Cambridge: Cambridge UP, 1979).

[4]The word "conservative" is often used interchangeably with "nationalist," especially when dis-cussing rightist politics and culture within the context of late nineteenth- and early-twentieth century Germany. In my view, nationalism per se is but one element in conservative ideology.

[5]Ernst Jünger, *In Stahlgewittern: Aus dem Tagebuch eines Stoßtruppführers* (Berlin: Mittler, 1922), 182. Tr. by Basil Creighton as *The Storm of Steel* (New York: Fertig, 1929), 235. Jünger made significant revisions to most of his wartime texts. For the final versions, see *Werke* (Stuttgart: Klett, 1960–1965). 10 vols.

war, and obsessed with the rise of National Socialism, Anglo-American critics tend to see the nationalistic and communal ideology of the conservative war narratives only as proto-fascist. Such a limited view dangerously falsifies both the *Weltanschauung* of the war narratives and the historical context of the so-called conservative revolution. Like the Weimar Republic itself, modern historical and cultural criticism of that period is complex and fragmented. Political and social histories of Weimar concentrate on the origins and rise of conservative ideology and of the conservative parties and paramilitary organizations, set alongside the disastrous economic events of the interwar years. Cultural histories, on the other hand, tend to focus on the artistic avant-garde. What is largely missing is an examination of conservative cultural attitudes and practices, their historical continuity, and the ways in which those views shaped political and social thought. Weimar's "culture wars" lie at the core of the period's complexity, and are fundamental to any understanding of its political, as well as cultural, development.

The widespread neglect of the German war narratives (and the poetry, for that matter) in the English-speaking world can likewise be attributed to differences in the war myth. The last comprehensive examination of these works in English is Pfeiler's *War and the German Mind* (1941), in which the author frankly admits that he is attempting to explain, in the wake of the Second World War, why the Germans are the way they are. Most English criticism concentrates on the only well-known German text, Remarque's *All Quiet on the Western Front*. Although there is valuable critical material in German, much of it is difficult to obtain, and naturally inaccessible to non-speakers of German. Thus my emphasis on the conservative narratives is partly dictated by their dominant position both in terms of quantity (they far outnumber the liberal narratives), and of intellectual history, and partly to redress the neglect of English-speaking critics.

The primary goal of this study is to reexamine and reassess a wide range of German First World War narratives (from a corpus of hundreds of texts) within the historical and cultural contexts of Imperial Germany and the Weimar Republic. Part of the uniqueness of the German war narratives stems from their having been written by men raised in Wilhelmine Germany, but reflecting their war experiences through the dark lens of the Weimar Republic. As the question of authenticity lies at the center of these discussions, I have chosen to deal exclusively with combat narratives written by former combatants, encompassing novels, memoirs, diaries and composite narrative forms. These I have supplemented with art, film, periodicals and ephemera (particularly posters and postcards) whenever they illuminate the subject at hand. I have likewise generally limited myself to the geographical heart of the war, the western front, because it was regarded by all sides as the key to victory, and because it became the nexus of Great War myth-making. It is nevertheless important to recall that Germany fought on several fronts, and that a sense of encirclement and divided effort colored the German reaction to the war. Finally, to ensure maximum accessibility, all quotations are in English, using published translations whenever they exist. For specialists, the original German is available in the notes.

With those points in mind, the first two chapters examine the historical and philosophical background of German cultural nationalism, the structure of Wilhelmine society, and most importantly, the upbringing and education of what is usually called the "war generation." Chapter 3 examines in considerable detail the major themes that comprise the war experience, as seen through the narratives. Chapters 4 and 5 are devoted respectively to narrative structure (including a discussion of the Bildungsroman) and to the imagery and symbolism characteristic of the German narratives. The final chapter delineates the creation and reception of the war narratives in the context of the political fragmentation and culture wars of the Weimar Republic, with special emphasis on the role of the war narratives in the conservative movement of 1929–1933.

Although the reader may find some of these narratives aesthetically weak and many others philosophically repugnant, no genuine understanding of the two world wars or of Germany in the interwar period is possible without them. The creation and exploitation of the German war myth is one of the keys to German history in the twentieth century.

A note on editions and translations: Many works cited in this study exist only in the original edition and are therefore out of print and available only through libraries. In most cases, I have used the earliest edition available to me. When no early edition was obtainable, I have used a later reprint or the author's collected works.

In order to make this study accessible to non-specialists, I have used the following system for titles and quotations. Titles of works that have not been translated are given in German throughout, with a translation of the title at the first reference. Titles of works that have been translated are given in German first, then in English. Thereafter, I have generally used the English title. Quotations in the text are in English. The quotations in the original languages (in most cases, German) are in the notes, with page references to the original edition cited. I have quoted from published English translations of the narratives when those exist, and the page numbers refer to the specified translation. Many of the German narratives were translated shortly after their appearance in German, usually by British translators, who rendered German trench slang into British trench slang, occasionally with unintentionally amusing results. In those cases, I have retained the British terminology and spelling. Where no published translation exists, the translation is mine. In those cases, the page numbers refer to the cited German edition.

1: The Spirit of August

In the first hot days of August, 1914, most of Europe went to war. Bands played, young men rushed to volunteer, and troop trains rolled, while white-clad girls decked soldiers, guns and trains with flowers. Europe, after forty years of peace, embraced war with a rush of patriotic enthusiasm unparalleled in its history. This "spirit of August" (*der Geist des Augusts*) was all the more astonishing for its suddenness. The mounting international tensions that followed the assassination of the Archduke Franz Ferdinand on 28 June had been punctuated by large anti-war demonstrations in France and Germany, and by pacifist sentiments in the British press.[1] But in the first days of August, doubts and hesitations vanished in a wave of national exaltation that silenced pacifists and convinced reluctant German Social Democrats to vote war credits in the Reichstag.[2]

Besides its suddenness, universality was the most striking feature of the August war enthusiasm. European writers were intoxicated by the demise of a "world grown old and cold and weary," in Rupert Brooke's famous formulation. The war was almost universally welcomed as a spiritual awakening, the salvation of man from narrow social and economic interests, and the unification of the nation in spiritual solidarity, whether one called it *union sacrée* or *Gemeinschaft*. Stromberg has examined in detail the "ideas of August" common to the major belligerent nations, and has remarked on the similarities of content and mood. While acknowledging that universality, it is nevertheless important to note that the philosophical certainties differed from nation to nation, as did the relative importance of the ideas and the language in which they were couched. In short, each nation harbored its own form of nationalism.[3] If only as prelude, the spirit of August is as much a part of the myth of the war as is the experience of the trenches. In the case of Germany, two concepts dominated the August rhetoric: the rediscovery of national community (*Volksgemeinschaft*) and the foundation of that community in unequaled German spirituality and idealism, that is, in German *Kultur*. As Jost Hermand has pointed out, Germans believed that a war

[1]Roland N. Stromberg, *Redemption by War: The Intellectuals and 1914* (Lawrence: Regents Press of Kansas, 1982), 40. See also Modris Eksteins, *Rites of Spring: The Great War and the Birth of the Modern Age* (New York: Anchor/Doubleday, 1989), 62–63, and Jean-Jacques Becker, *1914: Comment les Français sont entrés dans la guerre* (Paris: Presses de la Fondation nationale des sciences politiques, 1977).

[2]Stromberg, 46–50, Eksteins, 63.

[3]On attitudes in Britain, see Paul Fussell, *The Great War and Modern Memory* (New York: Oxford UP, 1975), 18–35, and Hynes, 3–95. I have borrowed Hynes's phrase "the myth of the war," by which he means the imaginative construct, based primarily on the literature of the war, that we designate as the experience of the First World War. For attitudes toward the coming of war in France, see Becker, *1914*.

that had begun so idealistically, so purely, could only end in the victory of such values as "community, self-sacrifice, cultural consciousness, aspiration toward higher things and the like."[4]

The focus on abstract national values is singularly characteristic of the rhetoric of August, and is invoked by virtually all the pro-war apologists. They had precious little use for sober discussion of economic or political war aims, and instead reminded their readers of the national need for "a place in the sun" (one of Kaiser Wilhelm's favorite phrases), for the preservation of the English way of life, or for the avenging of an invaded *patrie*. The language is invariably vague and elevated, but no where more so than in Germany. With an unshakable belief in the superiority and uniqueness of German spirituality and the culture it had created, the German witnesses of August 1914 speak, almost to a man, the language of the spirit.[5] Ernst Troeltsch, recalling the outbreak of war at a distance of ten years, evokes the "flood of spirituality that ran through the nation."[6] The metaphysical world again shone forth, and young men were inspired by Kant, Fichte, Hegel and Schleiermacher. For Troeltsch, the most powerful experience of 1914 for the German people was a return to a belief in "die Idee und den Geist" (the idea and the spirit). Both the philosophical diction and the choice of philosophers are telling indicators of the rejection of pragmatic concerns. Only Germany could have produced Otto Baumgarten's 1927 contribution to the Carnegie Institute's social history of the war, entitled *Spiritual and Moral Effects of the War in Germany*.[7] Baumgarten's goal is to condemn the German obsession with spirituality as a cause of the war; he does so in the pre-war diction of Troeltsch and Thomas Mann.

The "spiritualization" of the war weaves through most of the texts about August 1914, including the literary ones. Few of the combat writers who are the major focus of this analysis have provided an account of those events.[8] Other than Serenus Zeitblom's gently bewildered recollection in chapter 30 of Mann's *Doktor Faustus*, in which many of Zeitblom's conservative feelings and arguments echo those Mann expressed in his 1914 essay "Gedanken im Kriege"

---

[4]Jost Hermand, *Der alte Traum vom neuen Reich* (Frankfurt am Main: Athenäum, 1988), 94. " . . . Gemeinschaftlichkeit, Opferbereitschaft, Kulturbewußtsein, Streben nach Höherem usw . . . . "

[5]The development of the German notions of spiritual and cultural superiority, an aspect of the historical *Sonderweg*, will be discussed in chapter 2.

[6]Ernst Troeltsch, *Deutscher Geist und Westeuropa* (1925; reprint, Aalen: Scientia, 1966), 37–39. " . . . eine Welle des Übersinnlichen ging durch die Nation . . . . "

[7]Otto Baumgarten, *Geistige und sittliche Wirkungen des Krieges in Deutschland*, Wirtschafts-und Sozialgeschichte des Weltkrieges, Deutsche Serie (Stuttgart: Deutsche Verlags-Anstalt, 1927).

[8]Most of the combat narratives begin with training or the trip to the front. A number were also written by men who were too young to enlist in 1914, and therefore entered the war later. See, however, Franz Schauwecker, *Aufbruch der Nation* (Berlin: Frundsberg, 1930), 7–34. Tr. by R.T. Clark as *The Furnace* (London: Methuen, 1930), 1–29.

("Thoughts in War"), the most interesting literary locus, both for content and narrative style, is Ernst Gläser's novel *Jahrgang 1902 (Class of 1902).*[9] The narrator-protagonist belongs to the class of 1902 (that is, those born in 1902), and is therefore twelve at the outbreak of war. He provides the reader with a child's-eye-view of adult behavior, bringing the double vision of innocent child and cynical adult to bear on life in a small German city from 1914 to 1918. The pertinent passages are a virtual catalogue of the received patriotic ideas of 1914, and a remarkable account of the actions and reactions of the cultivated bourgeoisie, arranged and commented on by the "innocent" child.

In July of 1914, the protagonist and his mother are vacationing at a Swiss hotel that boasts an international clientele. His best friend and daily companion is a French boy named Gaston. Toward the end of July he begins to notice changes in the behavior of the guests. During the evening dances on the terrace, what had earlier been a "multicolored international mixture" turns into a sorting of the guests according to the colors of their national flags.[10] The English separate themselves from the Germans, with whom they had previously enjoyed watching the Alpine sunsets. The Austrian gentlemen, who had earlier danced with the lively French ladies, now dance with the German ones, who, unfortunately, are much stiffer. There is much receiving and sending of telegrams, followed by an express letter from the narrator's father urging them to return home immediately. But it all makes no impression on his mother. "My mother laid the letter aside among her others and said that she wished they would leave her in peace with their fatuous politics; a new book by Hofmannsthal had just appeared, and she was more interested in that."[11]

The narrator's mother represents the stereotypical apolitical bourgeoise, uninterested in politics even when events might endanger her, but enthusiastic about writers. When the boy announces to her that Austria has declared war on Serbia, she, skillfully dissecting a roast chicken, replies "But what is Serbia to me . . . ?"[12] By this time the Austrians have already left, the French are singing the Marseillaise in the dining room, and Gaston has been forbidden to speak to the narrator.

When the narrator and his mother finally return to Germany, war has been declared and the trains are jammed with people hurrying home. While still in

[9]Ernst Gläser, *Jahrgang 1902* (Berlin: Kiepenheuer, 1929). Tr. by Willa and Edwin Muir as *Class of 1902* (London: Secker, 1929).

[10]Gläser, 162–163. "Hatten vorher in buntem Gemisch Angehörige verschiedener Nationen zusammengesessen, Ausflüge gemacht, abends auf der Terrasse getanzt, so begann um diese Zeit eine Sortierung unter den Gästen, je nach der Farbe, die die Fahne ihres Landes trug" (178–179).

[11]Gläser, 164. "Meine Mutter legte den Brief zu den anderen und sagte, man solle sie endlich mit der blöden Politik in Ruhe lassen, es sei ein neues Buch von Hofmannsthal erschienen, das interessiere sie mehr" (180).

[12]Gläser, 165. "Aber was geht mich Serbien an . . . ?" (181).

Switzerland they share a compartment with an elderly German professor who lectures them on the war. Although the passage is a long one, it is worth quoting in its entirety.

On the back of his hotel bill he had added up the numerical strength of the European armies, and balanced them against each other. He compared the two totals and assured my mother that the spiritual qualities of the German troops compensated for the numerical superiority of the Russians. For in this war spiritual qualities alone would decide the day, and Germany's spiritual qualities were the best in Europe. As a university professor he knew that our youth were ready for the fray, full of ideals. At last the hour had come when our people could enter on its great world mission. He himself had been almost into despair by the crass materialism of the last few years — particularly in the lower classes — but at last life had regained an ideal significance. The great virtues of humanity, which had found their last refuge in Germany — fidelity, patriotism, readiness to die for an idea — these were triumphing now over the trading and shop-keeping spirit. The war was the providential lightning flash that would clear the air; after it a new German people would arise, whose victory would save the world from mediocrity, brutalizing materialism, western democracy and false humanitarianism. He could see a new world, ruled and directed by a race of aristocrats, who would root out all signs of degeneracy and lead humanity back again to the deserted peaks of the eternal ideals. Those who were too weak must perish by the wayside. The war would cleanse mankind from all its impurities. The future belonged to Siegfried; in this war Hagen would be slain.[13]

This amazing diatribe is a virtual inventory of the standard patriotic ideas of the day, with extra lashings of Sombart, Nietzsche and *völkisch* ideology, all ren-

---

[13]Gläser, 171–172. "In unserem Abteil saß ein älterer Herr. Er begann sofort mit uns zu reden, als seien wir gute Bekannte von ihm. Auf der Rückseite seiner Hotelrechnung hatte er die Kriegsstärke der europäischen Armeen addiert und gegeneinander abgewogen. Er verglich die beiden Salden und sagte zu meiner Mutter, der Geist der deutschen Truppen mache die ziffernmäßige Überlegenheit der Russen wett. Denn in diesem Kriege entscheide allein der Geist und Deutschlands Geist sei der beste Europas. Er wisse das als Universitätsprofessor, unsere Jugend sei schwertbereit und voller Ideale. Endlich sei die Stunde gekommen, wo unser Volk seine große Weltsendung antreten könne. Er selbst sei schon fast verzweifelt gewesen über den krassen Materialismus der letzten Jahre — besonders in den unteren Volksschichten — endlich habe das Leben wieder einen idealen Sinn. Die großen Tugenden der Menschheit, die in Deutschland ihren letzten Hort hätten, — Treue, Vaterlandsliebe, Todesbereitschaft für eine Idee, triumphierten jetzt über den Händler- und Krämergeist. Der Krieg sei der rettende Blitz, der die Atmosphäre reinige, aus ihr entstiege ein neues deutsches Volk, dessen Sieg die Menschheit vor Verflachung, Vertierung im Materiellen, westlicher Demokratie und falscher Gefühlsduselei rette. Er sähe eine neue Welt, den Adelsmenschen herrschen und gebieten, der alle Degeneration ausrotte und die Menschheit wieder in die Firnhöhe ewiger Ideale zurückführe. Wer zu schwach sei, bleibe auf der Strecke. Der Krieg säubere die Menschheit von schlechten Stoffen. Siegfried gehöre die Zukunft, in diesem Krieg würde Hagen erschlagen." (188–189).

dered in the ironic elegance of the German subjunctive of indirect discourse.[14] A close examination yields, first, the old chestnut about the spiritual superiority of the Germans overcoming the mere numerical superiority of the Entente, embodied by the Russians. Although Gläser, writing a decade after the war, is fully aware of the irony of the professor's sums, the strength of the German spirit was an article of faith from the General Staff down, though the General Staff no doubt had a slightly more realistic view of the military situation, as the younger Moltke's continued tampering with von Schlieffen's plan attests. Moltke nonetheless maintained that "Germany alone can help mankind to develop in the right direction. For this reason Germany will not be vanquished in this war, it is the only nation which can at present take over the leadership of mankind towards higher goals."[15] Troeltsch also decries mathematical calculation: "Our opponents counted square kilometers, size of populations, and the financial power of the Entente and counted on victory with the oft-repeated triumphant words: 'it's mathematical!' We said: 'God cannot want, nor do we want our extirpation from the future power of the world of nations,' and that was our mathematics."[16] The sort of reckoning that both Troeltsch and Gläser's fictional professor derogate smacked of the material, counting-house approach to life that was anathema to the cultivated German. Embodied in Werner Sombart's antithesis of *Händler* (shopkeepers) and *Helden* (heroes), the opposition of the commercial, represented by England, and the spiritual, represented by Germany, is deeply embedded in late nineteenth-century German thought.[17]

On a deeper level, it also reflects the German belief in its civilizing mission to the world, most often embodied in Geibel's lines "And the world may again be healed through the German spirit."[18] Like Moltke's belief in German leadership of mankind, Geibel's conviction rests on the abstraction of spiritual superiority. Such superiority emerges most clearly in necessity, as Thomas Mann

[14]Völkisch ideology proclaimed the superiority of a *Volk* (people) unified by their "essence" and living in their natural landscape, to which the individual soul is connected.

[15]Qtd. in Fritz Fischer, *War of Illusions: German Politics from 1911–1914*, tr. Marian Jackson (New York: Norton, 1975), 549.

[16]Troeltsch, 37. "Unsere Gegner zählten Quadratkilometer, Bevölkerungsmaße und Finanzkraft der Ententevölker und vertrauten auf den Sieg mit den stets wiederholten triumphierenden Worten: c'est mathématique! Wir sagten: 'Unsere Austilgung aus der zukunftsstarken Völkerwelt kann Gott nicht wollen und wollen wir selber nicht,' und das war unsere Mathematik."

[17]Werner Sombart, *Händler und Helden* (München: Duncker, 1915).

[18]Geibel, "Deutschlands Beruf," in *Geibels Werke*, ed. Wolfgang Stammler (Leipzig: Bibliographisches Institut, 1918), 2:219–220. The poem dates from 1861. "Und es mag am deutschen Wesen/ Einmal noch die Welt genesen." See also Klaus Schröter, *Literatur und Zeitgeschichte: Fünf Aufsätze zur Deutschen Literatur im 20. Jahrhundert* (Mainz: Hase u. Koehler, 1970), 12. A shorter English version appeared as "Chauvinism and its Tradition: German Writers and the Outbreak of the First World War," *Germanic Review* 43.2 (March 1968), 120–135.

wrote in "Gedanken im Kriege," "we are in need, in deep need, and we welcome it, because that it is that has raised us so high."[19] As in 1813, so again in 1914.

The spiritual struggle of what Mann calls this "morally oriented people" (21) rests, according to Gläser's professor, in its devotion to idealism rather than materialism, and it is precisely that idealism that makes German youth ready to "bear the sword." Hatred of materialism was an essential tenet of German nationalism, especially of the *völkisch* side of the house, including the Wandervogel. Even Mann described the pre-war era as "wolfish mercantile" (13), and insisted that what people felt in August was "purification, liberation . . . and an enormous hope."[20] The hope was that the war would wash away the dross of materialism, including all manifestations of an urban, industrialized society, leaving a purified, rural, spiritual Germany. Keller remarks on the reappearance of the German god of war — Wotan — as the great purifier.[21] Mann declares that war was "the unprecedented, powerful and rapturous unification of the nation in its readiness for the most extreme test,"[22] and the fictional professor maintains that the war is lightning that will clear the atmosphere. One could multiply examples ad infinitum, so common was the theme.

Gläser's professor uses diction that was, in 1914, already cliché, as the author's skillful parody suggests, but which survived substantially unaltered until 1945. The metaphor of lightning is a characteristically trite descendant of the Romantic-organic paradigm of life and history, with, of course, a glancing reference to Germanic mythology. The talk of "degeneration" and the "cleansing of humanity" originates with the social-Darwinist current of nationalist thought, which focused on the preservation of German racial purity through eugenic schemes, and the conquest of sufficient *Lebensraum* for the expanding Germanic race.[23] The invocation of the great Germanic folk hero Siegfried who, it is worth remembering, was betrayed and murdered, rounds out the professor's

[19]Thomas Mann, "Gedanken im Kriege," in *Friederich und die große Koalition* (Berlin: Fischer, 1916), 17. "Wir sind in Not, in tiefer Not. Und wir grüßen sie, denn sie ist es, die uns so hoch erhebt."

[20]Mann, "Gedanken," 14. "Krieg! Es war Reinigung, Befreiung, was wir empfanden, und eine ungeheuere Hoffnung."

[21]Ernst Keller, *Nationalismus und Literatur: Langemarck, Weimar, Stalingrad* (Bern: Francke, 1970), 35-37.

[22]Mann, "Gedanken," 15. "Es war der nie erhörte, der gewaltige und schwärmerische Zusammenschluß der Nation in der bereitschaft zu *tiefster Prüfung-* . . . ." (emphasis in original).

[23]Hermand, *Der alte Traum*, 47–99. See also George L. Mosse, *The Crisis of German Ideology* (New York: Grosset, 1964), 88–145; Fritz Stern, *The Politics of Cultural Despair* (Berkeley: U of California P, 1961, and the chapter on Houston Stewert Chamberlain in Roderick Stackelberg, *Idealism Debased* (Kent: Kent State U P, 1981).

monologue in fine style. The narrator, noting the professor's gray face and weak frame, can't understand his preoccupation with Siegfried.[24]

The narrator's mother, on the other hand, is enraptured. She suddenly begins to take an interest in the war. The author speculates that it is because the man is a university professor, and because his interpretation has nothing to do with politics. When he predicts that the war will give a strong impetus to art, the narrator's mother is completely won over. "She believed in the war as she would have believed in a new poet."[25]

The cultural patriotism to which the narrator's mother succumbs finds its most interesting expression in the occasional verse of the first months of the war. Rose estimates that one and a half million occasional poems were written in 1914.[26] Elizabeth Marsland has remarked on the homogeneity of First World War patriotic poetry, particularly in the abstract idealization of the nation, the superiority of each national culture and the presence of God as an ally.[27] The transfer of the war from the political to the cultural stage is nevertheless particularly notable in Germany. In Lissauer's 1914 "Führer" (Leaders), for example, the rhetoric of war conscripts the cultural "greats" of the past into the spiritual battle against Germany's enemies. Lissauer also wrote the most famous—or infamous—German poem of the war, the "Haßgesang" (Song of Hate), whose refrain contains the phrase "Gott strafe England" (God punish England), and which is one of the most virulent expressions of German animosity against England.[28] "Führer" opens with an image of great clouds of celestial warriors encamped on the borders of Germany. These "spiritual" troops are the greatest names in German culture:

> Luther, the trooper of God, armed with his great Bible,
> Bach leading hymns of praise at the organ,
> Kant, armed with duty, armed with sternness,
> Schiller, swinging his powerful orations like a
>   crushing sword, . . . [29]

[24]Gläser, 173; German edition, 189–190.

[25]Gläser, 173. "Sie glaubte an den Krieg wie an einen neuen Dichter" (189).

[26]William Rose and J. Isaacs, eds., *Contemporary Movements in European Literature* (London: Routledge, 1928), 56–58.

[27]Elizabeth Marsland, *The Nation's Cause: French, English and German Poetry of the First World War* (London: Routledge, 1991), 59, 71.

[28]Marsland, 62–64.

[29]Helmut Lamprecht, ed., *Deutschland, Deutschland: Politische Gedichte* (Bremen: Schünemann, 1969), 288.

The roll call of "warriors" continues in the next stanza with Beethoven, Goethe, and Bismarck, "of the eternal union the eternal chancellor." It then concludes:

> Behold them glimmering in the distance,
> Dürer and Arndt and Hebbel, Peter Vischer and Kleist
> and Stein.

> Encircling Germany, they stand their high watch,
> The general staff of the spirit, holding sway over
> the battle.[30]

This descendant of what Patrick Bridgewater calls "the windy rhetoric of the patriotic verse of the Romantic era"[31] is difficult to render into tolerable English, but the thrust of the poem is that the great cultural figures (Bismarck presumably counts as a cultural figure because his unification of Germany made "true" German culture possible) form a protective spiritual "general staff" that will control the outcome of the conflict. All of the cultural leaders are appropriately "armed," and their leadership is specifically warlike. They constitute a cultural Siegfried Line. German cultural superiority, as evidenced by the roll-call of spiritual greats, will ensure a German victory and protect German culture from the destructive forces of democracy to the west and Slavic barbarity to the east.

The metaphoric union of culture and militarism is striking, although by no means unique. Mann comes close to it when he calls German militarism the "manifestation of German morality."[32] Werner Sombart, writing a year later,

---

Luther, der Landsknecht Gottes, mit riesiger Bibel bewehrt,
Bach, vorbetend preisende Orgelgesänge,
Kant, gewappnet mit Pflicht, gewappnet mit Strenge,
Schiller, die mächtige Rede schwingend als malmendes
Schwert,

[30]Lamprecht, 288–289.

Beethoven, von kämpfenden Erzmusiken umdröhnt,
Goethe, kaiserlich ragend, von Tagewerksonne gekrönt,
Bismarck, großhäuptig, geharnischt, pallaschbereit,
des ewigen Bundes Kanzler in Ewigkeit.

Seht sie gedrängt verdämmern in Ferneschein,
Dürer und Arndt und Hebbel, Peter Vischer und Kleist und
Stein.

Rings über Deutschland stehn sie auf hoher Wacht,
Generalstab der Geister, mitwaltend über die Schlacht.

[31]Patrick Bridgewater, *The German Poets of the First World War* (London: Croom Helm, 1988), 16.

[32]Mann, "Gedanken," 21.

gives the concept a more concrete expression: "Militarism is Potsdam and Weimar in the highest unity. It is *Faust* and *Zarathustra* and Beethoven Quartets in the trenches. For both the *Eroica* and *Egmont Overture* are true militarism."[33] Horst Wessel, the Nazi hero, eerily echoes Lissauer's and Sombart's paeans to *Kultur*: "The SA is marching for Goethe, for Schiller, for Kant, for Bach, for Cologne cathedral and the Bamberg Rider, for Novalis and Hans Thoma, for German culture, whether you believe it or not."[34]

Whatever the style and level of German arguments for war, they were far less important in August 1914 than a single, overriding emotion: the German people were caught up in an all-encompassing feeling of national unity.[35] The political unification of the German nation in 1871 was regarded by many as incomplete and superficial. German nationalism, with its Romantic roots, had always aimed at a unity more spiritual than political.[36] Thus the political union of 1871, coinciding as it did with the period of Germany's most rapid industrialization and urbanization, appeared to disintegrate into the disunity and disorder of party politics.[37] When the declaration of war came, it was accompanied by an instantaneous outpouring of national feeling. The response of Schauwecker's young volunteer to the old woman who inquires whether he isn't afraid of getting shot is typical: "Who thinks about that . . . There is only one thing to think about — Germany!"[38] Richard Dehmel, in "Lied an alle," blesses the war as "the sober hour, / that has finally united us in steel."[39] Countless patriotic poems of 1914 echo the same thought (cf. Bröger, "Bekenntnis eines Arbeiters"; Schröder, "Deutsches Lied"; Flex, "Deutsche Schicksalsstunde"). Significantly, such poems come not only from the predictable sources, but also from poets who were later known for "anti-war" poems.[40] The eyewitnesses agree that an extraordinary spirit of unity and comradeship prevailed throughout Germany, transcending political and class differences. The Reichstag deputies joined in the

[33]Sombart, *Händler und Helden*, 85. "Er [Militarismus] ist Potsdam und Weimar in höchster Vereinigung. Er ist 'Faust' und 'Zarathustra' und Beethoven-Partitur in den Schützengräben. Denn auch die Eroica und die Egmont-Ouvertüre sind doch wohl echtester Militarismus."

[34]Qtd. in J. M. Ritchie, *German Literature under National Socialism* (London: Helm, 1983), 86.

[35]Keller, *Nationalismus und Literatur*, 38; Walter Falk, *Der kollektive Traum vom Krieg* (Heidelberg: Winter, 1977), 8–10, and Walter Laqueur, *Young Germany: A History of the German Youth Movement* (London: Routledge, 1962), 61.

[36]Hermann Glaser, *The Cultural Roots of National Socialism*, tr. Ernest A. Manze (Austin: U of Texas P, 1978), 164.

[37]Hermand, *Der alte Traum*, 47–52.

[38]Schauwecker, *The Furnace*, 29. "Wer wird denn jetzt daran denken, jetzt gibt es nur eins: Deutschland" (34).

[39]Lamprecht, *Deutschland*, 291. "Sei gesegnet, ernste Stunde,/ die uns endlich stählern eint;"

[40]Thomas Anz and Joseph Vogl, eds., *Die Dichter und der Krieg: Deutsche Lyrik 1914–1918* (München: Hanser, 1982), 239–240.

general spirit by declaring the *Burgfrieden*, eschewing party politics for the duration of hostilities, and by voting the war credits. Kaiser Wilhelm proclaimed from the throne (4 August) "I know no more parties, I know only Germany."

Again, Ernst Gläser captures the spirit of the time in *Class of 1902*. As the narrator and his mother continue their journey home from Switzerland they have a long wait at one of the stations. The waiting room is jammed with people, but everyone is happy. When the Kaiser's telegram to Russia is read, everyone sings "The Watch on the Rhine." Workers are calling everyone "brother" and drinking the beer a gentleman buys for them. The professor remarks on how "uplifted and united" the people are and on how all the class distinctions are disappearing.[41]

Once on the train again, the boy is astounded by the friendliness and goodness of all the people. "We all knew one another. Strangers shared their food together, exchanged cigarettes, presented the children with chocolate."[42] It was as if he had "a thousand mothers and a thousand fathers."[43] His mother, completely overcome by emotion, weeps and says "Our dear German people, how terribly we have misunderstood their real nature."[44] Significantly, the emphasis in these passages is on the substitution of familial (some would say *völkisch*) unity for political and social diversity. Economic distinctions vanish in a great flood of soulful unity.

The general enthusiasm for the war was shared by soldiers. The soldiers in Gläser's book are so happy that the narrator can't decide if they're going on vacation or to a carnival.[45] The holiday atmosphere, due partly to the beautiful summer weather, seems, in retrospect, ironic or at least unseemly. But it is useful to recall that virtually everyone was convinced that it would be a quick, victorious war, with the troops home by Christmas.[46] For Gläser's young narrator "the world lay transfigured. The war had made everything beautiful."[47] In the sense that carnival and holiday represent a release from the restraints of daily existence, and an opportunity for adventure, some of the more tasteless displays

---

[41]Gläser, *Class of 1902*, 173. "'Sehen Sie das Volk,' sagte der Professor zu meiner Mutter, 'wie es begeistert ist und einig unter sich.' ... 'Ist das nicht wundervoll?!' sagte der Professor, 'alle Gegensätze heben sich auf!'" (190–191).

[42]Gläser, 176. "Jeder kannte den anderen. Fremde Menschen teilten sich ihre Brote, tauschten Zigaretten, schenkten ihren Kindern Schokolade" (192).

[43]Gläser, 177. "Es war mir, als hätte ich tausend Mütter und tausend Väter ..." (194).

[44]Gläser, 178. "Unser gutes deutsches Volk, wie sehr haben wir uns in seiner Seele getäuscht!" (195)

[45]Gläser, 177. "Fuhren sie in die Ferien oder auf eine Kirmes?" (194)

[46]Ecksteins, *Rites*, 101–102, Fischer, *War of Illusions*, 542–549, J.M. Winter, *The Experience of World War I* (New York: Oxford UP, 1989), 38–39, and J.-J. Becker, *The Great War and the French People* (Leamington Spa: Berg, 1985), 3–4.

[47]Gläser, 178. "Die Welt lag verändert. Der Krieg hatte sie schön gemacht" (195).

of enthusiasm become comprehensible. For example, the rhymes and jokes chalked on the sides of the railway carriages during the mobilization are sometimes cited as evidence of blood-thirsty German militarism.

Chicken fricassee in Paris —
Bear fricassee in Petersburg!

Menu for next week:
French bone soup
Russian brains in the German style
Serbian cutlet in the Austrian Style
English Beefsteak with Russian Eggs and French Gravy.[48]

From a critical standpoint the level of the humor is best passed over in silence, but the rhymes provide a glimpse of the morale of the troops during the mobilization, and are more indicative of their youth and schoolboy mentality than of any especially gruesome militarism. Secondly, the young soldiers, particularly the volunteers, shared a strange sense of relief and of liberation from the restraints of bourgeois life. The war was seen as an escape from a stable, predictable world, as a way out of problems, and as "some kind of solution" that youth needs.[49] For the members of the Wandervogel (the most important and influential of the youth organizations), the war represented a chance to feel at one with the Fatherland and with one's comrades, far from the class distinctions and limitations of Wilhelmine society. The schoolboy-soldiers who chalked their boasts on railway carriages were members of the first literate mass armies.[50] The

---

[48]Albrecht Armin, *Die Welt in Flammen* (Leipzig: Verlag "Die Welt in Flammen," 1914), 64, 199. Volume 1 of *Illustrierte Kriegschronik*, number of volumes unknown, 1914–1918.

"Hühnerfrikassee in Paris — Bärenfrikassee in Petersburg!"(64)
"Küchenzettel für die nächste Woche:
Französische Knochensuppe
Russisches Gehirn auf deutsche Art
Serbenkotelett auf österreichische Art serviert
Englishes Beefsteak mit russischen Eiern und
französischer Tunke" (199)

Postcards bearing such "menus" were popular throughout the war. See Paul Vincent, *Cartes postales d'un soldat de 1914–1918* (Paris: Gisserot, 1988), 98–105 for French examples. Some German examples are shown in Hans Weigel, Walter Lukan and Max D. Peyfuss, eds., *Jeder Schuß ein Russ, jeder Stoß ein Franzos* (Wien: Brandstätter, 1983). Their title comes from the most popular patriotic rhyme of the mobilization.

[49]Ludwig Renn (pseud. of Arnold Friederich Vieth von Glossenau), *Krieg* (Frankfurt a.M.: Frankfurter Societäts Druckerei, 1929), 12. Tr. by Edwin and Willa Muir as *War* (London: Secker, 1929), 16.

[50]Marsland, *Nation's Cause*, 44–46, Hynes, *War Imagined*, 28. See also Benedict Anderson, *Imagined Communities: Reflections on the Origin and Spread of Nationalism* (London: Verso, 1983) on the importance of the vernacular in nationalism (chapter 3).

product of forty years of European peace and the social and intellectual parameters it created, they welcomed the war as the great adventure of their time. Ernst Jünger spoke for his generation:

> We had left lecture-room, class-room, and bench behind us. We had been welded by a few weeks training into one corporate mass inspired by the enthusiasm of one thought . . . to carry forward the German ideals of '70. We had grown up in a material age, and in each one of us there was a yearning for great experience, such as we had never known. The war had entered into us like wine. We had set out in a rain of flowers to seek the death of heroes. The war was our dream of greatness, power and glory. It was a man's work, a duel of fields whose flowers would be stained with blood. There is no lovelier death in the world . . . anything rather than stay at home, anything to make one with the rest . . . [51]

They did not stay at home, and they were to have experiences of which no one had ever dreamed.

---

[51]Jünger, *Storm of Steel*, 1. "Wir hatten Hörsäle, Schulbänke und Werktische verlassen und waren in den kurzen Ausbildungswochen zusammengeschmolzen zu einem großen, begeisterten Körper, Träger des deutschen Idealismus der nachsiebziger Jahre. Aufgewachsen im Geiste einer materialistischen Zeit, wob in uns allen die Sehnsucht nach dem Ungewöhnlichen, nach dem großen Erleben. Da hatte uns der Krieg gepackt wie ein Rausch. In einem Regen von Blumen waren wir hinausgezogen in trunkener Morituri-Stimmung. Der Krieg mußte es uns ja bringen, das Große, Starke, Feierliche. Er schien uns männliche Tat, ein fröliches Schützengefecht auf blumigen, blutbetauten Wiesen. Kein schönrer Tod ist auf der Welt . . . . Ach, nur nicht zu Haus bleiben, nur mitmachen dürfen!" (1).

Das Aufgebot unserer. Feinde zur Rettung europäischer Kultur.

"The offering of our enemies for the salvation of European culture."
A German response to Allied accusations of barbarism. Postcard, 1914.
Published in Weigel et al., Jeder Schuß ein Russ.

"Weekly menu, 1914."
The dishes are enemy soldiers served up in national gastronomic styles.
From Weigel et al., Jeder Schuß ein Russ.

2: The Children's Crusade

Who were they, then, these youthful soldiers whom Gläser's patriotic professor describes as "ready to wield the sword" and "full of ideals"? Statistics from the German army, and from the armies of the other nations that fought in the First World War clearly show that the millions of soldiers who served in those armies included all eligible age groups (roughly 18–45 in most of western Europe), as well as younger and older men who lied or otherwise wrangled their way into the service. It is therefore difficult, as Robert Wohl has shown,[1] to designate a specific cohort of men as the "generation of 1914," the "war generation" or even the "lost generation." The majority of the more than nine million men who died in the war (two million of them Germans) were under age 30, and most were also from the working and peasant classes.[2] The popular image of the "war generation" nevertheless focuses on young men with at least secondary educations, often still students, from comfortable middle-class backgrounds. The universality of this "type" and its literary elevation to the status of myth is one of the striking commonalities of the literature of the First World War. Its significance lies in the *idée reçue* that because such young men represented the "cream" of their generation and the future of their nation their loss was more than usually tragic.[3] The poignancy is reinforced by the fact that for the cohort of soldiers who went directly from school to war, war was their introduction to life.[4] Unlike older men who had established professions and families to return to, the younger soldiers who survived returned to a void. If their experience — and experience of the front is the defining element of their lives — was to have any significance, individually or collectively, they had to create that meaning themselves.

This helps to explain why the vast majority of extant combat narratives (as well as lyric poems) were produced by men from a narrow stratum of society. These young men were the future ruling class of their nations, and had been so educated. Much has been made of the First World War as the first war fought

[1] Robert Wohl, *The Generation of 1914* (Cambridge: Harvard UP, 1979).

[2] Winter, *World War I,* 206–7.

[3] See Wohl, 208–209 on the "generation of 1914" as a specific social group, and 114–15 on British middle and upper-class losses, which serve as the paradigm for postwar views in the English-speaking world. German postwar views differ significantly, as we shall see.

[4] Wohl, *The Generation of 1914,* 64, 222.

by mass armies of literate men,[5] and it did indeed produce a greater quantity of accounts than any previous war, but the combat narrative belongs almost exclusively to the bourgeoisie and a few members of the aristocracy.[6] In only two senses can the literature of the war be regarded as a "mass" literature: first, because masses of people read it, and secondly because it attempts to convey the experience of the front, an experience which young intellectual writers shared with the mass of front soldiers, and for whom they became spokesmen. It is a rare combat narrative, especially in Germany, that does not claim to represent the experience of *all* that nation's front soldiers. The degree to which a nationalist consciousness — by which I mean the privileging of national feeling and culture — dominated late nineteenth-century European thought has been well-documented.[7] National feeling was shared by a wide range of social classes and age groups, but was especially marked in the middle classes, who perceived that their well-being was linked to that of the nation.[8] The upper classes shared a traditional patriotism tied more to reverence for throne and altar and for the person of the monarch, (where one was present), than to an abstract concept of the nation. Where there was no reigning monarch, as in France, upper-class loyalties gravitated to the traditional institutions historically linked with monarchy, the army and the church.[9]

The patriotic enthusiasm of the students who volunteered and marched off to war in 1914 is likewise a donnée of most studies of the period.[10] But their patriotism was not that of their elders, though it was perhaps closest to being so in Britain, where, at least for the middle and upper classes, the industrial revolu-

---

[5]Samuel Hynes, *A War Imagined: The First World War and English Culture* (New York: Athenaum, 1991), 28; Elizabeth A. Marsland, *The Nation's Cause: French, English and German Poetry of the First World War* (London: Routledge, 1991), 44–46.

[6]Among the few texts produced by members of the working class, Theodor Plievier's *Des Kaisers Kulis* and Adam Scharrer's *Vaterlandslose Gesellen* are the most notable.

[7]Of the enormous literature on the subject, Anderson's *Imagined Communities* is particularly illuminating. See also Marsland, *The Nation's Cause*, chapter 2, Eric Hobsbawm and Terence Ranger, eds. *The Invention of Tradition* (Cambridge: Cambridge UP, 1983), and Eric Hobsbawm, *Nations and Nationalism since 1780* (Cambridge: Cambridge UP, 1990), 101–130.

[8]See Anderson, *Imagined Communities*, 66–78 and Marsland, *The Nation's Cause*, 42–44. On France, see James F. McMillan, *Dreyfus to De Gaulle* (London: Arnold, 1985), 30–37 and 46–60, and Wohl, *The Generation of 1914*, 5–41. For Germany, see especially Hermand, *Der alte Traum*, Mosse *Crisis*, and Gerhard Ille and Gunter Köhler, eds., *Der Wandervogel* (Berlin: Stapp, 1987) on the nationalism of the youth movement before and during the war.

[9]On the forms of French patriotism, see Robert Tombs, ed., *Nationhood and Nationalism in France: From Boulangism to the Great War, 1889–1918* (London: Harper Collins, 1991), Jacques Meyer, *La Vie quotidienne des soldats pendant la Grande Guerre* (Paris: Hachette, 1966) and Stéphane Audoin-Rouzeau, *14–18: Les Combattants des tranchées* (Paris: Colin, 1986).

[10]Becker, *1914*, 21–43. See also Wohl's chapters on France, England and Germany in *The Generation of 1914*.

tion had not ruptured the sense of historical and natural continuity, nor destroyed the public school ethos of national service. The high ideals of chivalry, patriotism and the "sporty heroics" of pre-war and wartime boys' fiction mirror the general attitudes.[11] In France the situation was quite different, as J. J. Becker has pointed out.[12] While their elders concentrated on *revanche*, the famous Agathon survey of 1913 established that young men longed for a national renewal based on spiritual regeneration that would free France from German influence, and were prepared to sacrifice their lives to that end in a war they thought inevitable.[13] While the limited field surveyed by the *enquête* (15- to 25-year-old Parisian male students in the *lycées*, universities and the *Grandes Écoles*) restricts its universality, it is precisely those limits that make it particularly valuable for this study, as it focuses on the specific segment of society under consideration here. In Germany, similarly, young men rejected the traditional *Thron und Altar* nationalism of the generation of 1870 in favor of devotion to mystical, pseudo-medieval idealized images of the German *Volk* and *Reich*, which we shall shortly examine in more detail. In the above examples, the characteristic departure from the older generation involves a movement toward more abstract and spiritual forms of patriotism, which eventually came to shape the depiction of the war and its significance.

The most misleading popular myth of the First World War is that of the disillusioned young soldier, his patriotism destroyed, the ideals and values for which he fought as irrevocably lost as his friends lying dead in the trenches. Wohl maintains that the war generation is "lost because its history is overlaid with myth," and sets out to restore its historicity.[14] My purpose is to explore the myth — a myth largely created through the literature of the war, interwoven with other forms of cultural expression and overlain by the aesthetics of politics. The origins of that myth — a myth that profoundly shaped both popular and elite perceptions and actions between the wars — are embedded in pre-war culture. The uniqueness of each national response to the war is at least partly dependent on the national and nationalist cultures from which the writers emerged.

The analysis of German cultural and intellectual history that follows emphasizes the uniqueness — what has been called the "peculiarity" — of German history.[15] The notion that the German pattern of historical development differs from that of the rest of western Europe (especially from that of England and France),

[11] Mary Cadogan and Patricia Craig, *Women and Children First: The Fiction of Two World Wars* (London: Gollancz, 1978), 71–76.

[12] Becker, *1914*, 43.

[13] Wohl, 5–9, 213; Becker, *1914*, 31–33, 39–42.

[14] Wohl, 2.

[15] David Blackbourn and Geoff Ely, *The Peculiarities of German History: Bourgeois Society and Politics in Nineteenth-Century Germany* (Oxford: Oxford UP, 1984).

that Germany followed a special path, originates in the political writings of the German Romantics. Until the end of the First World War — and indeed for Germans of a conservative inclination, until the end of the Second World War — the German *Sonderweg* posited a positive model of development, buttressing the Second Empire with an aura of spiritual legitimacy and historical continuity, and supplying conservatives of the Weimar Republic with persuasive arguments for rejecting the "alien" forms of republicanism. After the collapse of 1945, the *Sonderweg* was seen only in a negative light. Beginning in the sixties, German historians attempted to account for National Socialism as the direct descendant of German Romantic nationalism and the ideologies it spawned.

In the eighties and nineties, the very existence of a German *Sonderweg* has come under attack.[16] This is not the place to join that debate, for the existence of a positive German *Sonderweg* was rarely questioned by the writers who grew up in the Wilhelmine era. They believed that Germany's remarkably rapid development as a nation was ordained by God or fate, *Schicksal*, and were convinced that their special path was a great and beneficial one that had raised the German people to heights of spiritual culture unmatched by other nations. One needs only dip into Sombart's *Händler und Helden* or the students' letters from the front collected by Phillip Witkop to perceive the underlying certainty, at least among the educated classes, of Germany's unique place in the scheme of things.[17]

The German belief in the *Sonderweg* is genuinely unique in two ways. In the first place, it survived the First World War. The majority of the German combat writers never succumbed to the devastating disillusionment common to the veterans of Britain and France. Their belief in the uniqueness of their nation mutated under the pressure of trench warfare, but it never faltered. Secondly, most of the combat writers likewise perceived no profound war-induced break in historical continuity. The notion of a pre-war world and a postwar world divided by the abyss of the war — a notion widespread in the rest of postwar Europe — made few inroads in conservative German thought. The break with the past was not the war, but the Weimar Republic, regarded by conservative Germans as an alien, un-German imposition on Germany's special status that had to be undermined and destroyed, as indeed it was. The reasons for the survival of the *Sonderweg* lay in the qualities of German intellectual and cultural history that the soldiers of the First World War carried with them to the

---

[16]The curent debate on the *Sonderweg* is examined in Blackbourn and Ely 1–35. See also Helga Grebing, ed., *Der "deutsche Sonderweg" in Europa 1806–1945: Eine Kritik* (Stuttgart: Kohlhammer, 1986) which has a good introduction, and D. Bracher et al., *Deutscher Sonderweg — Mythos oder Realität?* (München: Oldenbourg, 1982).

[17]Phillip Witkop, *Kriegsbriefe gefallener Studenten* (1916; reprint, München: Muller, 1928). Tr. by A.R. Wedd as *German Students' War Letters* (London: Methuen, 1929).

trenches and dugouts of France and Flanders, and the manner in which the past shaped the interpretation of the war experience.

The German literature of the First World War presents the reader with virtually a single protagonist: the young, idealistic bourgeois student. By patriotism or historical accident, he is whisked from his desk in the *Gymnasium* or university classroom into the trenches, where he learns lessons inconceivable to chauvinistic professors who had fought in the war of 1870. In the process of becoming a *Frontschwein* the student-soldier never completely loses the intellectual baggage of his earlier life, although he may, in despair, declare it dead or meaningless. What sort of mental baggage, what framework of ideas, did these very young men take into war with them? What had been given them by their families, their churches, their schools, their reading? Why did they go so enthusiastically into war, the troop trains decked with flowers and chalked with jingoistic schoolboy rhymes?

The answers are complex, and reach far back into German intellectual history, but one may use Gläser's fictional professor, himself a representative figure as only a caricature can be, as a point of departure. He states categorically that the nation's young men are full of ideals and ready to fight for them. It is idealism, German Romantic idealism, that is the root system of nineteenth- and twentieth-century German ideology. From those roots spring the patterns of education and *Bildung* (that uniquely German educational ideal) and, most significantly for the present inquiry, German nationalism — in short, the entire edifice of German thought from the end of the eighteenth century to the middle of the twentieth.

Idealism

The fundamental tenet of idealism, particularly in the German context, is the belief that truth and value lie not in the material world, but in the world of mind and spirit.[18] As German Romantic idealism has been thoroughly examined elsewhere,[19] it will suffice to review two influential concepts. First, the belief that truth lies in the realm of spirit produces a corresponding elevation of spirit over matter, and the consequent glorification of the mind and its creations.

[18]The German term is *Geist*, which may be variously translated as spirit, mind, intellect, imagination, soul, etc. I have generally used the English word "spirit" to designate aspects and activities of the mind as distinct from physical activity and material existence. *Geist* is burdened with a heavy load of philosophical and cultural connotation that can only be suggested in English.

[19]Nicolai Hartmann, *Die Philosophie des deutschen Idealismus* (1923; reprint Berlin: de Gruyter, 1960) is, despite its age, an excellent introduction to the subject. In English see Glyn Tegai Hughes, *Romantic German Literature* (New York: Holmes, 1979) and Marshall Brown, *The Shape of German Romanticism* (Ithaca: Cornell UP, 1979). Hajo Holborn's *Germany and Europe* (Garden City: Doubleday, 1970) provides a useful overview of the impact of idealism on German politics.

What the Romantics glorified in the spirit was not merely its intellectual capacity, but its emotional capacity, so that Romanticism, in its quest for spiritual truth, followed the path of the emotional and the irrational. Rationality was shunned as a part of the material world, and worse, as a foreign French imposition. The course of German intellectual history in the nineteenth and twentieth centuries is an exemplar of the triumph of the irrational, as Glaser, Hermand, Sontheimer and others have succinctly shown.[20] Langbehn, Möller van den Bruck and the National Socialists stand at the terminus of a journey that began with Novalis, Fichte and the Schlegels.

With the inclination toward irrationalism, the predominance of the spiritual in German thought created a dualistic vision of the world that penetrated into every corner of German life. The dichotomy of spirit and matter produced, on the one hand, the abiding German reverence for the products of the spirit — music, philosophy, literature, art — in short, culture. The German word *Kultur* carried the connotation of a "high" culture rooted in the fundamental life of the *Volk*, or people. Our modern phrase "popular culture," with its implications of a divided society, would have seemed nonsensical to a cultured German of 1914. In *The Cultural Roots of National Socialism*, Herman Glaser argues that the genuinely high intellectual and cultural level of the Romantic period was perverted and trivialized in the nineteenth century into what he calls "living-room culture."[21] Pachter argues that middle-class culture consisted of correct German, the classical authors, and serious music.[22] Pachter's definition brings to mind Remarque's Paul Bäumer, who on one level is genuinely representative of his generation of bourgeois upbringing. On home leave from the front, profoundly altered by his experiences of war, Paul contemplates his parents' changeless home with bemused irony. The mahogany piano and his collection of butterflies are in their accustomed places.[23] In his own room his bookshelves hold only collected editions of the classics (188). In an earlier reference, he tells us that the drawer of his writing table holds "the beginning of a play called 'Saul' and a bundle of poems . . . we all did something of the kind."[24]

One finds further affirmation of the value of culture and of spiritual well-being in the Witkop collection of letters. Although Paul Fussell cogently argues

---

[20]Hermann Glaser, *The Cultural Roots of National Socialism*, Tr. Ernest A Manze, (Austin : U Texas P, 1978) and Kurt Sontheimer, *Antidemokratisches Denken in der Weimarer Republik* (München: Nymphenburger Verlagshandlung, 1962).

[21]Glaser, *Cultural Roots*, 95.

[22]Henry M. Pachter, *Modern Germany* (Boulder: Westview, 1978), 37.

[23]Erich Maria Remarque, *Im Westen nichts Neues* (Berlin: Propyläen, 1928), 162. Tr. by A.W. Wheen as *All Quiet on the Western Front* (London: Putnam, 1929), 178.

[24]Remarque, *All Quiet*, 27. "Es ist für mich sonderbar, daran zu denken, daß zu Hause, in einer Schreibtischlade, ein angefangenes Drama 'Saul' und ein Stoss Gedichte liegen. . . . Wir haben ja fast alle so etwas Ähnliches gemacht . . . " (23).

that it is unwise to take soldiers' letters home at face value,[25] these letters, when compared with other sources, seem a fair reflection of attitudes among young male intellectuals. In the autumn of 1914, R. Fischer wrote to his family in Freiburg,

> Spiritually I am pretty well all right again and proud to be allowed to help and to fight for parents, brothers and sisters, for the dear Fatherland and for all that has stood highest in my estimation — for we are fighting for poetry, for art, for philosophy and culture. It is tragic, but magnificent . . . . So be happy in Freiburg as we are at the Front.[26]

What strikes the modern reader here is Fischer's anxious assurance to his parents that he is "spiritually" all right, as if that has greater significance to him and to them than his physical safety, which is never mentioned. In his enumeration of what he is fighting for, the predictable family and country barely precede what is "highest in his estimation": German culture. Sombart's definition of German militarism and Horst Wessel's manifesto on the goals of the Nazi party (quoted in the previous chapter) are but echoes of Fischer's convictions. In a similar vein, Franz Blumenfeld, a law student, worries about the coarsening of his spirit and finer feelings:

> One thing weighs on me more from day to day — the fear of getting brutalized. . . . I have no fear, none at all, of bullets and shells, but only of this great spiritual loneliness. I am afraid of losing my faith in human nature, in myself, in all that is good in the world! Oh, that is horrible! . . . it is much harder for me to endure the incredibly coarse tone that prevails among the men here.[27]

The fear of being spiritually coarsened appears frequently in letters and memoirs, often produced by the gulf between social classes. Many bourgeois student-soldiers first encountered men from the rural peasantry or the urban proletariat in the army. Even youth organizations such as the Wandervogel were almost entirely urban and middle class, despite their rhetorical glorification of the peasantry and calls for the union of young people from all classes.[28] Blu-

---

[25]Fussell, *Great War*, 181–83.

[26]Witkop, *Students' War Letters*, 15. "Seelisch bin ich wieder ziemlich in Ordnung, bin stolz, mitwirken zu dürfen für Eltern, Geschwister, fürs liebe Vaterland, für alles was mir bisher das Höchste war. Für Dichtung, Kunst, Philosophie, Kultur geht ja der Kampf. Er ist traurig, aber groß. . . . Seid also frölich in Freiburg, wie wir im Feld es sind" (19).

[27]Witkop, 20. "Eines drückt mich von Tag zu Tag mehr, ich fürchte mich so vor der inneren Verrohung. . . . hab' ich gar keine, aber auch gar keine Angst vor allen Kugeln und Granaten, sondern nur vor dieser großen inneren Vereinsamung. Ich fürchte, meinen Glauben an die Menschen zu verlieren, an mich selbst, an alles Gute in der Welt! Ach, das is sehr schrecklich! . . . viel schwerer ist mir, den unglaublich rohen Ton zu ertragen, der zwischen den Leuten hier herrscht" (23).

[28]Laqueur, *Young Germany*, 10–12; Ille and Köhler, *Der Wandervogel*, 30–86. The Wandervogel was the most prominent of the German youth groups, founded in the Steglitz suburb of

menfeld writes home later that he is getting on better with the men, that they are more agreeable, and that it may be due to his influence. A similar passage appears in Walter Flex's *Der Wanderer zwischen beiden Welten*, his idealized account of the life and death of his friend Ernst Wurche. Wurche embodies the high-minded lieutenant and former Wandervogel who improves his men by example and uses disapproval to coax them out of telling dirty jokes.[29] These texts illuminate the middle-class commitment to spiritual and cultural values, and the literature of the First World War that is a significant product of those values.

Beyond the reverence for culture, the dichotomy of spirit and matter in German thought also created an anti-materialistic bias that permeated not only philosophy and the arts, but political, economic and social life. Romantic theory dictated that nature, the organic embodiment of the divine, was the natural home of the spirit, and those who lived at one with nature partook of that spirituality. The natural goodness of agrarian peasants and the rightness of their way of life was an idea whose early influence only increased over a century and a half. Oddly enough, Rousseau's philosophy found more fertile soil in Germany than in France, bringing with it the fulsome praise of the noble savage and the noble peasant.

The antithesis of the ideal life of the countryside was the rational, legalistic life of the city dweller. The urban population, especially the comfort-loving bourgeoisie, was regarded as the victim of an unnatural contractual society based on logic and therefore divorced from the life-giving forces of nature and the irrational. The rapid industrialization of Germany after 1840 failed to dislodge this Romantic paradigm; indeed it reinforced it. Industrialization and technology produced growing material comfort for the urban population, undermined the economic and social status of the peasantry, and simultaneously failed to convince anyone that the urban material life was worth leading.[30] So firmly fixed was the anti-material, anti-technological, anti-urban stance of German thought that it became a predictable standard of Wilhelmine propaganda. The derogation of England as a materialistic nation of shopkeepers with a "counting-house mentality" appeared with increasing frequency in the last years before the war. Sombart made it the thesis of his *Händler und Helden*. Once the war began, the allied superiority in numbers and war materiel was dismissed by

Berlin at the turn of the century. The Wandervogel fostered emotional bonding between members, and encouraged adolescent boys to discover the German landscape, rural traditions, and the German medieval heritage of folklore and folksong.

[29]Walter Flex, *Der Wanderer zwischen beiden Welten: Ein Kriegserlebnis* (1915; reprint Heusenstamm: Orion-Heimreiter, 1979), 16–18. Laqueur states categorically that had Wurche lived, he would have been right-wing after the war (*Young Germany*, 46–7).

[30]Sontheimer, *Antidemokratisches Denken*, 308–316, 322–327; Mosse, *Crisis*, 13–30; Rolf Dahrendorf, *Society and Democracy in Germany* (London: Weidenfeld, 1968), 50; Koppel S. Pinson, *Modern Germany* (New York: Macmillan, 1954), 271–72.

Germans as "mere" material, more than outweighed by the German superiority of spirit.

The other, more creative aspect of Romantic idealism was its organic view of life. For the Romantics, life, whether that of natural things or of men and societies, followed an organic pattern of development. That organic model of the universe replaced the mechanistic, clockwork model favored by Enlightenment thinkers. The essential difference is that the organic model presumes universal and eternal change in the form of growth and development, while the mechanistic model does not. The eternal but "finished" universe of the Enlightenment was supplanted by a universe of eternal metamorphosis. The concept of transformation inherent in the organic model of existence enabled the Romantics and their intellectual heirs to see the world and themselves in a constant state of natural, and therefore positive, change. It is important to note that organicism implies a positive result. That is, the change is occurring according to a natural order that embraces all life. Within the parameters of organicism, all change, even destruction and death, is a necessary part of a developmental cycle which may also lead to rebirth. Herder's organic model of history established a pattern of historical thought that lasted through the Second World War.[31] Most Germans, as Hermand observes, have a tendency to cyclical thought.[32]

As an essential component of the idealistic *Weltanschauung*, organicism pervaded German thought on human and historical development throughout the period under discussion. Herder's organic model of human history and Hitler's belief in government as perpetual revolution merely represent the historic poles of the concept.[33] For the First World War writers, it provided an intellectual framework into which they could fit their experiences and which would endow those experiences with coherence and meaning. As we shall see in a later chapter, the writers were able, with a few exceptions, to perceive their war experiences as a necessary stage in their individual and collective (that is, national) transformation and rebirth, thereby largely avoiding the alienation and the sense of a break in historical continuity so typical of the British experience of the war.

Nationalism

The precise form of German nationalism resulted from the historical coincidence of Romantic idealism with the 1813 Wars of Liberation from Napoleon. For the Germans, the Wars of Liberation represented freedom from foreign occupation, and above all, freedom from the dominance of foreign ideas. When they ejected the French from their soil, they simultaneously rejected what the French represented: the Enlightenment, the French Revolution, and the entire

[31] On organicism in Weimar, see Sontheimer, *Antidemokratisches Denken*, 322–327.

[32] Hermand, *Der alte Traum*, 68.

[33] J. P. Stern, *Hitler: The Führer and the People* (Berkeley: U of California P, 1975), 114–115.

complex of political and philosophical ideas embodied in those historical events. The historical conjunction of Romantic philosophy and the defeat of the French led to the demise in German thought of the Enlightenment beliefs in the rights of man and in a state based on a social contract. In its place, the Germans substituted a quasi-religious belief in the German nation as an organic community of German-speaking people governed by a natural leader.

This profoundly anti-gallic concept of nationhood, with its roots in the idealist emphasis on the spirit and on the organic model of the world, found its first and greatest spokesman in Johann Gottlieb Fichte. Fichte's *Reden an die deutsche Nation* (*Lectures to the German Nation*, 1808) provided the ammunition needed by German Romantic nationalists in their rebellion against French ideas. The classic locus for the origins of Romantic nationalism is Fichte's seventh lecture. Working from the organic paradigm, Fichte identifies the Germans as the "ursprünglich lebendige Volk" (original living people), and contrasts them with the "dead" foreigners.[34] What distinguishes the Germans, the "Urvolk" (original people) from all other peoples, he goes on, is their belief in the absolute originality, freedom, organic development and eternal progress of their race. Those who believe in the status quo, or even in reaction, or who put "eine tote Natur" (a dead nature) in control, are "undeutsch und fremd" (un-German and foreign), and from them Germans should uncompromisingly separate themselves.

Although these passages have been widely analyzed, a few comments are appropriate. First, at the very core of German nationalism in the nineteenth and twentieth centuries lie the twin convictions of German uniqueness and German spiritual superiority. Because they are the *Urvolk*, the Germans are blessed with a spiritual depth and purity unknown to other superficial or even "dead" peoples (particularly the French). Such distinctions, clearly directed against the rationality that German thinkers perceived as a French monopoly, underlie the vicious debates on *Kultur* and *Zivilisation* that enlivened Wilhelmine and wartime *Kulturkritik*.

Secondly, the German spirit is seen as organic and vital, constantly growing and metamorphosing. As elaborated by men such as Lagarde and Langbehn, this *Lebensphilosophie* became a cornerstone of German thought, equally applicable to individual and nation. On a personal plane, the belief in the progressive development of the *Volk* encompasses the development of the individual, who is the microcosm of the nation, and whose maturation is inseparable from that of the *Volk*. In literary terms the pattern is significant, for it permits the creation of representative characters whose experience exemplifies that of the nation. That exemplary experience, in the case of the war literature, becomes the only accept-

---

[34]Johann Gottlieb Fichte, *Reden an die Deutsche Nation* in *Die Deutschen Romantiker*, Gerhard Stenzel, ed., (Salzburg: Bergland, n.d.) 2:389–426.

able version of the war experience, automatically rejecting and devaluing any other construction of the experience of the war.

Vitalist philosophy is also pertinent to the third Fichtean idea, the mystical unity of the *Volk*. For Fichte, national unity is predicated on a mystic, spiritual union of will and purpose, rather than on contractual obligations between individuals or groups. The only valid social organization is one based on a mystical unity with one's people, an ideal that is irrational rather than logical.[35] It is also what Viereck calls the "mathematical fallacy" of Romantic nationalism: the assumption that the whole is greater than the sum of its parts.[36] Like Troeltsch's denigration of allied "mathematics," this fallacy stems from the underlying conviction that the only unity is spiritual and has nothing to do with practical political arrangements. The lasting importance of the "spirit of August" for German writers testifies to the critical significance of mystical nationhood. These convictions colored German thought to 1945, and influenced the First World War soldier's reaction to the experience of comradeship and to its opposite, the war of materiel.

Finally, Fichte's rejection of foreign ideas and customs, understandable in the context of the Wars of Liberation, retained its validity long after the historical situation had changed, because his rejection was based on something more fundamental than hatred for a conqueror's ways. He identified the German *Volk* with the life force, so that anything foreign automatically became dead — not life-creating, but life-destroying. That position ensures that foreign ways are more than undesirable; they are a threat to the very existence of the *Volk*. Fichte's ideas reinforced German xenophobia, which had manifested itself long before Romanticism, and likewise encouraged the mindless glorification of all things German. As Glaser puts it, "the word 'German' gilds everything."[37]

The dangerous conjunction of xenophobia and patriotism was sealed by the victory over French arms in the Wars of Liberation, a triumph that confirmed in concrete terms the spiritual superiority and mystical power of a growing *Volk* over a "dead" foreigner. Every German political and military victory thereafter, especially that of 1871, automatically assumed the status of a moral and spiritual triumph. So when defeat came in 1918, the first reaction was bewilderment that a superior people could be defeated by inferior ones, followed by the reduction of the defeat to the material plane (the "undefeated" army overcome by mere materiel) or to some betrayal of that army by nefarious forces in the homeland (the *Dolchstoß* or stab-in-the-back). As Otto Baumgarten put it in his 1927 study of the moral effects of the war: "In us lived the obstinacy of the idea in the

---

[35]Helmuth Plessner, *Die verspätete Nation* (Stuttgart: Kohlhammer, 1959), 48. See also Hermand, *Der alte Traum*, particularly 47–73, and Sontheimer, *Antidemokratisches Denken*, chapter 9.

[36]Peter Robert Viereck, *Metapolitics* (New York: Knopf, 1941), 29.

[37]Glaser, *Cultural Roots*, 97.

face of brutal reality. Thus in the normal German way it was unthinkable that the Reich which had risen to world power through the victories of 1864, 1866, and 1870 could be defeated by mere numerical superiority! . . . And what was unthinkable, unimaginable, could not be real."[38] The German reluctance to accept 1918 as a defeat had its roots in a century of Fichtean nationalism.

After a series of political reverses that only served to strengthen its ideology, German nationalism triumphed with the 1871 proclamation of the German Empire in the Hall of Mirrors at Versailles. From that date nationalist thought, in its myriad forms, permeated nearly every facet of German life. The language of government and politics was overtly chauvinistic, as was that of most newspapers. Education (to which I shall shortly return) became progressively nationalistic in this period. The Pan-Germans and other conservative extremists, although clearly minorities, exerted a disproportionate influence in government and society.[39] In a general sense, it was the *völkisch* movement that exercised the greatest influence on German nationalist thought in the Wilhelmine era.

Völkisch ideology, that form of German nationalism focused on the idealization and pre-eminence of the *Volk*, occupied an eminent and influential position within German conservatism from around 1870 to 1945. Resting on Fichte, Langbehn and Lagarde, *völkisch* ideology emphasized the mystical unity of the *Volk* and the bonding of the individual to the *Volk* through an irrational union with the spiritual forces surging through the *Volk*. The *völkisch* movement has been thoroughly analyzed, but the extent of its influence in the pre-war years warrants a brief discussion of its major tenets.[40]

The core of *völkisch* ideology, as already noted, is the oneness of the individual with the *Volk* and therefore with the natural life forces of the cosmos. The individual must live in harmony with these life forces which make individual and communal development possible, or be forever sundered from the *Volk* (hence the frequent designation of *völkisch* thought as "vitalist"). That vitalism, in turn, is rooted in the Romantic-organic paradigm of the world. "Rootedness" was a key concept, and one that exerted great influence on nationalist thought to the end of the National Socialist era. The notion of "rootedness" — as always, the diction is organic — conveys the mystical correspondence of individual-

[38]Baumgarten, *Wirkungen des Krieges,* 9. "In uns lebte der Trotz der Idee gegen die brutale Wirklichkeit. Es war doch für normale deutsche Art undenkbar, daß das durch die Siege von 1864, 1866, 1870 zur Weltmacht aufgestiegene Reich der bloßen numerischen Übermacht unterliegen würde! . . . Und was undenkbar, unausdenkbar, das konnte nicht wirklich werden."

[39]Pinson, *Modern Germany,* 309–311; Hermand, *Der alte Traum,* 47–83. On the Pan-German movement, see Roger Chickering, *We Men Who Feel Most German* (Boston: Allen and Unwin, 1984). On militarism, see Thomas Rohkrämer, *Der Militarismus der "kleinen Leute:" Die Kriegervereine im Deutschen Kaiserreich 1871–1914* (Munich: Oldenbourg, 1990), especially 175–252.

[40]Most of the following discussion is drawn from Mosse, *Crisis,* Stern *Politics,* Stackelberg, *Idealism Debased,* and Hermand, *Der alte Traum.*

Volk-landscape-cosmos, that harkens back to the Romantic dream of a medieval utopia, in which man was rooted in his natural agrarian landscape and in a stable, hierarchical social order. Novalis's *Die Christenheit oder Europa* is the best-know Romantic vision of the Golden Age.[41]

But the *Volk*'s intimate accord with nature should not be confused with an undifferentiated love of the natural world. On the contrary, the spirit of a *Volk* is linked to, and determined by, its specific landscape. The landscape assumes vast significance because it both embodies and creates the fundamental cultural values of the *Volk*, and is specific only to that *Volk*. To any other, it is emotionally and physically alien. The worst disaster that can befall a *Volk* is to be cut off from its roots, for to be "rootless" is to be spiritually dead. To borrow Mosse's example, the Jews, a desert people, are seen in *völkisch* thought as arid, barren, shallow and lacking creativity and profundity. In contrast, the Germans in their dark, misty forests are spiritually "deep, mysterious, profound."[42] This curious and inherently racist German version of the pathetic fallacy shaped the interpretation and presentation of history and culture in German society.

A striking instance of the intrusion of *völkisch* ideology into expressions of patriotism is the erection of the great nationalist monuments in the late nineteenth century. Such monuments reflect the arrival of what Anderson calls "official nationalism," that is, the forced merger of nation and dynastic empire.[43] In Germany, official nationalism arrived in 1871 with the proclamation of the German Empire, which also coincided with the widespread creation of national traditions, as Hobsbawm has correctly argued.[44] The problem of the Second Empire was how to interpret history in a way that bestowed legitimacy on the newly-created Empire. *Völkisch* nationalism provided one answer through its forceful belief in historical continuity within the *Volk*. A rooted *Volk* could trace its history into the remote past, and observe the unchanging endurance of a people amid its own forests, rivers and mountains. The connection of the landscape to the soul of the *Volk* is deepened by legendary heroic deeds enacted in that landscape. The defeat of the Romans by Arminius in the Teutoburger Wald provides an exemplary instance of the *völkisch* reinterpretation of history. The 1875 monument to Arminius, built in the new German Empire's first flush

---

[41]On the nationalist utopias of the nineteenth and twentieth centuries, see Hermand, *Der alte Traum*. Peter Fisher provides an interesting analysis of popular utopian and fantasy fiction in Weimar in *Fantasy and Politics: Visions of the Future in the Weimar Republic* (Madison: U of Wisconsin P, 1991).

[42]Mosse, *Crisis*, 4–5. Obviously, the presumed "rootlessness" of the Jews contributed to the persistent anti-Semitism of the Second Empire. That anti-Semitism became more virulent in the Weimar Republic when Jews became associated with the material urban modernism that *völkisch* ideologists despised. See *Crisis*, 126–145.

[43]Anderson, *Imagined Communities*, 80–102.

[44]Hobsbawm, *Tradition*, 263–269 and 273–277.

of national enthusiasm, was meant to evoke the sacred power of the ancient hero on the very site of his victory. The monument, in the depths of a German forest, visually couples the hero, the victor over an alien culture attempting to impose itself on a Germanic *Volk*, with his physical place in the German landscape.[45] Thanks to the Romantic idealization of German legends, and their association with specific landscapes, Germany became full of sacred sites that appealed to the mystical nationalism and *völkisch* sense of community characteristic of the period.[46] Nineteenth-century Germans, faced with the problems of industrialization and modernization, fled into what Keller calls "mythical nationalism."[47] Like the erection of national monuments, the late nineteenth century saw the foundation of national holidays that centered on public ceremonies. The period witnessed the creation of Bastille Day in France and Thanksgiving in the United States, as well as that most national of German holidays, Sedan Day.[48] The notion of a festival to link past victories with more recent ones was proposed in Germany as early as 1814 by Ernst Moritz Arndt (the leading patriotic poet of the Wars of Liberation), who suggested that the Battle of Leipzig be commemorated by festivals held at a monument to the victory of the Teutoburger Wald. The monument was to be surrounded by a sacred space planted with oaks, which are an important symbol of strength and continuity in many observances.[49] Sedan Day celebrations, meant to symbolize the Prussian-Protestant unity of the new Germany, generally included church services and military parades, supplemented by speeches, choral music and gymnastic exercises.[50]

The idealized medieval past of a peasant *Volk* living symbiotically with the land embodies the antithesis of the modern, industrialized state that Germany was becoming in the course of the nineteenth century.[51] Virtually all the con-

[45]For other examples see Mosse, *The Nationalization of the Masses* (New York: New American Library, 1975), especially the chapters on monuments and the "aesthetics of politics."

[46]The creation of national monuments to the dead of the First World War reflected nationalism in a different manner and will be discussed in chapter 6. George Mosse, *Fallen Soldiers: Reshaping the Memory of the World Wars* (Oxford: Oxford UP, 1990) provides an insightful guide.

[47]Ernst Keller, *Nationalismus und Literatur: Langemarck, Weimar, Stalingrad* (Bern: Franke, 1970), 234.

[48]Hobsbawm, *Tradition*, 276–282.

[49]Max L. Baeumer, "Imperial Germany as Reflected in its Mass Festivals," in Volker Dürr, Kathy Harms and Peter Hays, eds., *Imperial Germany* (Madison: U of Wisconsin P, 1985) 62–74. See also Hobsbawm, *Tradition*, 277.

[50]Baeumer, "Imperial Germany," 65–6. See also Gerhard Ille "Schülernot und Jugendkult im deutschen Kaiserreich. Zur Situation der bürgerlichen Jugend um 1900," in Ille and Köhler, *Der Wandervogel*. Ille includes a photo of the 1903 Sedansfest at the Oberrealschule in Steglitz (33), and the program of the 1897 festivities at the Gymnasium (35).

[51]Dahrendorf, *Society and Democracy in Germany*, 35-47; Ecksteins, *Rites of Spring*, 67–70.

stituent elements of an urban, industrial society were anathema to *völkisch* thinkers. Industrialization, with its creation of masses of "uprooted" workers lured from their rural occupations by the promise of "mere" lucre and jammed into urban centers, was only the first of a horde of enemies identified by the *völkisch* ideologists. The leftist ideologies of the urban proletariat (socialism, Marxism) were viciously and consistently attacked by *völkisch* ideologists, as were the most egregious examples of urban life, the Jews. Anti-Semitism is an essential rather than an incidental tenet of the *völkisch* movement. As noted above, conservative thinkers despised Jews as the prototypical parasitic people, and the apparent Jewish preference for urban life, material gain, the liberal professions, and leftist politics only exacerbated their hostility.

Anchored in the basic dichotomy of rooted rural life vs. rootless urban life, and in the dichotomizing mentality present in much German thought, *völkisch* thinkers logically scorned most manifestations of urban life in a modern industrialized state. Factories, which uprooted men from the traditional way of life of the countryside, despoiled the landscape and relied on industrial technologies, were consistently vilified.[52] Technological advances from telephones to machine guns were consigned to the same ideological rubbish heap. The later German reaction to war materiel, exemplified by artillery and machine guns, is to a considerable extent the result of the conservative deprecation of technology and materialism. As Herf correctly notes, the confrontation between technology and the traditions of German nationalism was at its sharpest in Weimar and was a legacy of the *Materialschlacht* of the First World War.[53]

The materialism that appeared in the wake of the industrial revolution was, like its technology, more roundly condemned in Germany than elsewhere. The traditions of German idealism, and of its descendant *völkisch* ideology, ensured that materialism appeared to pose a particularly insidious threat to the idealist values of German *Kultur*. The members of the bourgeoisie were regularly condemned for their materialism, and their consequent betrayal of everything sacred in the German cultural heritage. The German youth movement, especially the Wandervogel, was born as a youthful rebellion against the materialism of the older generation. As Laqueur notes, their revolt was Romantic, and therefore idealist and anti-materialist, and was directed primarily against the protestant middle-classes.[54] By the outbreak of war, it was widely believed that the emotionalism and idealism of the war would cleanse the German soul of the dross of materialism.

---

[52]On the complex history of conservative thought and technology, see Jeffrey Herf's superb study *Reactionary Modernism* (Cambridge: Cambridge UP, 1984).

[53]Herf, 19.

[54]Laqueur, *Young Germany*, 4–6; Ille, "Schülernot," Günter Köhler, "Der Steglitzer Wandervogel 1896–1914," 54–85 and "Darstellung und Charakterisierung der Entwicklung des Wandervogel bis zum Ersten Weltkrieg" 86–98, all in Ille and Köhler, *Der Wandervogel*.

Despite the rapid and thorough industrialization of Germany after 1840, the nation failed to modernize in social and political terms. Calling Germany a "belated nation" (Plessner's phrase) has become a truism of German historiography. The retention of a semi-feudal social structure and the anti-Enlightenment bases of German nationalism ensured the rejection of political modernism with its democratic ideals and institutions. The *völkisch* ideologies, predictably, condemned the rational, contractual society (*Gesellschaft*) as inferior to the organic community of the *Volksgemeinschaft*. The former was capable of producing only a superficial, trivial *Zivilisation* (always a pejorative in the nationalist context), while the latter created the depth, breadth and authenticity of a true, rooted *Kultur*. The famous quarrel of the Mann brothers on this point was only a late formulation of a longstanding debate.[55]

The superiority of *Kultur* was so firmly seated in the German mind that when German writers referred to "European" culture, they meant German culture plus classical antiquity. Thus one can find such sentences as this one, in the introduction to a chronicle of the war obviously intended for bourgeois consumption: "Brazenly strikes the heavy hammer of fate against the proudly towering temple of European culture. As its guardian and protector the German people (*Germanentum*) fight the bitter struggle against Gallic revenge, Slavic barbarism, and the English shopkeeper's spirit."[56] While the inflated bellicose rhetoric, though far from rare, is especially typical of 1914, the sense of beleaguered superiority is characteristic of pre-war thought. The German conviction of encirclement (*Einkreisung*) by hostile but spiritually inferior forces owes much more to cultural perceptions than to political realities, as does the paranoid xenophobia of the Weimar period. As was the case with Gläser's fictional bourgeois lady, politics per se were of no interest, but political ideas masquerading in cultural dress were vastly more persuasive than facts, figures and rational discourse.

---

[55]Sombart's *Händler und Helden* is one of the classic formulations of the argument. The quarrel between the brothers Mann began early in the war and outlasted it. They were reconciled on this point only in 1922. See T. Mann, *Briefe I* (Frankfurt am. Main: Fischer, 1961).

[56]*Der Krieg: Illustrierte Chronik des Krieges, 1914* (Stuttgart: Frankh'sche Verlag, 1914) 1:1. "Ehern schlägt des Schicksals schwerer Hammer gegen den stolzragenden Tempelbau europäischer Kultur. Als sein Hüter und Schirmherr ficht das Germanentum den bittern Kampf gegen gallische Rachsucht, slawische Barbarei und englischen Krämergeist." The German obsession with *Kultur* was evident to many foreign observers. During the war purported German atrocities in Belgium and France led foreign cartoonists to equate the much-vaunted German *Kultur* with barbarism. See especially John Grand-Carteret's collection of European cartoons on the subject in a volume from the series Caricatures et images de guerre called *La Kultur et ses hauts faits* (Paris: Chapelot, 1916) 29, 35, 49 and 76.

Education

The young soldiers of 1914 had grown up in the stability of a unified German Empire. For many, the empire represented the fulfillment of the dreams of generations of nationalists.[57] For others, the unity was material and superficial, lacking true spiritual wholeness. Nevertheless, the authority of the Prussian state that had brought about that unity was bolstered by traditional Prussian ideals of duty to state and monarch, and by the equally important traditions of order, discipline and avoidance of politics, particularly among the bourgeoisie.[58] In spite of liberal and socialist discontent, the population of Wilhelmine Germany was overwhelmingly nationalist, idealist and apolitical. Middle-class boys absorbed the pervasive nationalism at home, at the great national festivals, and preeminently at school.

The national system of public education, which had been centralized in Berlin in 1871, formed the most important conduit for the inculcation of nationalist ideas in young minds. One of the enduring legacies of the European nationalist revival movements of the late nineteenth century was the establishment of national systems of public education, among whose goals was the implantation of patriotic nationalism. Such tendencies were as obvious in France as in Germany, while Britain was far less systematic and centralized than the continental powers.[59] Public school systems, especially those serving the bourgeoisie, were inevitably nationalistic, given the parallel rise of nation states, of the bourgeoisie and of what Benedict Anderson calls print-capitalism. As Anderson points out, " . . . an illiterate bourgeoisie is scarcely imaginable. Thus in world-historical terms bourgeoisies were the first classes to achieve solidarities on an essentially imagined basis."[60] What Anderson is suggesting is that the national state as an "imagined community" is far more dependent upon a literate bourgeoisie, and therefore upon education, than upon political or even social institutions. The bourgeois investment in the national state consequently secured the virtual inevitability of national and nationalist education.

Education, Eksteins maintains, was the most important human component of Germany's rise to industrial and military preeminence in Europe by 1914. In some parts of Germany, compulsory elementary education predated the 1870s

---

[57]Ecksteins, *Rites,* 67; Hermand, *Der alte Traum,* 47–56.

[58]The transmission of Prussian values and the co-optation of the Prussian national image (especially of Frederick the Great) by the German Empire is ably explored in S. D. Stirk, *The Prussian Spirit, 1914–1940* (Port Washington, N.Y.: Kennikat, 1969).

[59]See Mary Cadogan and Patricia Craig, *Women and Children First: The Fiction of the Two World Wars* (London: Gollancz, 1978) for a discussion of British attitudes. On French views see Marieluise Christadler, *Kriegserziehung im Jugendbuch: Literarische Mobilmachung in Deutschland und Frankreich vor 1914* (Frankfurt am Main: Haag, 1978).

[60]Anderson, *Imagined Communities,* 74.

by several decades.[61] The German bias toward spiritual values and the commitment to individual spiritual development in the characteristic German form of *Bildung* (part of the Classic-Romantic heritage), were evident in the educational ideals and practices of the Empire. In 1908, for example, the regulations for elementary schools aimed at providing "valuable and worthy content" for the mind, not at the teaching of critical thinking.[62] The curriculum included the teaching of the scriptures, "at least twenty" hymns, fluent reading and writing in German, the principle works of the poets and some information on their lives, arithmetic, geometry, history, geography (aimed at providing a knowledge of near surroundings and historical phenomena), drawing, singing and gymnastics, with, for females, needlework and domestics.[63]

The last decade of the nineteenth century saw substantial reforms in the secondary system, leading first to the modernization of the system, and second to the ever-increasing penetration of Romantic nationalism into its curriculum. Prior to 1901 only the classical *Gymnasia* could grant leaving certificates for entrance into the university, thus effectively curtailing the growth of the modern languages and of technical occupations. Studies at the classical *Gymnasium* were meant to increase aesthetic and literary culture and "exert a formative influence on the intellectual faculties."[64] For a nation in the grip of the most rapid industrialization in Western Europe, such aims were clearly inadequate for the technological and social needs of the country, and pressure for reform was correspondingly high. In 1890, and again in 1900, national conferences on the reform of secondary education triggered lengthy quarrels between the "ancients" and "moderns," but in 1901 all three types of high school (classical, modern and technical) were allowed to grant the coveted leaving certificates.

The rout of the partisans of classical education had been partly accomplished by the personal intervention of Wilhelm II in both conferences. He encouraged modernization, but above all urged that the character of secondary study should be uniformly German, national and patriotic. He insisted, predictably, that the study of modern life and modern history, that is, the war of 1870 and the founding of the Second Empire, were far more valuable for the education of youth than the study of classical antiquity. Wilhelm's insistence opened the way for the study of the modern nationalist historians, notably Treitschke, and to the teaching of historical figures and events from a nationalist perspective — Arminius, the Saxons, Barbarossa and the Wars of Liberation to name but the most important. Along with German history, German lan-

---

[61]Ecksteins, *Rites of Spring*, 71.

[62]Friederich Paulsen, *German Education: Past and Present*, tr. T. Lorenz, (London: Unwin, 1908) 250. This volume provides a valuable contemporary survey of education under the Second Empire.

[63]Paulsen, 253.

[64]Paulsen, 201.

guage and literature occupied an ever larger place in the curriculum at the expense of both modern and ancient languages.[65]

By the beginning of the twentieth century, the German Empire had become, in the elder Moltke's words, "the educator of the nation." Under an authoritarian Ministry of Education, German education aimed to instill a sense of "work and serious performance of duty . . . diligence, punctuality, love of order, cleanliness and virtue."[66] The main subjects of the *Gymnasium*, as one critic later put it, were "patriotism, Latin and Greek."[67] Rooted in Fichte and Turnvater Jahn, this combination of individual and national goals was, ultimately, intended to produce not only good citizens, but good soldiers. *Gymnasium* students were pressured by teachers and parents to volunteer for military service, rather than waiting for the usual conscription. Such volunteers were required to serve only one year and earned thereby the socially important position of reserve officer.[68] The nationalism had become not only militant, but militaristic. German education, as Christadler's title suggests, was "education for war" (*Kriegserziehung*).[69]

At this point, a brief comparison with the English ethos of the gentleman educated on the "playing fields," be they at Eton or elsewhere, is illuminating. Although there are some concrete points in common — the emphasis on physical exercise, the inculcation of steadfast loyalty to one's comrades, the sense of belonging to a larger group — the irrational metaphysics behind the German scheme are entirely absent from English thought. There is no English counterpart to Fichte or Jahn, nor an English equivalent to the German concept of authority. Moreover, as Cadogan and Craig have noted in their analysis of British adolescent reading material, the values asserted by such fiction include patriotism, chivalry and decency, qualities also emphasized in German works, but also the more English virtues of fair play and "sporty heroics."[70] Such values accord well with the apocryphal story of the British regiment that initiated its Somme attack by kicking a football across No Man's Land. The importance of sport, and of war as sport, can scarcely be overstated in the context of First World War Britain.[71] The *Turnvereine* and *Schutzvereine* of Germany come

[65]V. H. Friedel, *Pédagogie de guerre allemande* (Paris: Fishbacher, 1918), 136. As Friedel's book was published during the war, his views must be regarded with some scepticism. See also Glaser, *Cultural Roots,* 118; Christadler, *Kriegserziehung,* 9–13, and Ille and Köhler, *Der Wandervogel,* 32–33.

[66]Qtd. in Ille and Köhler, *Der Wandervogel,* 31.

[67]Qtd. in Ille and Köhler, *Der Wandervogel,* 30.

[68]Ille and Köhler, *Der Wandervogel,* 37. At the outbreak of war, young men who volunteered for service (*Kriegsfreiwillige*) also received preferential treatment.

[69]See Ille and Köhler, 150.

[70]Cadogan and Craig, *Women and Children First,* 71–81.

[71]Fussell, *Great War,* 25–29.

from a more earnest patriotic tradition conditioned by historical disunity, regionalism, and the persistence of folk customs.

In that tradition, authoritarianism shaped every aspect of German society, from the paternal authority of the father within the family to the authority of a minister over his flock, a teacher over his students, or the Kaiser over his subjects. Ludwig Renn, who later became a communist, venomously castigated that tradition in *Nachkrieg* (1930, translated as *After War*, 1931), his novel of postwar Germany, and drew the link between education, the army and political responsibility:

> The cursed drill in the army was to blame for one's not being able to speak one's mind. . . . And even as a child they bedeviled you with obedience and love to your parents and the priest and the teacher. A funny kind of love that made you stupid! One must root out all these feelings that were inoculated into one. And the older generation were already on the pounce to set up all this authority again.[72]

It is worth noting in this context that Renn (a pseudonym) came from an aristocratic military family, and is clearly railing against his own authoritarian upbringing, one that was certainly similar to that of many young men from the aristocracy and the *Bildungsburgertum*.[73]

For the students of the German Empire, the authority of the school teacher, especially the secondary school professor, was very broad. Professors had a great deal of security, and the German respect for learning ensured that they were treated with deference. Wilhelm II enhanced the new social prestige of schoolmasters by his assertion that they were the educators of the nation.[74] Hermann Glaser has drawn attention to the reactionary professorial spirit, sundered from the ideas of the Enlightenment and steeped in the irrationality of Romantic nationalism.[75] They supplemented the nationalist curriculum with their own conservative and often militaristic views. Ernst Gläser ridicules both the patriotic professor on the train, and his narrator's preposterous gymnastics master, who is the only teacher excused from military service because he is

---

[72]Ludwig Renn, (pseud. of Arnold Friederich Vieth von Glossenau) *Nachkrieg* (Berlin: Agis-Verlag, 1930; reprint, Berlin: Aufbau, 1985). Tr. by Edwin and Willa Muir as *After War* (London: Secker, 1931), 176. "Das kam von dem verfluchten Drill beim Militär, daß man so einem Krautkopf nicht die Wahrheit sagen konnte! Und schon als Kind haben sie einen eingefuchst auf Gehorsam und Liebe gegen die Eltern und Pastor und Lehrer! Das ist doch eine komische Liebe, die einen dumm macht! Man muß dieses eingebleute Gefühl zerstören! Dabei sind die Leute von gestern eben wieder im Begriff, diese Autorität neu aufzurichten" (450).

[73]See Ille and Köhler, *Der Wandervogel*, for a description of the Bildungsburgertum of Steglitz at the turn of the century. See also Tom Taylor, "Images of Youth and the Family in Wilhelmine Germany: Toward a Reconsideration of the German Sonderweg," *German Studies Review* 15 (winter, 1992):55–73.

[74]Rudolf Schenda, *Die Lesestoffe der kleinen Leute* (München: Beck, 1976), 82–83.

[75]Glaser, *Cultural Roots*, 107–109.

"indispensable for the military training of the young."[76] The most familiar literary example is easily the ranting schoolmaster Kantorek in Remarque's *All Quiet*, who shepherds his whole class of boys to volunteer.[77] His radical militarism is even more vividly portrayed in the 1930 film of the novel.

While French and English school systems could also be accused — and were — of indoctrinating their students with nationalistic ideas, German nationalism, as taught by authoritarian professors, had one unique characteristic: the belief that struggle was an inherent part of individual and national life. Drawing, as always, on vitalist ideas, life was seen as a constant battle for survival and war as an essential component in that general struggle.[78] Like the German *Volk*, battle was identified as an irresistible force of nature. Typically the Wars of Liberation and of 1870 provided historical confirmation of Romantic metaphysics. Struggle, and its most extreme expression, war, were elevated to the level of metaphysical and natural necessity; through the teaching of patriotic pedagogues, war became a national necessity. In his 1912 book *Der vaterländische Gedanke in der Jugendliteratur*, Wilhelm Kotzde, after affirming the need for "vaterländische Erziehung" (patriotic education) and "ein deutsche Kultur voll Kraft und Männlichkeit" (a German culture full of force and manliness), insisted that war was "der Markstein deutschen Lebens" (the boundrystone of German life).[79] In short, struggle was both healthy and right, a necessary event without which nothing of value could be attained.[80] As Christadler correctly points out, the whole ideology of battle suggests that the surrounding world is hostile, and in effect rules out the possibility of a peaceful solution of differences, far less of peaceful coexistence. That, in turn, contributed significantly to the German eagerness for war in 1914, and the ecstasy with which the declaration was welcomed.[81]

The ideology of battle permeated both the content and language of German nationalism. It was particularly evident in the youth literature of the Wilhelmine period examined by Christadler. In that literature, the army was the "die Schule der Nation" (the school of the nation), war "ein Stahlbad auf dem Weg zum Erwachsensein" (a steel-bath on the journey to adulthood) and "eine Probe der Männlichkeit" (a test of manhood).[82] The 1870 war and the Wars of Liberation (whose centennial took place in 1913) were favored subjects.[83] The titles of

[76]Gläser, *Class of 1902*, 318.

[77]Remarque, *All Quiet*, 17–20.

[78]Christadler, *Kriegserziehung*, 71.

[79]Qtd. in Schenda, *Die Lesestoffe*, 84–85.

[80]Christadler, *Kriegserziehung*, 72.

[81]Christadler, 73.

[82]Christadler, 74.

[83]Christadler, 117.

many adolescent books display the bellicose idiom: "Der Kampf um . . . " (The Struggle for . . .), "Die Schlacht bei . . . " (The Battle at . . .), and, to glorify the offensive, "Der Sturm auf . . . " (The Storming of . . .).[84] Similar titles frequently occur as chapter headings in the conservative First World War narratives, and if any further evidence should be needed to establish the persistence of the diction of battle through the Second World War, one need only mention Hitler's *Mein Kampf* and the central position of the concept and terminology of struggle in National Socialist ideology.

In summary, then, by about 1910 the dominant direction of German education was, as Schallenberger expressed it, the "glorification of power, the heroism of war, and the absoluteness of the national idea."[85] This education for war worked primarily through the commitment to war as a necessary part of the natural order of things and through the omnipresence of German nationalism. Students bombarded at home and in the classroom with the traditional chauvinism of the Wilhelmine bourgeois and mythical images of the glory of war supplemented their Romantic nationalism with the *völkisch* ideas of the youth movement, especially those of the Wandervögel.

The German Youth Movement

The German youth movement, born in the Steglitz section of Berlin in 1901 as a protest against the materialistic bourgeois society of the older generation, exerted considerable and direct influence on its young members, and an extended, less easily documented influence on middle-class society. It was composed of a number of separate groups, most of which eventually joined together under the general aegis of the name Wandervogel. In the unpolitical German tradition, the movement sought to revitalize the individual spirit, and through it the national spirit. The heart of this youthful revolt lay in its Romantic qualities: idealism, vitalism, emotionalism, and irrationalism veneered with medievalism and love of country. In keeping with such ideals, the boys — and later, girls — yearned to shape their own lives "at their own initiative, on their own responsibility, and with deep sincerity."[86] This, the *Freideutsche* formula of 1913, reflects

---

[84]Christadler, 73, 79. On the European obsession with the offensive in the first decade of the century, see Stephen Van Evera, "The Cult of the Offensive and the Origins of the First World War," in *Military Strategy and the Origins of the First World War,* Steven E. Miller, ed., (Princeton: Princeton UP, 1985), 58–107, and Michael Howard, "Men against Fire: Expectations of War in 1914," in the same volume, 41–57.

[85]Qtd. in Christadler, 9. " . . . die Verherrlichung der Macht, Heroisierung des Krieges, Verabsolutierung der nationalen Idee."

[86]Laqueur, *Young Germany,* 31. The inclusion of girls in the movement largely took place after 1914; the inherent anti-Semitism of the movement never altered.

not only the basic Romanticism of the movement, but the importance of individual development, emotional sincerity and authenticity.[87]

As was the case in the French nationalist revival, the young generation was seen as a redeeming force in a degenerate society.[88] In Germany, however, that function was colored by the widely-held and influential ideas of social Darwinism. The application of Darwinian science to human society created a pseudo-science committed to frankly racist social ideals. Young people would obviously play a large role in the biological regeneration and strengthening of the *Volk*. The principles of natural selection and the struggle for existence also accorded well with the organic model of vitalist philosophy, particularly in its application to national history.[89]

The ideology of the Wandervögel was essentially *völkisch* in nature and particularly influenced by the ideas of Lagarde and Langbehn. The latter's emphasis on all facets of peasant life and on the natural harmony of the organic *Volk* encouraged the Wandervögel in their Romantic attachment to the fatherland. Their patriotism was emotional, vitalist and based on deep devotion to German nature.[90] Their activities centered primarily on the concept of *das Wandern*, rambling or hiking.[91] This organized exploration of the countryside (it is worth remembering that most of these boys belonged to the urban middle class) fulfilled three aims. First, it made possible the rediscovery of nature, specifically of the German landscape, and of the simple, rooted rural life of the *Volk* in its own landscape. Second, it created a situation in which an emotional and philosophical bond could develop between members of the group — a prototypical comradeship. In imitation of the wandering scholars of the Middle Ages, the Wandervögel revived medieval titles and customs to strengthen the bonds between them. Finally, they searched for the roots of German culture in folklore and folksong, which further linked them to the history of the *Volk* and the glories of the German Middle Ages. These activities converged to create a love of country that was based on personal experience, rather than on the conventional ideals of service to the *Reich* that shaped the patriotism of their parents.[92]

[87]The best recent examination of the history and ideology of the Wandervogel is Ille and Köhler, *Der Wandervogel*, cited above.

[88]Wohl, *The Generation of 1914*, 205–206; Ille and Köhler, *Der Wandervogel*, 40.

[89]Ille and Köhler, *Der Wandervogel*, 43–44. See Stachelberg, *Idealism Debased* for a detailed analysis of social Darwinism and the ideas of Houston Stewart Chamberlain, and Hermand, *Der alte Traum*, 71–83 for the spread of those ideas in *völkisch* ideology.

[90]Ille and Köhler, 43–47.

[91]*Das Wandern* connotes hiking and camping in the countryside without a fixed geographical destination, but with the intention of exploring the beauties of nature and the traditional life of the country. Although the Wandervögel claimed to be imitating the wandering scholars of the Middle Ages, the ramblings of the German Romantic poets are more pertinent.

[92]Laqueur, *Young Germany*, 5, 8–9; Mosse, *Crisis*, 173.

When the war came, the Wandervögel shared the general enthusiasm and the feeling of oneness with *Volk* and fatherland.[93] As Ille has shown, the prewar Wandervogel had universally tended to romanticize, sentimentalize and glorify war. The younger members were very fond of war games set in medieval times, while older members eagerly collected and sang battle and soldier's songs from the Thirty Years War and the Wars of Liberation. Such attitudes are also mirrored in the conviction that the war was a crusade of the "German" against Western civilization.[94] Once faced with modern warfare, disillusion was inevitable. A former Wandervogel who served in the war wrote that they believed before the war that "death in battle was the crowning point of life," but now "when the bullets whistle around one, then everyone thinks: if only it won't hit *me*, not me, or at least not this time."[95] Despite the realities of the war, the monthly *Wandervogel* magazine continued to publish patriotic songs and romanticized illustrations of cavalry.[96]

Some 14,000 Wandervögel saw service in the war, and twenty-five percent fell dead.[97] Ille states that by 1918 one-third of the Steglitz Wandervögel were dead.[98] The influence of the Wandervogel on those of its members who went to war is difficult to assess. There are ample letters, but with the exception of one narrative, there are only a few scattered references to the Wandervogel in the narratives of the First World War, and those are usually generalized to sleeping under the stars or singing folksongs, and may not refer to the youth movement at all. The one book, Walter Flex's memoir of his friend Ernst Wurche, *Der Wanderer zwischen beiden Welten* (The Wanderer between Two Worlds, 1915) is essentially a glorification of Wurche as the ideal Wandervogel, and thus as the ideal German. As a German theologian, Wurche also embodies the knightly and medieval ideals so dear to the Wandervögel.[99]

Although there is little concrete evidence, the influence of the Wandervogel may have worked on the young soldiers of 1914 in subtle ways. Alongside the militaristic nationalism learned in school and in society, and the Romantic idealism that supported it, those who had been involved with the youth movement had undoubtedly imbibed a more *völkisch* brand of nationalism formed on an emotional oneness with others and with the fatherland. There is plenty of evidence in descriptions of the German landscape to show that many soldiers were deeply and emotionally attached to the very land of home, and not merely to

---

[93]Laqueur, *Young Germany*, 87; Ille and Köhler, 154–158.

[94]Ille and Köhler, *Der Wandervogel*, 156.

[95]Qtd. in Ille and Köhler, 156.

[96]See the illustrations in Ille and Köhler, 170–192.

[97]Laqueur, *Young Germany*, 97.

[98]Ille and Köhler, 168.

[99]See Keller's excellent analysis of this text 41-52, and Ille and Köhler, 182–185.

some abstract idea of the nation. More importantly, the emphasis upon emotional belonging typical of the youth movement may have prepared young men for the experience of comradeship, and indeed to have predisposed them to place that affective bond at the center of their war experience. Their "education for war" had not prepared them for the realities of 1914, but it had schooled them to order their experience within a given philosophical framework. Unlike the thorough ideological disillusionment of their English opponents, the edifice of German philosophy never collapsed — it was just remodeled by the war veterans. The children of this crusade were slaughtered in their millions, but the survivors kept the faith.

LEUR FAÇON DE FAIRE LA GUERRE
Dessin de GEORGES SCOTT.

The French view of German Kultur.
Drawing by Georges Scott, L'Illustration, *29 August 1914 (165).*

3: The Experience of War

The Problem of Experience

Passionate — that means to live for the sake of living. But one knows that you all live for the sake of experience. Passion, that is self-forgetfulness. But what you all want is self-enrichment. C'est ça- You don't realize what revolting egoism it is, and that one day it will make you an enemy of the human race?

Clavdia Chauchat to Hans Castorp

This exchange takes place in Thomas Mann's *Der Zauberberg (The Magic Mountain)*, published in 1924, but begun before the First World War. In that seminal conversation, Mann confronts the central position of *Erlebnis* (experience) in German thought. One critic has suggested that knowledge is the subject of the novel; more properly, the subject is experience and its uses.[1] Clavdia, herself a creature of the passion she describes, defines and denigrates the German obsession with the cultivation of the self, and with the catalyst in that process, experience. Through her Mann distinguishes between experience qua experience, what Clavdia calls living for its own sake, and experience as an educational process contributing to greater individual development, that is, *Bildung*, a goal that she identifies with German egoism. As Bruford has demonstrated, *Bildung* —the unimpeded development of one's resources of mind — came to be regarded in Goethe's time as a form of salvation.[2] Such an endeavor must not be regarded as purely intellectual or rational, although it encompasses cultural learning. On the contrary, self-cultivation in the tradition of *Bildung* is to a great extent moral and emotional.[3] That is, it aims to build an ideal character through the agency of human experience. Within the context of German Romantic thought, experience (and this is the crucial distinction) forms the core of the spiritual and emotional education of the individual. No purely rational learning can generate the profound spiritual metamorphosis inherent in the organic concept of *Bildung*. Without experience there can be no *Bildung*. Just as

[1]W. H. Bruford, *The German Tradition of Self-cultivation: "Bildung" from Humboldt to Thomas Mann* (Cambridge: Cambridge UP, 1975), 206.

[2]Bruford, vii. Like the words *Bildung* and *Erlebnis*, *Erlösung* (salvation) carries considerable connotative weight, and is, also like the others, a key word in radical nationalist ideology. See Peter S. Fisher, *Fantasy and Politics: Visions of the Future in the Weimar Republic* (Madison: U of Wisconsin P, 1991), 101–102 for a discussion of its implications.

[3]Bruford, 5–28.

true *Bildung* comprises two complementary components, cultural learning and spiritual development, *Erlebnis* likewise exhibits an external, factual aspect and an internal, spiritual one, the latter being more significant than the former. The strong irrationalist currents of thought in the early twentieth century encouraged what Sontheimer calls the breakthrough of the category of experience. Man yearned, he says, to sense the mystical, supernatural powers flowing through the world, to penetrate to the essence of things, and to feel the "creative power of experience."[4] By the outbreak of the First World War, experience was not only individually, but collectively creative. One could share a common experience and the bond it created with one's *Volk*, or what is more pertinent to this inquiry, with one's fellow Wandervögel or one's comrades-in-arms.[5] This form of *Erlebnis* in turn contributed to a collective spiritual development that underlies the German literary interpretation of the First World War. The *Kriegserlebnis* that emerges from the German narratives is that of the *German* soldier. It embodies the German myth of the war as surely as the poetry of Sassoon and Owen embodies the English myth of the war.[6]

The centrality of *Erlebnis* in the German literature is such that Sontheimer can call it an *Erlebnisliteratur*, and sympathize with writers of the Second World War who had their own experiences, but not "das *eine* Kreigserlebnis" (the *one* war experience).[7] Many of the conservative narratives, significantly, are subtitled with some form of the word *Erlebnis*: "*ein Kriegserlebnis*" (a war experience), "*ein Fronterlebnis*" (an experience of the front), "*ein Erlebnis aus dem grossen Krieg*" (an experience from the Great War), and so on. A writer who uses such a term is attempting to convey two things to the reader: first, the completeness of the experience, including its transformative power, and second, the meaning of the experience on individual and collective levels. The wholeness and therefore the power of an *Erlebnis* depend on its being both a physical and a psychological event. The psychological component is indubitably the more important, but cannot exist apart from the physical experience. That wholeness endows it with immense transformative power for the man who undergoes the experience. He emerges from the experience as a changed man; the change is inward and positive, however terrible the experience itself may have been. Herf has correctly de-

---

[4]Sontheimer, *Antidemokratisches Denken*, 48, 53.

[5]Klaus Theweleit, *Männerphantasien* (Frankfurt am Main: Roter Stern, 1978) underlines the importance of large crowds sharing a great experience in the ideology and activities of the National Socialists, 2:137–138.

[6]Experience is less important in the English tradition than in the German, firstly because it is not a part of an organic schema of character development, and therefore sui generis positive and creative. Many British writers see the experience of war as inherently destructive. Secondly, there is less tendency in the British context to see experience as collective — except as collectively meaningless suffering.

[7]Sontheimer, 115.

fined the experience of the First World War as a cultic initiation that altered souls.[8] Günther Lutz, writing what purports to be an analysis of the war novels, but is actually a paean to the myth of the *Kriegserlebnis* (and to its foremost representative, Adolf Hitler), emphasizes the antinomy of outer and inner. The external history of the war is well-known, he says, but one must also know the "innere Entwicklungsgeschichte" (inner developmental history).[9] By implication, it is the inner development that matters, because that is where the "true" meaning of the war is to be found. Obviously, the emphasis on "inner" experience both subjectifies it and removes it from the "outer" realm of verifiable incident.

It is here that one must confront the vexed question of authenticity in war writing. Jean Norton Cru, in his formidable study *Témoins*, outlines the problem with French precision. "The public," he says, "accepts ordinary novels as fiction, but takes war novels seriously, as if they were depositions."[10] This tendency of the reading public to accept war narratives as "true" confers on such narratives an air of unimpeachable authenticity, an authenticity bolstered by the frequent use of first person narration and by realistic, even gruesome, description. In the case of the German narratives, the cultural primacy of experience reinforced belief in the genuineness of the original experience. And on that authenticity is predicated the meaning of the war for the nation and for the men who fought.

The question of meaning in war is invariably hedged about by the need to compensate for human loss and suffering, and to justify victory or defeat. For a victorious nation, the meaning of the war lies in the victory itself, which renders the suffering meaningful and tolerable while confirming national values. But for a defeated nation, the question of meaning becomes an imperative search for explanation and justification amid the ruin of belief. The need to justify and explain who they were and what they had become was particularly urgent for the defeated German soldiers, many of whom felt not so much defeated as betrayed. The pivotal impact of war was early recognized by Ernst Jünger in his famous essay "Der Krieg als inneres Erlebnis" (War as inner Experience, 1925): "The war, father of all things, is also our father; he has hammered, chiseled and tempered us into what we are. And as long as life's whirling wheel turns in us, this

---

[8]Jeffrey Herf, *Reactionary Modernism* (Cambridge: Cambridge UP, 1984), 32. In his *Die Literatur des soldatischen Nationalismus der 20er Jahre* (Kronberg: Scriptor, 1974), 9, Karl Prümm states that soldiers defined the war as "ihrem zentralen Bildungserlebnis" (their central educational experience.)

[9]Günther Lutz, *Das Gemeinschaftserlebnis in der Kriegsliteratur* (Greifswald: Adler, 1936), 9.

[10]Jean Norton Cru, *Témoins* (Paris: Les Etincelles, 1929) 50. "La publique prend des romans ordinaires pour fictions, mais prend des romans de guerre au sérieux et comme des dépositions."

war will be the axle around which it whirls."[11] Significantly, the question is not only of individual but of collective and national meaning. Although he was writing after the National Socialist accession to power, Werner Picht crystallizes the impact of the lost war when he says that, "no explanation of this time or our existence is thinkable that does not use the war as a point of departure. And the constantly renewed question of the war's meaning or meaninglessness has such fearful urgency because it is a question of the meaning or meaninglessness of our own existence."[12] By using the phrase "our existence," Picht reintroduces the question of authenticity. The veteran's present — that is, postwar — existence is explicable and meaningful only in relation to his experience of the war, and that experience is preeminently an inner, spiritual one.

The pivotal position of the *Kriegserlebnis* depends, to a great extent, on its simultaneous subjectivity and collectivity. The verifiable external facts of the experience are never really in question. An English account of the physical effects of shelling on the landscape or the human body does not differ significantly from a German or French one. Given the geography and climate of the western front, physical conditions were much the same for all the combatants. One trench was as muddy, one soldier as lice-infested and one shell as destructive as another. The accounts diverge in the soldier's psychological reaction to events. And in Germany, with its heritage of "inwardness" and irrationalism, the authenticity of the *Kriegserlebnis* lies in the soldier's feelings and emotional solidarity with his comrades. Since the experience is essentially an emotional one, its "truth," that is, its authenticity, is undebatable. One cannot establish the factual veracity of feelings; one can only, based on one's own experience, sympathize with them, or reject them as alien and "untrue."

The debate that erupted in 1929 over *All Quiet on the Western Front* centers on the veracity of the *Kriegserlebnis* the book depicts. Remarque's novel, and the narratives that followed it, were praised or attacked on the basis of whether or not they told the "truth" about the soldier's experience of the First World War. And that "truth" was, almost without exception, determined by the critic's own experience, or his political views, or both.[13] That critical stance produced a spate of claims to "truth" in war books of all sorts. Beyond the subtitles incorporating

[11]Jünger, *Werke*, 5:13–14. "Der Krieg, aller Dinge Vater, ist auch der unsere; er hat uns gehämmert, gemeißelt und gehärtet zu dem, was wir sind. Und immer, solange des Lebens schwingendes Rad noch in uns kreist, wird dieser Krieg die Achse sein, um die es schwirrt."

[12]Werner Picht, *Der Frontsoldat* (Berlin: Herbig, 1937), 11. "Keine Deutung dieser Zeit und unseres Dasein ist denkbar, die nicht von ihm [dem Weltkrieg] ausginge. Und das immer neue Fragen, das um seinen Sinn oder seine Sinnlosigkeit kreist, hat diese fast angstvolle Eindringlichkeit, weil es sich dabei um Sinn oder Sinnlosigkeit unserer eigenen Existenz handelt."

[13]See Michael Gollbach, *Die Wiederkehr des Weltkrieges in der Literatur* (Kronberg/Taunus: Scriptor, 1978) for a systematic review of the critical reception of the war narratives. For a more recent analysis, see Hans-Harald Müller, *Der Krieg und die Schriftsteller: Der Kriegsroman der Weimarer Republik* (Stuttgart: Metzler, 1986).

some form of the word *Erlebnis*, which are, in themselves, claims to authenticity, authors frequently supplemented their claims with a prefatory statement asserting the intention of "telling the truth" or, like Georg Bucher, providing "an undistorted picture of what the war in the West was really like."[14]

Such claims, not of verisimilitude, but of absolute truth, form the kernel of the debate on the significance of the war that was touched off by the publication of Remarque's *All Quiet*. The flood of criticism, accusation, counter-accusation, debate and character assassination swirled around whether or not Remarque had written a "true" book, not whether he had written a good one. I shall examine the political myth-making of the war books in the final years of the Weimar Republic in a later chapter, but the lasting heritage of the cult of the *Kriegserlebnis* is the reduction of literary criticism to political and ethical debate. Sixty years of such "criticism" has produced the inevitable division of the German war narratives into pro- and anti-war categories, and resulted in the elevation of *All Quiet* to the position of First World War novel par excellence. The simultaneous reduction of the so-called pro-war novels to pre-Nazi propaganda has sabotaged any serious examination of them as aesthetic or historical documents.[15]

A re-evaluation of the German First World War narratives must therefore begin with the *Kriegserlebnis* itself, and answer three questions: First, what was the German soldier's experience of warfare as depicted in these narratives? Second, what was the soldier's reaction to that experience? And finally, how did it change him, and what lessons did he draw from it? The remainder of this chapter will attempt to answer those questions.

Separations

The soldier on his way to war separates himself irrevocably from the life he has known. The young soldiers of the First World War were no exception. After the heady national exaltation of August, the war led to an inevitable and, in most cases, welcome departure from the confines of ordinary life. For a generation whose self-image included revolt against the industrialized, bourgeois society of their elders, the war represented the antithesis of those societal restrictions, and an opportunity to realize romantic-heroic ideals.

---

[14]Georg Bucher, *Westfront 1914–1918. Das Buch vom Frontkameraden* (Wien-Leipzig: Konegan, 1930). Tr. by Norman Gullick as *In the Line: 1914–1918* (London: Cape 1932), 14. " . . . war doch alles so geschrieben, wie die unverzerrte, traurige Wirklichkeit im Westen einst war" (Forword).

[15]The judgment of most English-speaking critics is shaped by the association of good writing with the anti-war stance typical of the British paradigm of war experience, for example, Sassoon, Graves et al.

In his perceptive *No Man's Land*, Eric Leed maintains that for the combatants, war is an initiatory experience which can only be shared with other initiates.[16] Initiatory rites in folklore often begin with a journey to an "otherworld" in which the candidate's courage is tested. If found worthy, he returns to his own world as an initiate, and thus a changed man.[17] This "there and back again" pattern so typical of folklore, *Kunstmärchen* and quest literature, and later of the German version of the Bildungsroman, is also typical of the German Great War narratives. Like the pattern of *Bildung* achieved through *Erlebnis*, the significance lies in its essential creativity. Although many men failed to survive the test of combat, the focus is on those who returned home with a new concept of life and society drawn from the experience of the labyrinthine "otherworld" of the trenches.

That experience begins with the distancing of the characters from familiar surroundings through the device of the journey to the front. In most accounts, the vast majority of which are chronological, the initiate's journey is both actual and spiritual. Those narratives which do not begin in the trenches, in medias res, open in basic training or, more frequently, on the train to the front. The use of trains is more than a literary device; the notoriously efficient German railways were the main means of transportation for both men and materiel. In *War by Timetable*, A. J. P. Taylor has advanced the famous argument that the rigidity of the railway timetables on which mobilization depended actually precipitated Europe into war, because the schedules couldn't be altered and they permitted such rapid mobilization that there was no time for diplomatic activity.[18] Whatever the validity of Taylor's arguments, Germany was fighting on two fronts, and the trains moved the men, animals, and materiel east and west. The journeys were usually long (several days to a week or more for the eastern front), bone-jarringly uncomfortable, and disquietingly unfamiliar. Unlike the comfortable railway journeys of the bourgeois past, the ride to the front is a journey into the unknown, whose successive stages gradually detach the protagonist from the certainties of the past. Such journeys often begin with a patriotic appreciation of the homeland. Kröner, for example, riding to the western front, describes at length the beauties of the German countryside and proclaims the Rhine to be the "most German" of all rivers.[19] For those on westward journeys,

---

[16]Eric J. Leed, *No Man's Land: Combat and Identity in World War I* (Cambridge: Cambridge UP, 1979), 12.

[17]Stith Thompson, *Motif-Index of Folk Literature*, 4 vols. (Bloomington: Indiana UP, 1975). See vol. 3, F0–F199 for "Otherworld Journeys," H1250–1299 for "Quests to the Otherworld," and H1400 for "Tests of Fear."

[18]A. J. P. Taylor, *War by Timetable* (London: McDonald, 1969).

[19]Richard Kröner, *Landser. Im Westen viel Neues. Das Buch des Frontsoldaten in vier Jahren Krieg* (Chemnitz: Pickenhahn, 1931), 11–12. The beauty of the countryside (used ironically or seri-

the Rhine became the Rubicon — an irrevocable step on the road to war.[20] Ludwig Renn, a more detached observer, provides the classic account of the long, slow train ride in *Krieg* (*War*, 1929). The soldiers ride in freight cars, while the officers rate a third-class carriage. The typical mobilization jokes are chalked on the sides of the carriages:

> Unusually favorable offer!!!
> Free Trips!
> Only risk, a few shots!
> Direct to Paris!![21]

When the train pulls out, the first concern of the men is whether they are going east or west; this time "it's going to Paris" (10), which is greeted with cheers and the singing of "Deutschland über alles." The soldiers sing patriotic and sentimental songs (a fixture of these accounts), play skat (the favored card game) and sleep between stops for food and coffee. Finally, in the night they cross the Rhine, and, inevitably, sing "The Watch on the Rhine" (12). Renn inquires of himself "Am I not lucky to experience a war? It is some kind of solution. What a pity for those whose youth passes without one!"[22] Renn's ironic self-questioning is unusual, as most of the texts are serious to the point of earnestness.

Another interesting description of a journey west is Thor Goote's account of his experiences as a driver of ammunition wagons in *Wir fahren den Tod* (We Drive Death, 1930). His seventeen-year-old protagonist, setting out for the western front in 1916 or 1917 shares a compartment with veteran soldiers who fall to discussing the war. A seasoned infantryman sees no way out of the war because they, the soldiers, have lost all contact with life. As they leave German soil, the boy feels that he has left solid ground behind him.[23] Finally, he sees a field of poppies and remarks that they are beautiful. His companion shakes his head and says only "blood" (23). Goote forcefully conveys the sense of a journey into an unfamiliar world governed by different laws — governed by death. This passage is almost unique in the German literature of the war for its symbolic use of poppies. The connection between poppies and blood is so ingrained in English readers by the British war poetry, and of course by McCrae's "In Flanders Fields," that it comes as a shock to realize that the metaphor was scarcely ever

ously) is a theme common to many Great War writers on all sides of the conflict. Historically, the late summer of 1914 was one of the most beautiful on record.

[20]In this case, the boundary is more symbolic than actual, as German territory extended well to the west of the river.

[21]Renn, *War*, 10. "Ungewöhnlich günstiges Angebot!!!/ Freie Fahrt!/ Einziges Risiko ein paar Schüße!/ Dafür direkt nach Paris!" (10).

[22]Renn, *War*, 16. "Bin ich nicht glücklich daran, einen Krieg zu erleben? Es ist doch irgendeine Loslösung. Wie schlimm für die, deren Jugend ohne das vergeht!" (12).

[23]Thor Goote, *Wir fahren den Tod* (Gütersloh: Bertelsmann, 1930), 12.

used by the Germans, who, for reasons that will emerge in a later discussion, preferred the symbolism of oak leaves and the steel helmet.[24] Here it serves as an ironic warning to the boy that his illusions about war will be drowned in blood and death. His feeling that he has entered a different world is reinforced when he reports; he is ridiculed for showing up in the old-fashioned spiked helmet at a time when steel helmets had become the standard issue (25-26).

If Goote relies on concrete imagery to convey his ideas, Franz Schauwecker, one of the most militantly nationalistic of the First World War writers relies on elevated, even bombastic diction and the metaphor of the journey of experience for the individual and for the nation. "This war, I feel, is a journey we have to make as individuals and as a community, a journey on which souls are parted and transfigured, on which they must triumph or go to earth."[25] His arrival at the front gives him a feeling of "impenetrable separation from home" and of being "Germany in exile . . . plowing through the flaming seas of war."[26] The journey to the Front therefore is a journey in physical and spiritual distance, severing the soldier from the familiar landscape and occupations of home and carrying him into a new world which is alien and dangerous, but which also holds secret knowledge that only the initiates can hope to comprehend.

In the Trenches

The generals did not plan on trench warfare. Nor did anyone else. On all sides, the general staffs had, on the contrary, planned quick, mobile, decisive campaigns. In a few areas — parts of Russia, Romania — significant mobility continued throughout the war. But on the western front, almost universally regarded as the key to victory, the initial war of movement stalled after the German defeat on the Marne in mid-September. The Schlieffen plan had envisioned a rapid, stunning victory in the West, enabling the ever-efficient railroads to trundle the troops across Germany to deal with the Russian army before it had fully mobilized. The German failures in leadership and the over-confident miscalculations have been examined for more than seventy years. For the literature of the war only two consequences are important: first, the material actualities of twentieth–century warfare, even in 1914, negated the theories of the

[24]See, for example, Bridgewater's discussion of Wilhelm Klemm's "Dörfer" in *German Poets of the First World War*, 89–91. On the British use of the poppy, see Fussell, *Great War*, 243–254.

[25]Franz Schauwecker, *Der Feurige Weg* (Berlin: Frundsberg, 1926). Tr. by Thonald Holland as *The Fiery Way* (London: Dent, 1929), 21. "Das fühle ich deutlich: dieser Krieg ist ein Erlebnis aller und jedes einzelnen zugleich, ein Erlebnis wie ein Kreuzweg, an dem sich die Geister scheiden und wandeln, wachsen oder zugrunde gehen" (16).

[26]Schauwecker, *Fiery Way*, 57. "Wolkenhoch, undurchdringlich schießt eine Mauer hoch zwischen uns und der Heimat. Wir sind ausgewandertes Deutschland, ein Volk von Männern . . . durch die flammenden Meere des Krieges pflügend" (43).

general staffs; and second, the failure of the German offensive created the military stalemate that we call trench warfare, and with it the war of attrition. Fischer quotes a letter from Karg-Bebenburg (a front officer) written on October 10, 1914, that exemplifies the realignment of attitudes that followed the defeats of the Marne and Langemarck:

> The brisk, merry war to which we have all looked forward for years has taken an unforeseen turn. Troops are murdered with machines, horses have almost become superfluous. . . . The most important people are the pioneers . . . the theories of decades are shown to be worthless, everything is done differently now.[27]

Here, in embryo, is the shape of things to come — a world in which the revered cavalry and its cherished horses were anachronisms, the despised engineers were indispensable, and the inglorious machine, in the form of the high explosive shell and the machine gun, was the real lord of the battlefield.[28] The "brisk, merry" war of brass bands, glory and having the boys home by Christmas was one of the earliest casualties of the war. For the Germans, with their rapid mobilization and intellectual dependence on highly mobile battle plans, the descent from the "merry" war must have seemed, both literally and figuratively, like a descent into the labyrinth. The labyrinth became, indeed, one of the commonest and most natural metaphors of trench warfare, and functioned as both a metaphorical description of the trench system and of the feelings of the men trapped in it.[29] For the "initiates" mired in the filth, terror and death of the trench labyrinth, the interminably stalemated war left two legacies — a deep sense of fellowship with fellow sufferers (including those on the other side of No Man's Land), and a profound alienation from everything and everyone who had not endured that experience.[30] The community of experience common to the soldiers in the trenches forms the basis for comradeship, the fundamental German phenomenon of the war. But the very extremity of that experience spawned a rejection of "normal" society in two forms: first the dismissal of past life and education as worthless, and second, a complete breakdown in communication and understanding between the initiates at the front and the uninitiated at home and in the rear echelons.

The failure of conventional education in the face of war's actualities is a recurring motif. Schauwecker speaks of the dryness and deadness of his education and of a knowledge of life and the world that was merely "gray and lifeless the-

[27]Qtd. in Fritz Fischer *War of Illusions: German Politics from 1911–1914*, Tr. Marian Jackson (New York: Norton, 1975), 544.

[28]As an indication of the command mentality of the period, it is worth noting that at least for the first half of the war, most of the major commanders on all sides were cavalrymen. Although the cavalry was useless, horses remained essential for the transportation of war materiel, as John Keegan has noted in *A History of Warfare* (New York: Knopf, 1993), 307–308.

[29]Leed, *No Man's Land*, 72–80.

[30]See Marsland, *The Nation's Cause*, 157–177 on the impact of this polarization on war poetry.

ory" promulgated by bloodless, crotchety old men.[31] Of his ten weeks' military training, Remarque writes,

> We learned that a bright button is weightier than four volumes of Schopenhauer.... After three weeks it was no longer incomprehensible to us that a braided postman should have more authority over us than had formerly our parents, our teachers, and the whole gamut of culture from Plato to Goethe.[32]

In Joachim von der Goltz's *Der Baum von Cléry* (The Tree of Cléry, 1934), the character Siebenreut marvels at the emptiness and pointlessness of the pre-war life of young people and muses on the blindness of the "Gebildeten."[33] But the destruction of "school learning" by war is most effectively expressed by a disillusioned lieutenant at Verdun in Werner Beumelburg's *Gruppe Bosemüller* (Group Bosemüller, 1930), which, taken with Schauwecker's books, forms a virtual compendium of conservative nationalist views on the war. Drained by the horrors of Verdun, Siewers, the new member of the group (aged 17), still can't conceive of life without hope. The lieutenant tells him "You can't talk like that anymore when you've been here three months. All school wisdom kicks the bucket here. The whole of so-called moral philosophy shatters before a burst of well-aimed machine-gun fire."[34] The effectiveness of this passage rests on Beumelburg's use of machine gun fire as the symbol of man-made, mechanical destruction. The typical rightist hatred of technology narrows in the war to a loathing of the destructive power of the machines invented by that technology, which is invariably seen as Western, and antithetical to the values of German culture.

The disillusionment inherent in the lieutenant's statement, at least so far as traditional values were concerned, was widespread. One should not, however, assume that it is identical to the profound and socially devastating disillusionment typical of the British reaction to the war. German disillusionment, which was more restricted and superficial than the British, centered on the annihilation of expectations of glory and heroism in a war of movement and individual

---

[31]Schauwecker, *Fiery Way*, 24–25. "Ja, bisher haben wir das Leben und die Welt nur in einer Theorie kennen gelernt, die grau und unlebendig uns mürrisch anstarrten, eine Versammlung blutlosen Nörgelgreise" (18). The underlying reference is to Goethe's characterization of theory in *Faust*.

[32]Remarque, *All Quiet*, 29–30. "Wir lernten, daß ein geputzter Knopf wichtiger ist als vier Bände Schopenhauer.... Nach drei Wochen war es uns nicht mehr unfaßlich, daß ein betreßter Briefträger mehr Macht über uns besaß als früher unsere Eltern, unsere Erzieher und sämtliche Kulturkreise von Plato bis Goethe zusammen" (25).

[33]Joachim von der Goltz, *Der Baum von Cléry* (Berlin: Gutenberg, 1934), 56–57.

[34]Werner Beumelburg, *Die Gruppe Bosemüller. Der große Roman des Frontsoldaten*. (Oldenburg i.O./Berlin: Stalling, 1930), 74. "So sprechen Sie nicht mehr, wenn Sie drei Monate hier sind. Alle Schulweisheit kriegt hier das große Kotzen. Die ganze sogenannte Moralphilosophie zerplatzt vor einem wohlgezielten Maschinengewehrgeschuß ..." (74).

combat. But not all expectations were destroyed. In fact, the fundamental philosophical framework of German thought was never undermined. With the exception of certain cases, the idealist structure remained sound. Even the most liberal of writers, Remarque and Köppen for example, cannot completely escape the idealist heritage, as will be apparent.

But on one score there was universal German disillusionment: the behavior of rear echelons, and the attitudes and actions of people at home. About fat, safe sergeants and war profiteers there were no illusions, as indeed there were none in any of the combatant armies. Hatred of the rear is a universal theme with cultural variations. To call a front line soldier a *Frontschwein* (front pig) was honorable, if earthy, but an *Etappenschwein* (headquarters pig) was the lowest form of life in the world of the trench soldier. In the eyes of the front soldier, the *Etappenschwein* was safe, warm, well-fed (always a sore point), cowardly and materialistic. His patriotism was of the "hurrah" variety, he actively sought decorations (derisively called *Zinwaren* [tinware] by the real front soldier) and he placed far too much emphasis on the fine points of military appearance and etiquette. In *Aufbruch der Nation* (translated as *The Furnace*, 1930), Schauwecker delineates the geography of front and rear.[35] His spokesman, Albrecht, having survived Verdun, decides to accept a chance to go to officer's training. His introduction to paperwork illuminates a flaw in the structure of the army: "And in its structure a crack — just a tiny one — appeared. It ran parallel to the front somewhere just outside of enemy fire. Here began the misunderstandings and the opposition between fixed principles and theory on the one side and moving life and experience on the other."[36]

In the German literature, the intractable mistrust and hatred between front and rear rests on two convictions. The first is that the rear troops, unlike the front line soldiers, are out of firing range, and are therefore in no physical danger. In the eyes of the front troops, that made them at least self-seeking, and at worst, cowardly. The second gap is that between theory and experience. The rear echelons only theorize about front-line battles; the front soldiers experience them. Here, again, the authenticity of the experience of battle is elevated above the theorizing of the inexperienced. Renn, meditating on the same situation, attributes the gap to the development of trench warfare: "The men behind ceased to understand the troops once we settled down to a trench war, and the

---

[35]The German title of this novel, *Aufbruch der Nation*, actually means the uprising or awakening of the nation, and does not correspond to the title chosen for the translation. The British publisher may have thought an accurately translated title too redolent of German nationalism to sell books in Britain.

[36]Schauwecker, *The Furnace*, 212. "Und doch war hier schon ein feiner Riß im Gefüge. Dieser Riß zog sich gleichlaufend der Front etwa dort entlang, wo der Bereich der feindlichen Geschütze aufhörte. Dort begannen die Mißverständnisse und die Gegensätze der starren Prinzipien samt der Theorie einerseits und des spannkräftigen Lebens samt der Forderung der Wirklichkeit anderseits" (239).

troops thought they knew best and were unwilling to be ordered about any longer because they bore the brunt of the sacrifice."[37]

Although a gap exists in every war between those who do the actual fighting and those who plan the operations, the stalemate of trench warfare undoubtedly exacerbated the differences, real and perceived. The geographical nature of the impasse, even if it did not create the concept of front and rear, surely raised it to the level of an *idée fixe*. On both sides, three parallel rows of trenches faced No Man's Land, whose four elements were "iron, blood, bones, and earth."[38] Behind the trenches, sometimes at a considerable distance, were headquarters and essential services. Long-range shelling sometimes brought rear areas under fire, but the one general rule remained: the closer to No Man's Land, the greater the danger. Actual fighting took place in the first line, and occasionally in the second.[39] Until the Germans developed their storm tactics (deep penetration at weak points, avoidance of heavily defended positions to maintain forward motion, followed by "mopping up" of strong points) in late 1916, gains were measured in yards, and breaking through into the rear areas, beyond the trench lines, was unheard of. "The barrier of the front," says Hein, "made the staffs safer than they would have been at home."[40] These geographical facts created a breech both spatial and psychological between front and rear. The spatial model was so compelling that the terminology is still in use, even when used to describe guerrilla wars that have no geographical front or rear.

The initiate's knowledge of front-line fighting and strength to endure the trench existence elevates him morally above the cowardly *Etappenschwein*. This theme of moral superiority is often coupled with that of martyrdom to further authenticate the front soldier's unimpeachable moral authority. When a staff officer takes up a front-line command, or when the staff does a tour of the trenches, their fear and ignorance of the realities of trench life make them the brunt of considerable ridicule from the *Frontschwein*. Renn's company is suspicious of a new lieutenant from the staff because he wears a monocle and carries a riding stick.[41] Both smack of superficial prewar notions of officership, and are

---

[37]Renn, *War,* 275. "Die hinten verstanden die Truppe nicht mehr, als es zum Stellungskrieg kam, und die Truppe glaubte alles besser zu wissen und wollte nicht mehr gehorchen, weil sie es ist, die die Opfer bringt" (229).

[38]Alfred Hein, *Eine Kompagnie Soldaten in der Hölle von Verdun* (Minden i.W.: Kohler, 1930), 257. Tr. F. H. Lyon as *In the Hell of Verdun* (London: Cassell, 1930), 289.

[39]Alongside the notoriously dangerous areas of Ypres, the Somme and Verdun, there were throughout the war so-called "quiet" sectors where offensive activity was minimal. Naturally, the level of fighting varied according to season, weather and the plans of headquarters. See Tony Ashworth's interesting analysis in *Trench Warfare 1914–1918: The Live and Let Live System* (New York: Holmes and Meier, 1980).

[40]Hein, *Verdun,* 295.

[41]Renn, *War,* 299.

of no use in the line. Beumelburg ridicules the fear of a group of staff officers on a tour of the line, one of whom ends up with a degrading tear in the back of his trousers. That same major has come equipped with a vast array of useless gear that Beumelburg enumerates in all its silliness: "Binoculars, folded up field stool, two revolvers, gas mask, raincoat, staff coat, food bag, cap, everything is there."[42] The superfluity of equipment contrasts sharply with the filthy, ragged and hungry front soldiers. Similarly, when Hein, a runner, delivers a message to headquarters, he refuses the fine dinner they offer him because they, the shirkers, have suggested that his motivation is to gain an Iron Cross.[43] On another occasion, he inquires if he and his comrades have done their duty and suffered for these "bellies on legs?"(234) Remarque also notes that it is "queer" that all pay-sergeant-majors are fat.[44] The bitterness over differing rations is understandable. Due to the Allied blockade, German troops were, after the first year of the war, very badly fed. That was particularly true in active sectors or during offensives, as rations had to be fetched at field kitchens well behind the front lines and hand-carried to the troops. During heavy shelling the rations and the ration carrier often failed to reach the troops. The many accounts of scrounging food while in rest billets further attest to the hunger of the troops. Food as a symbol of social division and disunity continues to crop up in passages about war profiteers and in postwar scenes of "hamstering" and black market activities.[45]

The maintenance of military customs and courtesies superfluous at the front is another mark of the rear echelon officer. The most famous example of the headquarters mentality is probably an incident in *All Quiet*. Paul Bäumer, at home on leave and brooding over his alienation from home and family, fails to see an approaching major and render the appropriate salute. Despite Bäumer's apology, the officer, in true headquarters style, demands name, regiment, and where he is quartered (he says between Langemarck and Bixshoote). The major's failure to comprehend just where that is emphasizes the gap between front and rear. The major, infuriated, won't stand for Bäumer's "front-line manners," makes him double back and salute, and only then releases him.[46] The rift between front and rear, obvious in these examples, reinforced the front soldier's sense of alienation from the rest of the world and his belief in the uniqueness and genuineness of his own experience of war. It also prepared the way for the

---

[42]Beumelburg, *Bosemüller*, 219.

[43]Hein, *Verdun*, 52.

[44]Remarque, *All Quiet*, 100.

[45]"Hamstering" is an anglicized form of the German verb "hamstern," to hoard food, and was in current British usage between the wars. Remarque's *Der Weg Zurück* (Berlin: Propyläen, 1931), tr. by A.W. Wheen as *The Road Back* (Boston: Little, 1931) and Renn's *After War* contain good examples.

[46]Remarque, *All Quiet*, 180–182.

profound sense of betrayal felt by most front soldiers after the Armistice. The treachery of the rear echelons, and worse, of the home front would become a critical tenet of the conservative right between the wars.

If the gap between front and rear was wide, the fissure between the front line troops and the homeland, the *Heimat*, was an unbridgeable chasm. For the German front soldier of the First World War, "home" existed in two forms: letters and leave. In both cases, the most significant factor is the soldier's feeling of separation from the homeland, the feeling that "the front becomes his homeland."[47] Letters from home, although greeted with enthusiasm, often brought either distressing news or, worse, were so filled with trivialities and silly complaints that they lost all meaning for soldiers in constant danger of death. As the war lengthened, and the Allied blockade of Germany tightened, the letters were full of complaints of shortages. Goltz opens *Der Baum von Cléry* with the words: "It was in the West, at the time when the troops sang no longer. When the men wrote in their letters: Do our children still have bread?"[48] The inability of civilians at home to understand the nature of trench warfare also led them to write letters insisting on peace only with German victory, long after most front soldiers had given up any hope of victory.[49]

Packages from home, especially early in the war, provide an even more striking picture of the disjunction between the two worlds. The most astonishing example occurs early in Schauwecker's *The Fiery Way*. During an attack on a Russian village, the narrator receives food packages from home. He compares the foil wrapped chocolates to magic bullets:

> ... shrapnel shells are iron cylinders stuffed with leaden bullets, powder and wax, and yet here is a slab of chocolate filled with cream. I open one box after another, and an almost unbearable contrast appears in the trench: lobster mayonnaise and mud, maraschino and grease, cigarettes and rifle oil, preserved strawberries and foot bandages, dates and lice, roast pigeon and knee-boots, which we call dice-boxes — enough to drive you silly![50]

The contrasts he draws are obvious enough to pass without remark, but the analogy of foil-wrapped chocolates to shrapnel shells demands some comment. Although I would hesitate to suggest that so earnest a writer as Schauwecker

---

[47]Picht, *Der Frontsoldat*, 32. "Die Front wird seine Heimat."

[48]Goltz, *Der Baum von Cléry*, 5. "Es war im Westen, um die Zeit, als keine Truppe mehr sang. Als in den Briefen der Männer stand: haben unsere Kinder noch Brot?"

[49]Schauwecker, *The Furnace*, 111.

[50]Schauwecker, *Fiery Way*, 86. "Schrapnells sind Eisenzylinder mit Bleikugeln, Pulver und Wachs gefüllt. Hier ist eine Schokoladenwandung mit Vanillecreme gefüllt. Ich öffne eine Schachtel nach der andern, und im Graben entsteht ein fast unerträglicher Gegensatz: Hummermayonnaise und Lehm, Maraschino und Affenschmalz, Zigaretten und Gewehrfett, eingemachte Erdbeeren und Fußlappen, Datteln und Läuse, gebratene Taube und Schaftstiefel, genannt Knobelbecher, zum Verrücktwerden!" (67)

had adopted an ironic attitude, this is very close to it. The similarity of appearance between the candy and the shells underscores their opposite functions. A little further on, Schauwecker creates another ironic juxtaposition of candy and soil.

> . . . I fetch out my spade and hew away at the gravel, most stubborn of soils, a truly refined mixture, gravel and mud, frozen, like a mixture of truffle chocolates with arrack and coffee-cream. Lord! I always have wanted to try something like that, and now we've got it! Hope you like it![51]

Here, the ironic contrast is clearer, since the confection of which the soil reminds him was an object of desire. Now he has the front version of his wish, and has ample opportunity to contrast its refinement with that of the chocolate.

Letters and packages may have reminded the soldier of the misery and danger of his existence, but compared to leave at home their effect was small.[52] Most protagonists discover the width of the gap between themselves and life at home on their first leave. Virtually all those writers who write of leave spent at home speak first of an inability to communicate with civilians, even their nearest relations. Renn, for example, worries over what to tell people at home and feels restless the whole time.[53] Remarque's Bäumer speaks of a veil between him and his family, and says that he "cannot get on with the people." They all talk too much for him, and exclusively of their own worries. If the questions are impossible to answer, those who pride themselves on not asking questions because such things "cannot be talked about" are equally intolerable to the soldier's alienated spirit.[54]

Many of the home leave chapters contain a café scene complete with armchair strategists and Pan-German annexationists.[55] The gap between the front soldier's personal experience of trench warfare on the one hand, and the elderly civilians' antiquated strategies and inaccurate notions of life at the front on the other quickly becomes a yawning chasm. The authenticity of the soldier's expe-

---

[51]Schauwecker, *Fiery Way*, 86–87. " . . . hole ich aus und haue den Spaten auf Kies, die teuflischste aller Bodenbeimengungen, eine wahrhaft raffinierte Mishung, Lehm und Kies und dann noch in gefrorener Form, entsprechend Trüffelschokolade mit Arrak und Mokkacreme, Herr du meine Güte! So was hab ich mir schon immer gewünscht, und nun haben wir den Salat . . . wohl bekomm's!" (67)

[52]Both German and British armies had systems of rotating leave in place early in the war. The French, unlike the others, acted on their expectation of a short war and granted very little leave until well into 1915. Poor leave arrangements are generally credited with contributing to the French mutinies of 1917. See J. M. Winter, *The Experience of World War I* (New York: Oxford UP, 1989), 135–136. On the French mutinies, see also G. Pedroncini, *Les Mutineries de 1917* (Paris: n.p., 1967).

[53]Renn, *War*, 162.

[54]Remarque, *All Quiet*, 178–187.

[55]Cf. Remarque, *All Quiet*, 184–186; Beumelburg, *Bosemüller*, 77–81.

riences is usually dismissed as too narrow a view, and he is verbally patted on the back and told he's doing a good, patriotic job. A friend of one soldier's father maintains that the war would have gone better if they hadn't complicated it with so many new inventions. His recipe for success is "in bed by ten, out of the feathers at six, wash, a proper breakfast. . . . All wars are won that way."[56] Similarly, Paul Bäumer's former schoolmasters argue about the overall picture (which Paul can't see), where to break through, and what to annex.[57]

Civilian ignorance of the realities of the front is a constant for the soldier on leave. Heinz, in Unruh's *Opfergang* (Way of Sacrifice, 1919), waiting for a train in Frankfurt, talks to a well-fed, well-dressed civilian who thinks the trenches must be very boring and rather nice in the spring weather.[58] The resentment the front soldiers feel for the comfortable, self-satisfied civilians quickly turns to enmity:

> Was it not proof that the nation was being torn in two? One half of it was sweating, toiling, marching, starving, freezing, fighting, guarding, bleeding, dying at the front; the other half sat at home, missed a few comforts, discussed the war and their own indispensability, and expected others to win the victory.[59]

Their enmity was particularly directed toward the war profiteers who increasingly displayed their new-found wealth as the general populace grew ever hungrier. Schauwecker's enumeration may be unusually bitter, but it is not unusual in content.

In summation, then, the experience of war at the front was such that it could only be understood by someone who had taken part in it. Consequently, the entire front generation was irretrievably cut off from the staffs in the rear and from the civilians at home. Their alienation from the rest of German society laid the foundation for the sense of betrayal they felt at the loss of the war, and undoubtedly provided fertile ground for the growth of the *Dolchstoßlegende*, or "stab-in-the-back" myth. Their particular enmity for war profiteers only increased the traditional suspicion of material gain and the "counting-house mentality." All of these factors alienated the front veterans from German society and from the realities of postwar German life, including democratic government. That alienation was to have far-reaching consequences.

[56]Beumelburg, *Bosemüller*, 80–81. "Abends um zehn ins Bett, morgens um sechs aus den Federn, gewaschen, ein ordentliches Frühstuck. . . . So sind alle Kriege gewonnen worden" (81).

[57]Remarque, *All Quiet*, 185.

[58]Fritz von Unruh, *Opfergang* (Berlin: Eriss, 1919), 201.

[59]Schauwecker, *The Furnace*, 133. "Gingen hier nicht Teile der Nation auseinander? Die einen schwitzten, rackerten, marschierten, hungerten, froren, kämpften, wachten, bluteten, starben an der Front; die andern saßen zu Hause, entbehrten einige Bequemlichkeiten, erörterten den Krieg und ihre Unabkömmlichkeit und warteten auf die Siege der andern" (146).

"A Gigantic Death Factory"

This phrase (from Werner Picht) is emblematic of the German reaction to the war of materiel, the *Materialschlacht*.[60] For them, the war of materiel represented the triumph of the substantial over the spiritual, and, by definition, the destruction of Germany as the embodiment of the spiritual. It therefore occupies a central position in German thought about the war.[61] An equivalent of the preferred English epithet, "war of attrition," is scarcely ever used in German. Although both phrases refer to the same period of the war, roughly from the first attack on Verdun in February of 1916 until the March offensive of 1918, the German term emphasizes the weight of the Allied materiel, while the English one focuses on human losses. Picht's phrase is characteristic of German thought in that it metaphorically combines the ideas of death and of modern industrial technology, here in the form of a factory. Similar phrases abound: the "meat grinder" and the "human sausage factory" referred to Verdun. The idealist dislike of materialism and industrial technology, inherent in German philosophy since the middle of the preceding century, turned to loathing when the machines became killing machines. The weapons of modern total warfare — high explosives, automatic weapons and interdiction of the enemy's supplies — intensified the deadlocked war by exponentially increasing the materiel expended and the human losses suffered. For the German soldiers at Verdun or on the Somme the increased intensity of warfare correspondingly increased their isolation from anywhere that was not the front and their alienation from anyone who was not a front soldier, while reinforcing their belief in the genuineness and uniqueness of the front experience.

More than any other experience of the First World War, the *Materialschlacht* marked the men who survived it. From the German side of No Man's Land, the *Materialschlacht* was about one thing — the astonishing quantity of materiel (weapons, ammunition, food, and even personnel) that the Allies had at their disposal. Germany fought on two fronts until December 1917, and with its ports blockaded by Britain, was limited to indigenous raw materials and what foodstuffs it could produce. For the German troops in the field, the war of materiel was about survival, specifically survival against three weapons: shells, machine guns, and hunger.

In 1914, German food supplies were adequate. Substantial food was imported from neutral countries and army rations were, by all accounts, adequate

[60] In this case, the German word *Material* refers to military goods, in the traditional distinction rendered by the French *personnel et matériel*. I have used the standard anglicized spelling "materiel" used in most military writing to designate that meaning, and to distinguish it from material objects, materialist thought, and the like.

[61] See Sombart's chapter on the German spirit, "Der deutsche Geist," in *Händler und Helden*, for a typical exposition abounding with cultural justifications, for example pages 53 and 71.

to good. Many texts mention meat and bean stews, sausages, bread and coffee. Renn remarks on the efficiency of the much-admired horse-drawn field kitchens.[62] But as the Allied blockade of German ports tightened, imports ceased, and shortages appeared in 1915. By 1916 they were severe. In Germany, food was rationed, but even the legal ration was often unobtainable. Profiteering and black-marketeering were rampant, rousing anger in civilian and soldier alike. The situation worsened with the crop failures of 1916 and breakdowns in the transportation system. The bitterly cold winter of 1916–17 was called the "Turnip Winter" because there was little other than turnips to eat. Civilians died of cold and hunger and the diseases brought on by virtual starvation. The food situation did not markedly improve until the blockade was lifted in July of 1919, by which time an estimated 800,000 people had died of starvation and related diseases.[63]

Food supplies at the front were only slightly better. Although the army had first rights to what was available, it was pitifully little. Many civilians genuinely believed that they were suffering so that the troops would have adequate food. Alas, it was not true. The combat narratives abound with complaints about rations, even if one makes allowances for the soldier's time-honored right to complain about army food. The staple of the front soldier's diet in the last three years of the war was a mixture of dried vegetables that the troops called "*Stacheldraht*" (barbed wire). It was, by all accounts, highly unpalatable. As supplies worsened, the beautiful bread baked in the field bakeries was cut with sawdust, wood pulp and other substitutes. Richard Hoffmann complains of ersatz everything : "The entire homeland was ersatz! Ersatz-battalions, ersatz-butter, ersatz-eggs, ersatz-coffee, ersatz-sugar, ersatz-shirts, ersatz-men. . . . The only thing that was still stable was the front."[64] After the Turnip Winter the men considered themselves lucky to have turnip marmalade for their ersatz bread.

Men in the rear, or front troops in rest billets, were slightly better off because they could forage in the surrounding countryside. Remarque makes much of Katczinsky's extraordinary ability to find food.[65] The men in the front line, on the other hand, couldn't move about. Technically, rations were brought up to them from the field kitchens, but, as noted above, ration parties sometimes

---

[62]Renn, *War*, 66.

[63]See Richard Wall and Jay Winter, eds., *The Upheaval of War: Family, Work and Welfare in Europe, 1914–1918* (Cambridge: Cambridge UP, 1988), especially the essay by Armand Triebel, "Variations in Patterns of Consumption in Germany in the Period of the First World War," 159–195. For a brief summary of the food situation in Germany, see Winter, *Experience*, 178–179.

[64]Richard Hoffmann, *Frontsoldaten* (Hamburg: Fackelreiter, 1928), 172. "Die ganze Heimat war Ersatz! Ersatz-Bataillion, E-Butter, Ei-E., Kaffee-E., Zucker-E., E.-Hemden, Männer-E. . . . Das einzige, was noch stabil war, war die Front."

[65]Remarque, *All Quiet*, 47, 61.

failed to get through (or got through only with cold food) when shelling was constant and heavy. Cooks who kept their kitchens well behind the lines for their own safety were a consistent source of irritation.[66] Troops in the line also carried "iron rations" (canned food), but the quantity was limited and such rations could be consumed by the men only when they were ordered to do so.[67] As a general rule, soldiers caught under heavy shellfire often went hungry.

The long period of semi-starvation took an especially heavy toll toward the end of the war. The great Hindenburg offensive of March 1918 broke through the trench lines and into untouched countryside beyond. It petered out for military reasons, primarily the exhaustion of the storm troops, lack of reserves and lengthening supply lines, but witnesses recorded a breakdown in discipline among troops moving into deserted towns. Soldiers who had existed on meager rations for years raided the wine cellars and kitchens of food and drink they hadn't seen since early in the war, and temporarily degenerated into a disorganized rabble. Beumelburg puts a better face on the event by maintaining that the soldiers had starved so long that their stomachs couldn't tolerate even simple things, but expresses astonishment at the Allied provisions and disgust for the American troops who were "satiated and abundantly equipped."[68]

Throughout the war a favorite prize in raids on British trenches was the British canned beef, known as bully beef. Its favor with the Germans rather mystified the British, who only tolerated it, and completely astounded the French, who called the canned beef "singe"(monkey). The British nevertheless felt some sympathy for the sufferings of the enemy across No Man's Land. In Ford Madox Ford's *Parade's End*, Tietjens meditates at length on the misery of the enemy as the war drew to its close:

> Even the rotten and detestable huns had it [Spanish influenza]! . . . The German men were apparently beastly underfed, and, at that, on substitute-foods of relatively small percentage of nutritive value. . . . It was a ghastly thought, that of that whole vast territory that confronted them, filled with millions of half-empty stomachs that bred disorders in the miserable brains. Those fellows must be the most miserable human beings that had ever existed. . . . you did not wish them much real harm. Nothing like having to live in that hell on perpetually half-empty, windy stomachs with the nightmares they set up! Naturally influenza was decimating them.[69]

Inadequate food was unquestionably a factor in the slow wearing down of the German army, but the essence of the *Materialschlacht* was the Allied superiority in weapons, and the way in which the capabilities of those weapons took

[66]Remarque, *All Quiet*, 12.

[67]Schauwecker, *Fiery Way*, 93–95.

[68]Werner Beumelburg, *Von 1914 bis 1939: Sinn und Erfüllung des Weltkrieges* (Leipzig: Reklam, 1940), 19–21.

[69]Ford Maddox Ford, *Parade's End*, (1924–1928; reprint, New York: Knopf, 1966), 628.

control of the conduct of the war. Artillery fire and machine gun fire share two characteristics: they kill at a distance, and they are the weapons of a fixed fighting line, of defensive siege warfare.

The machine gun of the First World War, heavier and less mobile than modern automatic weapons, was nonetheless the ideal defensive weapon. The British learned that to their detriment on the first day of the Somme, 1 July 1916, when waves of troops were mown down by German machine guns that the British believed destroyed in the bombardment that preceded the attack. The Germans had already learned about machine guns at Langemarck, in October of 1914. As the war progressed, it became standard procedure on both sides to replace a continuous trench line with a system of mutually supported strong points defended by machine guns.[70]

The horse-drawn artillery of the First World War, which was also mobile, was used primarily as a siege weapon. After the establishment of the trench lines made mobility largely superfluous, entrenched artillery was used to "soften up" opposing lines before an attack. The unsuccessful attacks — German, French, and British — of 1915 led commanders on all sides to a realization that the defenses of the enemy's trench system could only be broken by bombardments of hitherto undreamed-of length and intensity. The attacks of 1915 had been small in scale and none had achieved a breakthrough into open countryside. The Germans had tried using chlorine gas — near Ypres — but the British line had held, albeit with high casualties. Early 1916 brought the first bombardment that can properly be called part of the *Materialschlacht*. After a delay of nine days due to rain and then snow (throughout which the assault troops shivered in their trenches), the German attack on Verdun opened at dawn on February 21 with a nine-hour bombardment. Even for the shell-cratered western front it was of unprecedented ferocity. Portions of the French trench system were simply obliterated. Despite a covering of vegetation, the landscape around Verdun is still deeply cratered. But although the assault troops had to traverse badly broken ground, the early German assaults were very successful and proved that intense bombardment before an assault could destroy or at least demoralize the enemy.

Sir Alexander Haig, in command of the British Expeditionary Force, was not so fortunate as General Falkenhayn had been in the early days at Verdun. Haig preceded his attack on the Somme with a seven-day bombardment in which a million and a half shells rained down on the German trenches. But this time the bombardment not only failed to destroy the German positions, it also failed to cut the barbed wire. The attacking British troops, who had been told that the wire would be cut and most of the Germans would be dead, walked upright into the intact wire and were cut down by the German machine guns.

[70]See John Keegan's remarks on First World War firepower in *A History of Warfare* (New York: Knopf, 1993), 358–366, and his exemplary analysis of the Somme in *The Face of Battle* (New York: Viking, 1976) 204–284.

The deep dugouts of the German front line had protected men and weapons from the barrage, and when it lifted, there was time to carry the guns upstairs and cut down the orderly waves of attacking troops. By the end of the day, the British had sustained 58,000 casualties for minute territorial gains. It was one of the greatest military disasters in history.

This was the new modern warfare at its ugliest: mechanical slaughter of men by the hundreds of thousands with no human dimension. For the Germans, it represented technological triumph with a vengeance. Displaying the usual German bias against technology and the associated ideas of materialism, capitalism, and liberalism, one of Schauwecker's spokesmen — under shellfire — lambastes the technicians who have "only" made money and invented socialism (which he regards as inverted capitalism): "They remained bent over their machines, and now we are here helpless in what is a mechanical war among their wonderful tools, their famous technical work, which rules the roost, alas! from Verdun to Mesopotamia!"[71] The helplessness of men caught in the intractable power of the machines is a recurring motif not only in the war narratives, but also in society at large during the interwar period. But in the war books it is mostly used to emphasize the antithesis between spirit and matter, and to suggest that the inevitable result of technology, however innocent it may appear, is the technology of death, actual or spiritual. Hein, for example, contrasts the current duties of a young artillery major with his previous work as an archivist writing on the Thirty Year's War, when heroism had still existed. Now the major directs a bombardment, where "he was in command of machines, the machines were not inspired by the men who served them; the men became slaves of the machines. It was really nothing but a sum."[72] Here the *gebildete* man, the man who knows the worth of the spirit and the heroism that comes from it is reduced to being the slave of the guns. The author's choice of the Thirty Years' War is significant, as it was one of the historical wars favored by the Wandervögel as a source of folk songs and heroic stories.[73] Further, the major's adjustments of distance and trajectory to make the guns fire on target are really

---

[71]Schauwecker, *The Furnace*, 194. "Sie blieben in der Maschine stecken, und nun geraten wir ahnungslos in die Materialschlacht rein, in ihr vielgeliebtes Material, in ihre famose Technik, die ihnen durchgegangen ist, heidi, von Mesopotamien bis nach Verdun!" (218)

[72]Alfred Hein, *Eine Kompagnie Soldaten in der Hölle von Verdun* (Minden i. W.: Kohler 1930). Tr. by F. H. Lyon as *In the Hell of Verdun* (London: Cassell, 1930), 295. "Hier aber kommandierte er Maschinen. Nein, die Maschinen wurden nicht menschlich beseelt durch die Menschen, die sie bedienten. Die Menschen wurden Knechte der Maschinen. Es war wirklich nur eine Rechenaufgabe"(262–263). The diction in German is particularly telling here, especially the words "beseelt" (inspired — literally given a soul), and "Knechte" (servants). The image of the controlling or even devouring machine is also common in rightest fantasies of the Weimar period. See Fisher's analysis of *Metropolis* in *Fantasy and Politics* (Madison: U of Wisconsin P, 1991), 128–137.

[73]Ille and Köhler, *Der Wandervogel*, 156.

only a sum. The debasement of human slaughter to mathematical sums is particularly onerous because it smacks of the material and monetary, the spirit of the tradesman rather than that of the hero, to borrow Sombart's terminology. Schauwecker writes that "our battalion has twenty percent casualties. Percent! What an expression! reeking of counting house and ledger! Trade and Exchange! God punish England and Satan punish France!"[74]

Yet another theme that emerges consistently from the war of materiel is the defenselessness of men against an unseen enemy. The machine gun and the explosive shell do their work at a distance, reducing both perpetrator and victim to slaves of the machine. Schauwecker, lamenting the killing of one of his best men by a shell splinter, says "done for in seconds by a man ten miles away, and that's what they call heroism, pulling at a trigger-string and striking dead blindly, miles away. . . ."[75] The dehumanization of mechanical warfare renders individual courage and personal heroism superfluous and even idiotic. The lack of a tangible opponent makes any traditional meeting of the enemy, to which the idea of personal heroism is attached, meaningless. The spiritual values of Schauwecker and of most of the German writers makes them crave that, at the last, " . . . we ourselves may decide . . . not these tireless weights of steel, mass, machinery, money. There's no skill and no strength in that . . . ."[76]

Along with the hatred of the inhuman destructive power of the Allied materiel, the war of shell and machine gun evoked other themes of interest. The experience of being under shellfire is one of the common denominators of First World War narratives. The terror of being shelled is concentrated first in the fear of death or wounds, and second in the inability to escape or to fight back. Shelling represents the epitome of the frustrations engendered by the deadlock of the war: it was deadly, men were impotent beneath it, and escape was impossible. The deadliness of shell fire needs little comment. Of the 650,000 men killed at Verdun, the majority died of wounds inflicted by shell fire. The bizarre shapes and unpredictable behavior of shell fragments were a constant of trench life. Even on "quiet" days men were killed by random, unpredictable shelling from which there was little protection.

In fact, the only protection from the inescapable shelling was the earth itself. Both Remarque and Schauwecker, whose reactions to the war differ so mark-

---

[74]Schauwecker, *Fiery Way*, 191. "Unser Bataillon hat schon zwanzig Prozent Verluste. Prozent! Was für ein Ausdruck nach Kontor und Bilanz! Nach Handel und Wandel! Gott strafe England und der Satan Frankreich!" (151–152)

[75]Schauwecker, *Fiery Way*, 154–155. "In zehn Sekunden erledigt über fünfzehn Kilometer weg, und das nennt sich Heldenmut, reißt an der Abzugsschnur und schlägt blindlings tot, meilenweit . . . " (120).

[76]Schauwecker, *Fiery Way*, 188. "Daß Wir selber endlich entscheiden und nicht diese unablässigen Wuchten von Stahl, Maße, Maschine und Geld. Das ist ja gar keine Kunst mehr und keine Kraft . . . " (149).

edly, wrote paeans to the earth. For Remarque, the forces that sustain a soldier pour into him from the earth:

> To no man does the earth mean so much as to the soldier. When he presses himself down upon her long and powerfully, when he buries his face and his limbs deep in her from the fear of shell-fire, she is his only friend, his brother, his mother; he stifles his terror and his cries in her silence and her security; she shelters him and releases him for ten seconds to live, to run, ten seconds of life; receives him again and often forever.[77]

The passage continues with an ecstatic, almost expressionistic, glorification of the earth and its protective powers. Schauwecker catalogues the reduction of human life in the trenches to the most basic elements:

> ... hunger, thirst, shelter, wanderings, common life, watching, food, sleep. These were the main things. The real foundations of life became visible out here. They had returned to the last one of all, the soil under their feet. In peace there was no such experience.[78]

He goes on to compare Germany, embodied by her soldiers, to Antaeus, who regains his strength with each contact with his mother earth (93) and speaks later of the earth as his mother (188).

The inability to escape or even to protect oneself adequately from the "roaring iron hurricane" [79] bred in the troops who experienced it a deep resignation that modern psychologists would identify as a "victim" mentality. Certainly the word *Schicksal* (fate) appears with increasing frequency in those passages that deal with the time period from 1916 to the end of the war. The concept of fate plays an important role in German intellectual history, as I have noted, since German history was conceived as a vital organic development, leading to the eventual fulfillment of Germany's destiny.

By the time of the First World War, the notions of national destiny had merged with similar communal, *völkisch* ideas to link individual destiny with that of the immediate community, the *Volk*, and the nation.[80] In the absence of

---

[77]Remarque, *All Quiet*, 64. "Für niemand ist die Erde so viel wie für den Soldaten. Wenn er sich an sie preßt, lange, heftig, wenn er sich tief mit dem Gesicht und den Gliedern in sie hineinwühlt in der Todesangst des Feuers, dann ist sie sein einziger Freund, sein Bruder, seine Mutter, er stöhnt seine Furcht und seine Schreie in ihr Schweigen und ihre Geborgenheit, sie nimmt sie auf und entläßt ihn wieder zu neuen zehn Sekunden Lauf und Leben, faßt ihn wieder, und manchmal für immer" (54).

[78]Schauwecker, *The Furnace*, 91. " ... Hunger, Durst, Unterkommen, Wandern, Zusammenleben, Aufpassen, Brot, Schlaf. Das waren die Hauptsachen. Die wahren Grundbedingungen des Lebens zeigten sich hier unverhüllt. Man ging auf das Letzte zürück, auf den Boden unter den Füßen. Im Frieden hatte es dergleichen nicht mehr gegeben" (99). The last sentence actually reads: "In peace such experience no longer existed."

[79]Hein, *Verdun*, 343.

[80]Sontheimer, *Antidemokratisches Denken*, 308–313; 318–320.

either actual or imagined control over individual destiny, the German front soldiers resigned themselves to whatever their collective fate would be. The sense of resignation to the control of a higher power created by the war of materiel ensured that endurance and survival were the only remaining military virtues. Schauwecker draws a portrait of the *Frontschwein* after Verdun:

> ... but for most of them there remained from those days at Verdun a calmness amounting almost to indifference; they took no reck of their futures as individuals; they were resigned to walk in the shadow of destiny. They were isolated and they were powerless.[81]

Schauwecker's emphasis on the isolation, resignation and powerlessness of the troops is entirely consistent with what Leed calls the breakdown of the offensive personality.[82] It is also significant that Schauwecker identifies that as a collective event and as a function of their joint destiny. The loss of offensive spirit appears in many novels in the form of the leitmotif of troops singing. The singing of troops as a gesture of patriotic, and ultimately, offensive enthusiasm is common in accounts of the early part of the war. But with the coming of the *Materialschlacht*, the student-volunteers who went into the attack at Langemarck singing enthusiastically were no more.[83] Goltz uses the leifmotif of singing troops to introduce his novel, which opens in the summer of 1916: "It was in the West, at the time when the troops no longer sang."[84] Given the ubiquitousness of troops singing, even in the German poetry of the war, the absence of singing after Verdun is all the more notable.

From February 1916, the war of materiel became a war of endurance and survival. The diction becomes that of living through or outliving (*durchleben*, *überleben*) the experience. As early as January of 1915, Binding had noted in his diary "this is a war of attrition; the side that is used up first will lose it."[85] The

---

[81]Schauwecker, *The Furnace*, 202. "... aber den meisten verblieb von jenen Tagen vor Verdun eine fast gleichmütig erscheinende Gelassenheit, die mit keiner persönlichen Zukunft mehr rechnete und gefaßt in den Schatten des Schicksals trat. Sie waren einzelne, und so waren sie machtlos" (227). The last sentence of the German actually translates "they were isolated and therefore they were powerless."

[82]Leed, *No Man's Land*, 107.

[83]Wilhelm Dreysse, *Langemarck 1914* (Minden i.W.: Kohler, 1934?), 28–29. Bernd Hüppauf, "Langemarck, Verdun and the Myth of a New Man in Germany after the First World War," *War and Society*, 6:2 (September 1988): 70–103 provides an illuminating analysis of the legends of Langemarck and Verdun.

[84]Goltz, *Der Baum von Cléry*, 5. "Es war im Westen, um die Zeit, als keine Truppe mehr sang."

[85]Rudolf G. Binding, *Aus dem Kriege* in *Dies war das Maß. Die gesammelten Kriegsdichtungen und Tagebücher* (Potsdam: Rutten und Loening, 1940). Tr. by Ian F. D. Morrow as *A Fatalist at War* (London: Allen and Unwin, 1929), 48. "Es ist ein Abnutzungskrieg; wer eher abgenutzt ist verliert ihn" (274).

German word Binding uses, *abnutzen*, means to use up or wear out, and the German troops were progressively worn down through their own lack of materiel and the Allies' abundance of it. Bucher underlines the diminishing resistance of the front soldiers: "More and more the war was burning us up; we should never turn tail before the storm, though we might break under it singly, in hundreds, in thousands, while victory seemed ever farther away."[86] And several pages later: "It was as if we lived in a different world, in the abyss of death, where there were no longer telephones, signals and runners — only shells, gas, blood, agony, and death."[87] Goltz, in his turn, inquires what had happened to the spirit of August. The war had become, he concludes, " . . . a stubborn contest for the discovery of ever more horrible weapons. The worth of men still shows itself only in endurance. . . . Everything had become meaningless."[88] A 1916 letter from Friedrich Steinbrecher echoes Goltz's despair in concrete images:

> The poetry of the trenches is a thing of the past. The spirit of adventure is dead. . . . We have become wise, serious and professional. Stern duty has taken the place of a keenness sometimes amounting to passion — a frigid, mechanical doing of one's duty. . . . Formerly the [dugout] walls were adorned with pictures — now they are covered with maps, orders and reports. Formerly the men christened their dugouts, trenches and houses — now they are numbered 1, 2, A, B, etc. I sometimes feel so wintry inside. . . . Death is the only conqueror.[89]

---

[86]Georg Bucher *Westfront 1914–1918. Das Buch vom Frontkameraden* (Vienna-Leipzig: Konegen, 1930). Tr. by Norman Gullick as *In the Line: 1914–1918* (London: Cape 1932), 184. "Mehr und mehr glüht dieser Krieg in uns etwas aus; und dennoch: wir beugen uns dem endlosen, entnervenden Ansturm nicht, beugen uns ihm nie! Wir werden aber zerbrechen darunter, beim Einzelnen, beim Hundert, beim Tausend, wenn sich der Sieg in die Länge zieht" (206).

[87]Bucher, 191. " . . . wir befinden uns doch in einer ganz anderen Welt, im Rachen des Todes, wo es keine Telephone mehr gibt, keine Blinksignale, keine Meldeläufer — nur noch Granaten, Minen, Gas, Gas, Blut, Qualen, Tod!" (214–215).

[88]Goltz, *Der Baum von Cléry*, 169. "Der Krieg war ein sturer Wettkampf im Erfinden immer schrecklicherer Kampfmittel geworden. Der Wert des Menschen zeigte sich nur noch im Erdulden. . . . Sinnlos war alles geworden."

[89]Witkop, *War Letters*, 325. "Die Schützengrabenpoesie ist vorüber. . . . Wir sind klug geworden, ernst und sachlich. An Stelle vom Interesse, bisweilen Liebhaberei, ist Pflicht getreten, kalte, mechanische Pflichterfüllung. . . . Früher winkten Bilder von der Wand, jetzt überall Karten, Befehle, Meldungen. Früher tauften die Leute ihre Unterstände, die Gräben, die Häuser, jetzt numeriert man: 1, 2 . . . A, B usw. Mir ist manchmal so winterlich zumute. . . . Sieger ist nur der Tod" (292). Note the devaluation implied in descending from names to numbers.

Johannes Philippson, writing home in July of 1917, sums up the psychological state of the German soldier:

> . . . but we, who have seen the dark side, must substitute for that enthusiasm a deep-seated determination to stand by the fatherland whatever happens as long as it has need of us. We know that death is not the worst thing we have to face. Thoroughly to realize everything, and yet to go back [to the front], not under compulsion but willingly, is not easy. To try and deceive oneself by working oneself up into a state of excitement, is, I hold, unworthy. Only genuine self-command is any use to me.[90]

In the world of the *Materialschlacht* the offensive enthusiasm of 1914 lies far in the past, replaced by a determination, not to win, but to endure to the end, whatever the power of the opposing side. To use Picht's terms, the idea of a heroic death has disappeared to be replaced by the sacrificial death of a willing victim.[91] The readiness to sacrifice oneself (*Opferbereitschaft*) for the good of the group or nation is a persistent theme of this literature. The language in which it is usually couched makes use of much Christian terminology, particularly messianic diction associated with sacrifice, martyrdom and salvation.[92]

The contrast between the patriotic intoxication of the beginning of the war and the despairing service of the war of materiel is the contrast between nationalistic idealism and physical reality. Because of the preeminence of spiritual values in German thought, the apparent destruction of those values, of culture itself, by spiritless material weighed heavily on the minds of German soldiers. Goltz writes forlornly that even Nietzsche and *Faust* leave him cold.[93] The frustration bred a conviction that the coming defeat — and many front soldiers could see what was coming, even if the civilian population was protected from the truth by censorship — was the defeat of a morally superior people by a mor-

---

[90]Witkop, 369. "Bei uns, die den Ernst geschmeckt haben, muß an ihre Stelle die tiefgegründete Entschlossenheit treten, solange das Vaterland in Not ist, für es einzutreten mit allem. Der Tod ist das Härteste nicht, was einen treffen kann. All dessen voll bewußt sein und dennoch — nicht dem Muß sich fügend — sondern bereitwillig und gerne hinausgehen, das ist nicht leicht. Mit Rauschgefühlen sich daruber hinwegzutäuschen, halte ich für unwürdig, nur rechte Selbstbesinnung hilft mir" (338). The self-control of which Philippson writes is clearly related to Theweleit's thesis of "body armor." See also Waltraud Amberger, *Männer, Krieger, Abenteuer: Der Entwurf des "soldatischen Mannes" in Kriegsromanen über den Ersten und Zweiten Weltkrieg* (Frankfurt am Main: Fischer, 1984), 41–51 and Fisher, *Fantasy and Politics*, 221.

[91]Picht, *Der Frontsoldat*, 59. Cf. Sombart, *Händler und Helden*, 57–64, and Hüppauf's analysis of the soldier of Verdun in "Langemarck, Verdun and the Myth of a new Man" already cited.

[92]Religious imagery and terminology are also vividly present in the Weimar fantasy literature, as Fisher points out. See his chapter "Revanchism and Racism" in *Fantasy and Politics*.

[93]Goltz, *Der Baum von Cléry*, 80.

ally inferior, if materially stronger one. As usual, Schauwecker speaks for the conservative majority:

> But the worst of all was the feeling of inferiority which increased at a terrible rate. They knew that they were no worse soldiers than the enemy. On the contrary they knew well enough that they fought better and that the better leadership was on their side. But — and that burned them like a poisoned barb that stuck irrevocably — they saw themselves helpless because they were faced with a mere, dull, stupid superiority of men and material.[94]

All the frustration of defeated and disillusioned idealism simmers in this passage. For an army whose ideas on war were based on the primacy of the will to win and the conviction that greater spiritual strength would always carry the day, the crushing weight of Allied materiel constituted a bitter defeat.

But in German eyes it was only a partial defeat. The victory of materiel was precisely and only that. The German army might be physically destroyed, but it could not be spiritually defeated. However specious the logic, it provides the foundation for one of the most pervasive beliefs of the interwar years: the myth of the undefeated German army. That myth was untouched by the naval mutinies at Kiel and other ports, whatever their importance in the destruction of the Imperial government. In fact, Hindenburg and Ludendorff did everything they could to distance the army and themselves from events at home. The myth of the undefeated army was buttressed by two facts. First, the German army did not surrender in the field. The fighting ended with an armistice. Secondly, the army retreated to its own borders in relatively good order, despite revolutionary chaos at home and the formation of soldiers' councils and similar revolutionary actions in rear areas. By and large, the front line was held and withdrew in order. It is undoubtedly true that the collapse and surrender of the German army and even the invasion of the homeland were only a question of time, but to patriotic Germans faced with a defeat that many, even at the end, never expected, the honorable military armistice and the orderly retreat were further proof of German moral strength and spiritual fortitude.

The theme appears in countless works of all persuasions, though most frequently in the rightist narratives. Starting at the top of German society, Crown Prince Wilhelm bathetically glorifies the soldier-martyrs and by implication shifts responsibility for the defeat away from the army, and specifically away from the high command:

---

[94]Schauwecker, *The Furnace*, 271. "Das Schlimmste aber war das Gefühl der Unterlegenheit, das sich fürchterlich niedersenkte. Sie wußten es, daß sie keine schlechteren Soldaten waren als die Feinde. Im Gegenteil, sie wußten ganz genau, daß sie besser kämpften und daß die größere Leistung auf ihrer Seite war. Aber — und das brannte in ihnen wie ein vergifteter und steckengebliebener Widerhaken — sie sahen es hilflos mit an, wie sie der bloßen und stumpfsinnigen Übermacht des Materials und der Menschen unterlagen" (308).

The German grew accustomed to fighting against a two-fold and three-fold superiority, supported by the technical resources of the whole world. The German Western Front defended itself for years until it was ultimately reduced to a last few heroes, bleeding from a thousand wounds, left to their own resources and yet invincible in battle.[95]

The Prince includes all the typical components of the theme: German paranoia about "encirclement," the "mere" numerical and technical superiority of the enemy, insufficient support from the homeland, and the concluding, overblown image of a decimated and wounded, but still unbroken army. A page later he describes the army of 1918:

> Decimated units: Companies of ten and twenty men [full company strength was 110 men] with hollow cheeks and torn, muddy uniforms. No enthusiasm or belief in victory now. Their step is slow and they are bowed down. But in their eyes flame the courage of despair, unconquerable pride, contempt of death, rage and fury at the misery of the Fatherland.[96]

Although the affected pathos of these passages is difficult to stomach, the picture of a physically wrecked but spiritually intact army is characteristic of many German First World War narratives.

Herbert Sulzbach, an artillery officer who served throughout the war, expresses the same sentiments in his diary. On 15 October 1918, he fulminates against Wilson's desire to humiliate Germany, mourns the loss of Lille, Bruges, Ostend and Roubaix, and then despairs of morale. "My God, who would have thought it would end like this? Undefeated! We must have made a lot of mistakes on the home front."[97] A few days later he maintains that " . . . we soldiers are not going to engage in revolution. We have done our duty for four years and three months; for four years and three months we have fought victorious actions, for four years and three months we have scored achievements which are completely unparalleled in history, and we shall hold on in the same spirit for

---

[95]Kronprinz Wilhelm, *Meine Erinnerungen aus Deutschlands Heldenkampf* (Berlin: Mittler, 1923). Tr. as *My War Experiences* (New York: McBride, 1923) v. "Der Deutsche war es gewöhnt, gegen doppelte und dreifache Überlegenheit zu kämpfen. Zehnfacher, durch die technischen Kriegsmittel der ganzen Welt gerüsteter Übermacht hat sich die deutsche Westfront durch Jahre erwehrt, schließlich zusammengeschrumpft auf eine Schar von Helden, blutend aus tausend Wunden, auf sich allein gestellt und dennoch im Kampfe unbesiegt" (vii).

[96]Kronprinz Wilhelm, vi. "Die gelichteten Verbände, Kompagnien von 20 und 10 Mann, mit hohlen Wangen, in zerfetzten und verdreckten Uniformen. Nichts mehr von Begeisterung, kein Siegesgefühl. Ihr Schritt ist schwer, ihre Haltung müde. Aber aus den Augen blitzt der Mut der Verzweiflung, unbeugsamer Trotz, Verachtung des Todes, Wut und Erbitterung über das Elend des Vaterlandes" (viii).

[97]Herbert Sulzbach, *Zwei lebende Mauern. 50 Monate Westfront* (Berlin: Bernard und Graefe, 1935). Tr. by Richard Thonger as *With the German Guns* (Hamden, Conn.: Archeon, 1981) 232. "Herr Gott, wer hätte an ein solches Ende gedacht! Unbesiegt! Wir müssen innenpolitisch viele Fehler gemacht haben" (228).

longer still!"[98] Like the Crown Prince, Sulzbach emphasizes the endurance and thus the stronger spirit of the front line troops, but introduces the notion of "mistakes" in the homeland.

This brings us to the other potent fiction of the end of the war, the corollary to that of the unbroken army. The theory of the "stab-in-the-back" will be examined in detail in a later chapter, but a few comments are appropriate here. The phrase was apparently coined either by Hindenburg or someone close to him within a few days of the armistice. It had a long dishonorable life in conservative writing in the interwar years, to emerge as a cornerstone of National Socialist rhetoric against the Treaty of Versailles. As a ploy to relieve the General Staff of responsibility for defeat and transfer that culpability to the new civilian government, it succeeded beyond the Staff's wildest hopes. Since the General Staff held a low opinion of politicians and wanted nothing to do with the new Republic, the maneuver effectively distanced them from the civilian government, while simultaneously aligning them with the "heroic" common soldiers.[99] Whatever its origin and degree of falsity, this "stab-in-the-back" myth does not invalidate the general feeling of betrayal among the combatants. The alienation of the front-line troops from both the rear echelons and the homeland ensured that substantial bitterness toward those who could never understand the experience of combat already existed. That was devastatingly true when the combat in question was a four-year war of attrition that had accounted for nearly two million dead in Germany.

The myth also reinforced the soldiers' sense of their own heroism, strength, and devotion to duty. It implied that they still believed in the homeland, but that the cowardly homeland had perfidiously betrayed their martyrdom. Theweleit has precisely caught the tone of wounded sacrifice when he notes that "the 'stab in the back' shows that the soldier had not lain down, that he had stood, stern face to the enemy, so that he did not notice the traitor behind his back and nevertheless offered him a fine target."[100]

In its mildest form, the front soldier's bitterness was concentrated on those who stayed safely at home and made a profit out of it. In its more radical form, it became a diatribe against those who failed to properly value the endurance and sacrifices of the front soldiers. The word "conspiracy" quickly appeared. In his *In the Line*, published as an antidote to the "false" picture drawn by Remarque, Bucher touches on most of the main themes.

[98]Sulzbach, 234. " . . . wir Soldaten revolutionieren nicht, wir haben vier Jahre und drei Monate unsere Pflicht getan, vier Jahre und drei Monate gesiegt, vier Jahre und drei Monate Leistungen vollbracht, die ohne Beispiel dastehen, und wir werden es noch länger aushalten im gleichen Geist!" (230) In the 1935 edition, the words of the above text are spaced for emphasis.

[99]Lindley Fraser, *Germany between Two Wars: A Study of Propaganda and War-Guilt* (Oxford: Oxford UP, 1944), 15–17; Hans Ernest Fried, *The Guilt of the German Army* (New York: Macmillan, 1942), 36–37.

[100]Theweleit, *Männerfantasien*, 86.

Already the arguments of the pacifist conspiracy had begun insidiously to destroy our will to fight on. . . . It was a terrible irony that while we were clinging
to that strip of Marne soil, clinging to it desperately with all the strength that
remained in us, the homeland was sending men among us who whispered that
every shot we fired, every blow we struck at the enemy, made us contemptible
prolongers of the war. Yes, that was said of us — of us who had marched away
with the intoxicating enthusiasm of 1914, who had seen our comrades struck
down by the thousands, who had endured so much. Yes, that was what they
said of us. The thought was deadlier than the fiercest onslaught of an armed
foe.[101]

At the core of these passages lies the conviction that having done their utmost,
and having suffered terribly, the fault for the defeat cannot lie with the soldiers.
It must, therefore, lie elsewhere, with war profiteers, pacifists, communists,
Jews, politicians. In short, it lies with the enemy to the rear: the homeland. "We
had ceased to believe in our fighting power and felt that the homeland must
bear the blame."[102] The conviction of betrayal marked the majority of veterans
between the wars, seriously undermined their confidence in civilian government,
and permanently affected the shape of the war experience.

"Ich hatt' einen Kameraden . . ."

Easily the most popular song of the war, Uhland's lyrics, familiar since the
Wars of Liberation, touched a resonant chord among front soldiers. Alienated
from civilians and staff alike by the experience of the trenches and the *Materialschlacht*, embittered by what they perceived as a civilian betrayal of their sacrifice, front soldiers turned for emotional sustenance to those who were literally
closest to them and who had endured the same experiences: their comrades-in-
arms, their fellow front soldiers. Leed accurately states that if Germany produced "a liberal experience of war that emphasized the loss of youth, the death,
horror and pollution of war," it also produced "a conservative experience which
centered upon the experience of comradeship and community."[103] The liberal

---

[101]Bucher, *In the Line*, 270; 273. "An unserem Willen beginnen die Hetzreden unsichtbarer
Verschwörer zu wüten . . . . Hier klammern wir bei der Marne an mit letzter Verzweiflung, mit
dem Wenigen das noch in uns lebt. Klammern an, während die eigene Heimat Sendlinge
schickt, die uns durch flüsternde Hetzzettel sagen, daß jeder Schuß, den wir abgeben, jeder
Hieb, den wir austeilen, mit denen wir die 'Drüben' immer wieder von ihrem Ziel fernhalten,
uns zu verachtungswürdigen Kriegsverlängerern macht. Dies sagt man uns. Uns! die wir 14 haben vorbeirauschen sehen, die wir das reihenweise Hinsinken unserer Kameraden mit ange-
schaut, mitgefühlt haben. Uns sagt man das. Dies lähmt mehr, als das tollste Wüten des
bewaffneten Feindes. . . " (314; 318–319).

[102]Bucher, *In the Line*, 279. " . . . wir haben den Glauben an unsere Kampfkraft verloren, unser
Höchstes, Gewaltigstes! Wir selbst sind nicht schuld daran — Heimat!" (326)

[103]Leed, *No Man's Land*, 25.

experience typical of British First World War writers is represented in German writing, most notably by Remarque, Unruh, Arnold Zweig and Edlef Köppen, but the liberal vision is overshadowed by the sheer quantity of conservative texts. What is more, even the liberal texts significantly praise comradeship and its centrality to the war experience, albeit without mythologizing it. The emotional bond of comradeship and the import of that bond dominate the German war narrative and indeed all discourse about the war in the succeeding years.

How, first of all, can one define this much-vaunted phenomenon of comradeship? Within the context of the German experience of the First World War, comradeship may be defined as an affective sense of community between front soldiers, based on shared experience and suffering. Even Remarque, the most famous purveyor of the liberal version of the war experience, admits the value of comradeship. Although he identifies it as a "practical sense of esprit de corps," rather than giving it the philosophical gloss bestowed on it by conservative writers, Remarque still identifies comradeship as "the finest thing that arose out of the war."[104]

Comradeship is based on three factors. The first is the shared experience of the front, especially of the western front and the *Materialschlacht*. The experience of comradeship is quintessentially communal and exclusively male. Historically, the experience of combat in the First World War is entirely male. As Hynes has correctly noted, war was an exclusively male activity that inevitably excluded women and their concerns.[105] The existence and influence of the various male associations (*Bunde*) in nineteenth- and twentieth-century Germany provided an even stronger impetus toward the formation of a formalized bond between fighting soldiers. The historically important bond of comradeship can be traced at least to the Wars of Liberation — hence the popularity of Uhland's song — an importance only increased by the romantic patriotism of the Wandervogel and similar organizations. The strong German model of male bonding no doubt predisposed soldiers to form such bonds and to see true comradeship as a specifically German phenomenon.

Secondly, the bond of comradeship is based on emotion. From a rational point of view, insofar as men in danger who stick together and help each other are more likely to survive, comradeship has a pragmatic aspect. But the emphasis is always on feeling, which links it to the Romantic and *völkisch* ideas of unity and community discussed earlier. Moreover, the irrational basis of the commu-

---

[104]Remarque, *All Quiet*, 35. "Das Wichtigste aber war, daß in uns ein festes, praktisches Zusammengehörigkeitsgefühl erwachte, das sich im Felde dann zum Besten steigerte, was der Krieg hervorbrachte: zur Kameradschaft!" (29)

[105]Hynes, *A War Imagined*, 87–96. For a fine analysis of British women and war literature, see Sandra M. Gilbert and Susan Gubar, "Soldier's Heart: Literary Men, Literary Women, and the Great War," in *No Man's Land: The Place of the Woman Writer in the Twentieth Century* (New Haven: Yale UP, 1989), 2:258–323. See also Margaret R. Higonnet, ed., *Behind the Lines: Gender and the Two World Wars* (New Haven: Yale UP, 1987).

nal bond places it within the framework of German idealism and vitalism. Günther Lutz proclaims that those soldiers who did not experience comradeship failed to do so because for them the war was a purely material occurrence, not an inner experience involving the creation of new values.[106] Although Lutz's work was published after the National Socialist assumption of power, his emphasis on inward transformation is in total accord with earlier conservative writers, as is his dismissal of material events as unworthy of consideration.

Thirdly, the feeling of unity is based on immediate authentic experience and is therefore above conventional distinctions of class, occupation and region. A number of writers, Beumelburg for example, make a point of including men from different classes in the community of comradeship. Beumelburg's *Gruppe Bosemüller* includes both middle and working class men from all over Germany. Johannsen's four "Inseparables" include a student (the narrator) called the Philosopher, a factory foreman, and a peasant's son. Such a combination is paradigmatic for the conservative narratives and even for some of the leftist writers such as Renn and Remarque. For most writers, at least, the unity of "field gray" overcomes all bourgeois divisions of class and education.[107] Such divisions are obsolete, furthermore, because they belong to the world "behind the lines." In the front line, the soldier's feelings and behavior are predicated on a system of moral values superior to civilian conventions, because that system is born out of genuine experience and because its moral imperative is absolute. Social equality is insignificant; spiritual unity is everything. That is not to imply that there are no distinctions within the ranks of the field gray community. Most significantly, there is the distinction between leader and led, to which I shall return, but which, like comradeship itself, is based on the organic development of the individual within the community.

The German obsession with wholeness and harmony, on which so many critics have remarked, appears in the war narratives as a comradeship both actual and emblematic of the larger unity of the *Volk*. For Schauwecker, who consistently taps into conservative beliefs, the soldiers are "a great gray family lying in shell-craters and trenches."[108] By choosing the family as his metaphor, he sug-

---

[106]Lutz, *Das Gemeinschaftserlebnis*, 36.

[107]For a typical group of comrades, see the opening passages of Ernst Johannsen *Vier von der Infanterie: Ihre letzten Tage an der Westfront 1918* (Hamburg: Fackelreiter, 1929). Tr. by A. W. Wheen as *Four Infantrymen on the Western Front, 1918* (London: Methuen, 1930).The bourgeois soldier's distress at the behavior and talk of ruder men, of which I earlier quoted several examples from Witkop's collection of letters, is largely a phenomenon of the early part of the war. The communal living necessitated by trench warfare and the psychological stress imposed by the *Materialschlacht* seem to have eliminated many of the traditional prejudices. Many authors remark, however, on the reassertaion of class distinctions after the war, when the field-gray uniform of the front soldiers was put aside.

[108]Schauwecker, *Fiery Way*, 67. " . . . eine große, graue Familie in Granattrichtern und Chausseegräben . . . " (51).

gests that the front soldiers make up a natural, organic entity linked by sentiment and existing only at the front. Earlier in the same book, he calls them
"Germany in exile — ploughing through the flaming seas of war."[109] Here the
metaphoric language elevates the soldiers to the level of the nation — they are
not merely Germans, but Germany itself. The phrase "in exile" points to the
theme of alienation from home and from the material past. It implies a theme
that for Schauwecker and other writers lies at the core of their sense of comradeship: they, and only they, having suffered and sacrificed for the nation at the
front, are the true bearers of the spirit of that nation.

Schauwecker returns to the theme in *The Furnace*. Under shellfire, his *porte-
parole* meditates on the nature of comradeship and the nation:

> And now here I am with Radtke and Herse [his comrades] and all the rest —
> together. Now where it's life or death, where we squelch in filth and lie under
> fire and share mud, lice, bread and poverty — now at least we are really to-
> gether.... Here we have it, unity, whose sense we shall never lose, unique
> unity — the nation.[110]

The yearning for true communal unity (*Gemeinschaft*) that stands out in this
passage does so in contrast to the divisive materialism of the "enemy" to the rear,
the capitalist society of *Gesellschaft*. At the front "they stood alone, they stood for
the nation that was to come, the nation which must not fall into the unclean
hands of those behind the lines."[111]

In a subsequent chapter, I shall return to the salient theme of comradeship
as the model for a future national community, but at this point, a few remarks
will suffice. The future form of the nation envisioned by Schauwecker, Beumelburg, and many of the other conservative writers was that of an organic hierarchical community of *Volk*, based on natural sentiment and idealism, and
modeled on the experience of comradeship at the front. The Romantic commitment to a homogeneous, harmonious community, akin to Novalis's vision of
the German Middle Ages, rather than to a diverse, contractual society, became,
in the First World War, the glorification of a comradeship that mitigated the
individual's isolation and vulnerability by situating him in a unified *Gemeinschaft*. While Romantic and *völkisch* ideas of community clearly contributed to
the centrality of comradeship in the German war experience, the more immediate background of the youth movement predominates. It would be impossible

[109]Schauwecker, *Fiery Way*, 57.

[110]Schauwecker, *The Furnace*, 197. "Und nun bin ich mit Herse hier und Radtke und den andern allen zusammen. Mit einem Male, wo es auf Leben und Tod geht, wo wir im Dreck wa-
ten und im Feuer liegen und Dreck, Läuse, Brot und Durst teilen — nun, da, endlich da sind
wir zusammen.... Da haben wir sie, die Eine, die Unlernbare, die Unverlierbare, die Einmali-
ge, die Nation!" (220)

[111]Schauwecker, *The Furnace*, 201. "Sie standen hier für sich allein da und für die kommende
Nation, die nicht jenen da hinten in die unreinen Hände fallen durfte!" (225)

to prove that most young German soldiers had some familiarity with the youth movement, but many of the urban bourgeois soldiers — the ones most likely to write accounts of their war experience — must have been involved. The communal organization of such groups, and their devotion to the ideals of belonging, self-sacrifice and fellow-feeling would have established a mental model of comradeship. The development of the idea of comradeship into a philosophical paradigm for society in no way undermined its essentially emotional base. Laqueur notes that for the Wandervogel *thought* about the war was denigrated in favor of *feeling* at one with the Fatherland.[112]

The emotional nationalism common to the idea of comradeship, the youth movement, and earlier Romantic-nationalist movements (the *Turnvereine*, the *Bunde*, the *Burschenschaften*) explains the striking lack of influence by proletarian organizations on the front troops. The rational and international bases of marxism rendered it largely inimical to the broadly nationalistic front soldiers who needed emotional support more than dialectics. During the Kiel mutiny and the final retreat of 1918, when disorders broke out behind the front, and some soldiers' councils were formed on communist models, marxism probably achieved the height of its wartime influence. Many front troops, however, considered such actions typical of rear-echelon troops, and regarded them as a betrayal of their own sacrifices. In the first chapter of *After War* Renn draws a detailed picture of the return to a homeland in the throes of revolution, complete with mutinous troops and the beginnings of the Freikorps — the military units formed to fight for German rule on the eastern frontiers. Bucher, quoted earlier, is particularly venomous toward what he sees as a leftist conspiracy to betray the front soldiers.[113]

The unified community of the *Frontschweine* is characterized, first and foremost, by a sense of solidarity with other men in the same situation and undergoing the same series of experiences. That solidarity is achieved through the subordination of the individual will to the needs of the group. A concomitant loss of individuality is a frequent theme in the early part of many war books. Some regret the loss of the individual identity, but accommodate themselves to it, as does Vring's Private Suhren in the novel of the same name.[114] In Ernst Wiechert's *Jedermann: Geschichte eines Namenlosen* (Everyman: History of a Nameless Man, 1931), one of the most interesting and least known novels to come out of the war, the sensitive protagonist Johannes Karsten suffers from the

---

[112]Laqueur, *Young Germany*, 87.

[113]Bucher, *In the Line*, 270–273. The Freikorps were military units formed of volunteers, usually demobilized veterans, in the period just after the war. Their duty was to fight on the eastern frontiers of Germany to prevent the loss of German territory to the new Polish state, or to any other governments.

[114]Georg von der Vring, *Soldat Suhren* (Berlin: Spaeth, 1928). Tr. by Fred Hall as *Private Suhren* (London: Methuen, 1929), 16–19.

loss of individuality at the outset of his training. The title of the book suggests the sacrifice of self to the "field gray family," and the theme is picked up by Johannes when he says of an unpleasant army doctor, "That isn't Moldehnke, but a uniform, a rank. . . . All names have become a matter of indifference, and with those names, all memories. There are only service obligations and materiel."[115] His realization that the individual will be destroyed leads him to compromise when he goes to the front. He sees two duties: to maintain his "own face" and simultaneously to be "outside himself" (327). After this symbolic soldier completes his pilgrim's progress through the war, Johannes discovers that only his home has survived unchanged, and on that basis he and his two living comrades can begin to rebuild their individual lives (516-531).

Few writers show Wiechert's sensitivity to the conflict between individual and community. Arnold Zweig explores the war's effect on the individual personality in both *Education before Verdun* and *The Case of Sergeant Grisha*, but in both novels the primary focus is elsewhere. The conservative writers, as one might expect, welcome the sacrifice of self to community as a form of spiritual purification. Individual privileges destroy the community spirit, so the war is hailed as a great leveler in the service of a truly ideal spiritual community. Schauwecker experiences a thrill of fraternity during his training when a girl he knows doesn't recognize him among the other soldiers. He feels himself "one among millions. Comrade, soldier."[116] A number of writers mention the thrill of being addressed by the old hands as "comrade" for the first time.[117]

The sacrifice of self, even of one's life is rewarded by an intense emotional belonging and understanding among comrades. Ernst Johannsen's *Vier von der Infanterie* (1929, translated as *Four Infantrymen on the Western Front*, 1930) is focused on the "bitter comradeship" of the trenches.[118] For Johannsen the war has no meaning except the experience of comradeship to the death and beyond. He leaves a striking, if grandiloquent, description of comradely behavior, rendered more significant by Johannsen's position as a liberal writer whose novel inspired Pabst's anti-war film, *Westfront 1918*:

> This comradeship, these friendships have a reticence beyond refinement. A man had rather lose his tongue than speak of his affection, his love for his mates. He will fetch in a wounded man under the deadliest fire; yet when his best friend, his boon companion, is killed, he merely says, "Well, he's hopped it." They help one another as a mere matter of course; a glance, a curse, a nod,

[115]Ernst Wiechert, *Jedermann: Geschichte eines Namenlosen*, 1931, in *Sämtliche Werke* (Wien: Desch, 1957), 3:309–310; 319. "Es ist nicht Moldehnke, sondern eine Uniform, ein Dienstgrad. . . . Alle Namen sind ganz gleichgültig geworden, und mit den Namen alle Erinnerungen. Es gibt nur Dienstobliegenheiten und Material." (309–310)

[116]Schauwecker, *Fiery Way*, 14. "Einer von Millionen, Kamerad. Soldat" (9).

[117]See, for example Hein, *Verdun*, 17.

[118]Johannsen, *Four Infantrymen*, 41.

a cigarette perhaps, that is all the thanks. To the youngsters the old hands are considerate and fatherly. They are often sarcastic, often scrap among themselves, but it is without the spitefulness, the heartless brutality so common in quarrels between women. Their best and worst feelings alike they keep to themselves, or mask them in coarse language and jest. Bound together in danger and in death, enjoying privacy in nothing, yet each preserves a masculine incuriousness towards the personal intimacies of the other, and so there is always a strange aloofness and reticence between them.[119]

Much of the interest in this passage lies in its compression into a single paragraph of characteristic themes and behaviors from a wide range of German First World War books. Most significant among those is the affection engendered by the forced sharing of the status and powerlessness of victims.[120] Although repressed or concealed, the emotion is always there, and is viewed as an ennobling and purifying agent. For Johannsen and most of the others, comradeship is the purest and most ideal form of friendship because it depends entirely upon fellow-feeling from men in the same extremity of danger. It is therefore untainted by materialism, class prejudices, rivalry or any of the other ignoble traits typical of civilians.

The remark about women demands some comment, as do the observations of Johannsen's last paragraph. The behavior described by Johannsen (and by many conservative authors) coincides with the model of the "armored" male fascist personality elaborated by Theweleit. Waltraud Amberger, following Theweleit, describes the "manly" qualities of this personality as "discipline, hardness, propriety, order and self-control."[121] This "strong man" is presented as the antithesis to weak, passive, emotionally and sexually chaotic woman. Woman is the "other" who can have no place in the male society of the front. Women are

---

[119]Johannsen, 42–43. "Wieviel Zartheit ist in dieser Kameradschaft und Freundschaft. Lieber beißt sich ein Mann fast die Zunge ab, als daß er unter seinesgleichen zarte, feine Gefühle und Empfindungen äußert oder gar Tränen zeigt. Man schleppt Verwundete durch das schlimmste Feuer, wenn aber ein guter Bekannter oder der Freund gefallen ist, heißt es nur: 'Nun ist der auch hin,' oder 'Er sollte morgen im Urlaub fahren.' Sie helfen sich mit Selbstverständlichkeit, ein Aufleuchten des Gesichtes, ein Fluch, ein Nicken oder eine Zigarette als Symbole des Dankes. Zu den Jungen sind die Alten nachsichtig und väterlich. Sie ärgern sich oft, haben auch Krach miteinander, aber es fehlt dabei die weibliche Nadelspitze, die herzlose Brutalität, die im Streit unter Frauen so leicht zum Vorschein kommt. Das Schlimmste und Zarteste machen sie mit sich selber ab oder kleiden es in grobe Worte und machen Witze dabei. Verbunden durch Not und Tod, in steter Gemeinschaft miteinander, sorgt doch jene männliche Gleichgültigkeit gegen das Allerpersönlichste des andern dafür, daß immer ein gewisser Abstand bestehen bleibt" (31–32).

[120]Leed, No Man's Land, 210.

[121]Waltraud Amberger, Männer, Krieger, Abenteuer: Der Entwurf des 'soldatischen Mannes' in Kriegsromanen über den Ersten und Zweiten Weltkrieg (Frankfurt a.M.: Fischer, 1984), 43. Although portions of her argument are flawed by her intrusively radical feminist-marxist orientation, Amberger makes many valuable observations on the conservative combat narratives.

consequently reduced to two types: 1) the pure, for example mothers, sisters, nurses, and perhaps appropriately submissive and faithful wives and sweethearts, and 2) the impure, including prostitutes, working-class women, and any woman who doesn't fit into the first category.[122]

Alongside the obvious facts that women were not present in combat areas, and that the narratives under discussion are preeminently *combat* narratives, the conservative devaluation of women helps to account for the limited presence of female characters in the texts. The loyal wives, mothers and sisters who do appear contrast sharply with "available" women behind the lines, who largely serve as the object of "soldierly love-maneuvers."[123] Even liberal texts tend to categorize women in the same way, for example Remarque's *All Quiet*, which contrasts Bäumer's mother and sister with the willing Frenchwomen behind the lines. The salient exception is Arnold Zweig's tetralogy, which contains several central, well-realized female characters.

But for the vast majority of the German Great War writers, the experience of comradeship stands at the center of the soldier's universe, transcending and replacing all previous forms of friendship and love. It becomes, in effect, an all-encompassing *Weltanschauung* that dictates both present and future attitudes, and that represents the sole authentic experience of the war admitted by the nationalists. Hans Seldte, founder of Stahlhelm, the most important of the post-war veterans' organizations, conflates comradeship and the war itself into the transformation that was the *Kriegserlebnis*: "The war for us has become experience. War and comradeship. The war made us front soldiers into new men, into a people within a people."[124]

The transformative power of comradeship has its effect on one of Schauwecker's characters when he says " . . . I'd rather be with you and Radtke and Schramm and Gericke than with any of my friends from pre-war times, and . . . I never really realized that till now."[125] The feeling of comradeship transcends and obliterates not only previous notions of friendship, but also, in its unselfishness and readiness to sacrifice, any other values. Albrecht, another soldier in *The Furnace*, voices the author's sentiments:

> "Comradeship and you and the others, and the rage you feel when you see them [the enemy] shoot your neighbor. You go quite mad when you see them come on. You can't help firing when you see that. And then it is a question

[122]Amberger, 76–89.

[123]Amberger, 89.

[124]Qtd. in Sontheimer, *Antidemokratisches Denken*, 123. "Der Krieg ist uns zum Erlebnis geworden. Der Krieg und die Kameradschaft. Der Krieg hat uns Frontsoldaten zu neuen Menschen, zu einem Volk im Volke gemacht."

[125]Schauwecker, *The Furnace*, 186. " . . . ich mit dir und mit Radtke und mit Schramm und Gericke lieber zusammen bin als mit allen meinen Freunden vorm Kriege, und daß ich das bis dahin nie so gemerkt habe wie jetzt" (204–205).

neither of pay or promotion or anything which one could get in other circumstances. It is a question of the whole of everything." "Aye," said Herse
thoughtfully, "a man shouldn't think of his distillery."[126]

In short, all material considerations (pay, promotion, property) are as nothing
against the pervasive force of collective devotion. And within the confines of the
nationalist combat narrative, comradeship, and comradeship alone, is "the
whole of everything."

The collectivity of comradeship should not be confused with equality, for it
encompasses an authoritarian hierarchy of leadership. Leadership was, in fact,
an essential component, but in keeping with its irrational and *völkisch* bias, the
leader was a natural leader who shared the comradeship of his men. He was a
front soldier among front soldiers, the antithesis of the rear echelon officer who
was, in the novels, invariably interested only in collecting an Iron Cross and
going back to a safe job. Examples abound. Company commanders, usually
lieutenants or captains, gained the loyalty of their troops by protecting and car-
ing for their men, not by wasting them in futile attacks. Hein contrasts Lt.
Wynfrith, who spares his men and gets no reward for it, with Lt. Beekmann,
who leads wild charges and gets his men killed, but goes to the rear with the
Iron Cross First Class.[127] Beumelburg speaks of a lieutenant "that one reads
about in books: constant, tranquillity itself, always in control, always in the
trenches."[128] Goltz's Lt. Bruchner (promoted from the ranks) finds that only his
concern for his men makes the conditions, and life itself, bearable.[129] Goote's
Lt. Bang sums up the front soldier's view of leadership:

> For me the most important thing is always that we develop a spiritual unity,
> that we are not bound to each other by orders, but that we all act together be-

---

[126]Schauwecker, *The Furnace*, 167. "'Die Kameradschaft und du selber zusammen mit den andern und die Wut, die du kriegst, wenn du siehst, wie sie den Nebenmann zerschießen. Du
wirst ganz wild, wenn du sie ankommen siehst. Du kannst gar nicht anderes, als schießen,
wenn du sie ankommen siehst. Und dann geht es nicht um Geld oder Beförderung oder um
Sachen, die man auch anders haben kann. Es geht um das Ganze, um alles.' Tja . . . ,' meinte
Herse. 'Man darf wohl nicht an seine Destille denken'" (183–184).

[127]Hein, *Verdun*, 86.

[128]Beumelburg, *Bosemüller*, 10. " . . . ein Leutenant, wie er im Buch steht: hochanständig, die
Ruhe selbst, immer an der Spitze, immer in Stellung."

[129]Goltz, *Der Baum von Cléry*, 184. An almost fatherly attitude toward one's men is also typical
of young British officers. Owen's poems are filled with it, and Blunden describes himself as a
"shepherd." See Fussell, *Great War*, 270–279. The homoerotic tradition that Fussell goes on to
discuss seems largely absent from the German narratives, although there are a few specifically
homoerotic texts.

cause it isn't possible to do otherwise. I don't want to be your superior, but a comrade who leads.[130]

The vision of the leader (*der Führer* is the preferred term) as first among equals derives from the notion of organic communal development. The true leader is a natural leader who emerges from the community. He neither inherits his position nor is elected to it, but necessarily grows into it as the community grows. Such ideas received a forceful impetus from the historical realities of the war. The only leaders the front-line troops saw with regularity were their immediate superiors — platoon and company commanders. As the fighting wore on and the ranks of junior and company-grade officers were decimated, such men were increasingly promoted from the ranks. Combat commanders, in addition, usually remained combat commanders, while staff officers remained at headquarters. The company commander had more common cause with his own troops than with the *Etappenschweine* to the rear.

In addition to the powerful incentive of shared experience, the front troops' admiration for their immediate leaders was only enhanced by the ignorance, arrogance, and incompetence of the rear echelon commanders, who, for the most part, never fouled their clean boots in the forward trenches. The gap between front and rear discussed above was, if anything, exacerbated by the rank and attendant privileges of the headquarters officers. Their relative security and comfort, which in most circumstances might have stirred only a moderate degree of envy, provided in the long catalogue of botched offensives and carelessly wasted troops that was the First World War, an excuse for disgust, hatred, and feelings of betrayal. For many a *Frontschwein*, the colonel in his comfortable château was a more dangerous enemy than the Frenchman across No Man's Land.

This disillusionment with the higher leadership of the army, and the separation of that leadership from the communal experience of comradeship produced a new ideal of "natural" leadership which would be raised to the level of a cult in what seemed to many veterans the leaderless disorder of postwar republican Germany.[131] The unity of leader and led is a persistent theme of conservative writers haunted by the specter of Germany's historical disunity. German society before August of 1914 is often described as "atomized" — not only broken into individual particles, but lacking organization and direction. The organization was provided by the comradeship of the front line, and the direction by the leader of the comrades, seen as "the best comrade," the exemplar of the

[130]Goote, *Wir fahren den Tod*, 53. "Mir ist aber immer die Hauptsache, daß wir eine seelische Einheit bilden, daß uns nicht Befehle aneinanderbinden, sondern daß wir alle an einen Strang ziehen, weil es gar nicht anders sein kann. Ich will nicht Vorgesetzter sein, sondern Kamerad, der führt."

[131]In the general disillusionment with higher headquarters, only Hindenburg was excepted, as he was credited with "saving" the army. He was revered until his death in 1934.

others and of the ideal of comradeship. Only men who had experienced the comradeship of the war were capable of understanding the meaning of that comradeship, its corollary, leadership, and by extension the war itself.

The unshakable certainty of having participated in a unique, shared experience encouraged the veterans to see themselves as the segment of society destined to lead the rest of the *Volk* into a new age, as in Seldte's description of front soldiers as a people within a people. While many veterans' organizations preached similar ideas, the most famous *Frontsoldat* of them all made it into a cornerstone of his political ideology. Adolf Hitler, although most historians myopically focus only upon his political career and the genuine horrors of his régime, was a front soldier who, except for two periods of hospitalization — first for a shrapnel wound in 1916, and then for a gassing in October of 1918 that temporarily blinded him — served virtually the entire war on the western front as a dispatch runner (*Meldegänger*). Since shelling inevitably destroyed the telephone lines that were the major means of communication between the front line trenches and headquarters, messengers were most essential in the most dangerous sectors. Hitler received the Iron Cross First Class in 1918 for bravery (he had already received the Iron Cross Second Class in 1914). At war's end, he was in the hospital recovering from the gas attack.

Such was Hitler's experience of the war, an experience that would mark his personality as it marked millions of others. For the rest of his life, he thought and spoke of himself as a soldier who was ready to sacrifice himself for his country. Indeed, the vocabulary of sacrifice (*Opfer*) is omnipresent in the conservative war narratives, and later in National Socialist rhetoric. In his address to the German people at the outbreak of the Second World War, Hitler called himself the "first soldier of the Reich" and spoke of resuming the uniform that was "most sacred and dear" to him. As John Keegan has correctly noted, he wore a version of the soldier's field gray tunic throughout the war, and finally committed suicide with a service pistol.[132]

More significant yet was Hitler's appropriation of the *Kriegserlebnis* as a foundation of his political action. Specifically, the characteristic ideals of comradeship, leadership and sacrifice became the model for a new German state envisioned as the apotheosis of comradeship. Günther Lutz states that "the war experience is today both ideal and model," and adds that National Socialism can be understood *only* as the communal experience (*Gemeinschaftserlebnis*) of the front.[133] In addition to his *In the Hell of Verdun*, Alfred Hein wrote a small book for children called *Das kleine Buch vom grossen Krieg* (The Little Book about the Great War, 1937), in which two children of a veteran learn about the experience of the war from their father, their teacher, assorted relatives, and an uncle who is in the SA. Although it is a blatant piece of political indoctrination, the con-

---

[132]John Keegan, *The Mask of Command* (New York: Penguin, 1987), 235.

[133]Lutz, *Gemeinschaftserlebnis*, 9.

stantly repeated emphasis on comradeship, fellow-feeling among people of the same *Volk*, and the importance of sacrifice of self to the common good reveals the links between the conservative version of the war experience and the ideology of National Socialism. At the end, the children demonstrate their understanding of the lessons of their elders by joining the Hitler Youth.

J. P. Stern, in his perceptive analysis of Hitler, maintains that the key to Hitler's use of the *Kriegserlebnis* is his elevation of personal experience to the arena of public affairs.[134] By claiming that through his *Kriegserlebnis* he had personal knowledge of the "little man's" sufferings and needs, he transformed himself into the nation's representative by the "authenticity" of that experience. Thus his validation for claiming to lead the German people was the genuineness of his experience and his feelings about that experience. The reliance on experience automatically and conveniently eliminates any need for systematic thought or a coherent political program. It also eliminates philosophical argument; one cannot argue about feelings.

Hitler's use of the "authentic experience" as a point of departure for political action is but the culmination of a movement that began with the Romantic nationalism of Fichte and Jahn. The irrational bases of comradeship as experienced during the First World War bear a close resemblance to the Romantic notions of the organic unity of the *Volk*. As was historically the case in German nationalism, the intellectual foundation of the state was a tangle of ideas that ultimately relied on the primacy of the irrational.

"There must be a reason . . ."
The Uses of Experience

My discussion has thus far concentrated on the experience of the First World War — its physical realities and the reactions, individual and collective, to those realities. But an analysis of the experience itself fails to answer the question that haunted the combatants and has bedeviled students of the war ever since: Why? What did the war mean, and how did the combatants arrive at that meaning? Did the men who fought learn anything from their experience, and if so, what? Or was it a meaningless slaughter of the innocents? I am not here referring to the belated analyses of historians, generals and politicians, who, for the most part, spent the war far from the trenches. The critical question is what the combatants made of their own experiences.

The British literary reaction to the war is, for the most part, a bitterly ironic denunciation of its massive human cost. One need only recall Sassoon's vitriolic condemnation of incompetent generals and uncomprehending bishops, or the bitterness of Owen's "old lie" to grasp the sense of irremediable and meaningless

---

[134] J. P. Stern, *Hitler: The Führer and the People* (Berkeley: U of California P, 1975), 23–24. I have been indebted to Stern's acute analysis throughout this section.

loss that characterizes the British and French war literatures.[135] Although the proponents of similar views are in the minority and the tone is entirely different, the literature of disillusionment also existed in Germany. The leading spokesman of the German "lost generation" was Erich Maria Remarque. The now-famous epigraph of *All Quiet on the Western Front*, which triggered an immediate sympathetic response in the English-speaking world, earned him as much opprobrium as praise in his native country. His book, he said, " . . . is to be neither an accusation nor a confession, and least of all an adventure, for death is not an adventure to those who stand face to face with it. It will try simply to tell of a generation of men who, even though they may have escaped its shells, were destroyed by the war."[136]

Despite the disclaimer, the book is both a confession and an accusation. As one of the earliest of the major war novels in Germany, Remarque's claim to speak for a generation physically or psychologically destroyed by the fighting placed him at the center of the expanding reexamination of the war. His contention that his generation was wasted in a war created by their elders was welcomed by many veterans. But it was indignantly rejected by even greater numbers of front soldiers, with accusations that Remarque had depicted a "latrine war" from a "worm's-eye" or "frog's-eye" view, and had completely ignored the spiritual aspect of the experience in order to describe the war in the crudest material way. The opening pages of the book, which center on a frank description of communal field latrines, were frequently cited as an example of Remarque's "latrine" vision.[137] The similarity of Remarque's experience of the war to that of many British writers largely accounts for the adulation with which the book was received in Britain, and for its continuing popularity in the English-speaking world as "the" novel of the First World War.

Although Remarque occupies the chair of minority spokesman, he was by no means the only German writer nor, indeed, the first to focus on the loss, horror, and insanity of the war. The heavily pacifistic expressionists had opposed the war from the beginning. The last and most extreme of a series of literary revolts beginning with *Sturm und Drang*, and equally dependent upon the subjectivism and radicalism of the earlier movements, the expressionist movement peaked between 1910 and 1918, and declined rapidly after the conclusion of the war. Most of the early war books in Germany — books written during or just

[135]In Britain and France there were minority voices who attempted to bestow on the war a meaning other than meaningless loss. But, as in Germany, the prevailing myth was too strong. Although the respective national myths were virtual opposites, the loss of minority views beneath the monolithic unity of those myths is similar. See Hynes, *A War Imagined*, 449–455 for the British minority writers.

[136]Remarque, *All Quiet*, 5. "Dieses Buch soll weder eine Anklage noch ein Bekenntnis sein. Es soll nur den Versuch machen, über eine Generation zu berichten, die vom Kriege zerstört wurde — auch wenn sie seinen Granaten entkam" (Dedication).

[137]On the reception of *All Quiet* see Gollbach, *Die Wiederkehr des Weltkrieges*, 275–309.

after the war, as distinguished from the much greater number that appeared between 1928 and 1935 — are either expressionistic or influenced by the expressionists. These books share a number of typical characteristics: revolt against the war and established authority, extreme contrasts, a utopian vision of human brotherhood, and a messianic belief in the ability of spirit to transform social and political realities.[138] The political wing of the expressionist movement was in the vanguard of anti-war sentiment throughout the war, particularly during the early years when opposition was almost unheard of. Even the Democratic Socialists and other leftist parties had joined in signing the disavowal of political strife — the *Burgfrieden* — in the first patriotic flush of 1914. They also voted the necessary war credits in the parliament, thereby proving their patriotism, but incidentally damaging their future credibility in the Weimar Republic.

On the literary side Fritz Pfembert's leftist journal *Die Aktion*, primarily a vehicle for expressionist work, published anti-war and avant-garde material until its dissolution in 1917, most notably the war poems of Stramm, Stadler and other "advanced" poets. The war verse of these poets is only now becoming known, largely because it was submerged by the tidal wave of patriotic occasional verse at the beginning of the war (one critic estimated over one million poems in the last five months of 1914), and in the twenties by the general disparagement of experimental verse in the rising tide of conservatism.[139]

The most important expressionist war narrative is Fritz von Unruh's *Opfergang* (Way of Sacrifice) written in the field in 1916, but not published until 1919. Its publication was forbidden during the war because of its pacifistic and humanitarian views. The title itself is ironic. The German word *Opfer* was much used by writers during the war in its positive patriotic sense of "sacrifice." In letters and diaries soldiers often speak of being "opferbereit," ready to sacrifice their lives for the good of the fatherland. These youthful writers of 1914–1918 were following a well-established, patriotic tradition in their use of the word. Prussian writers, especially, had enshrined the idea of sacrifice to king and country in the mythos of the Prussian, and later, German, state. Frederick the Great for example was glorified as the symbol of heroic sacrifice to duty.[140] But *Opfer* can also carry the far less heroic meaning of "victim," and there is little doubt that Unruh saw the war less as a way of sacrifice than as a parade of victims. For Clemens, one of the characters, the skulls of the regiments of men

[138]Walter Sokel, *The Writer in Extremis: Expressionism in Twentieth-Century German Literature* (Stanford: Stanford UP, 1959), 2.

[139]For an appreciation of the German war verse see Marsland, *The Nation's Cause* and especially Bridgewater, *German Poets of the First World War*.

[140]See Stirk, *The Prussian Spirit*, for an analysis of Frederick the Great as the embodiment of Prussian virtues. A famous National Socialist poster depicts Hitler as the heir of Frederick and Bismarck.

marching into Verdun (the locus of the book) were part of a charnel-house ("ein Beinhaus").[141]

Indeed, the controlling symbols in Unruh's book are the charnel-house, the madhouse, and the theater. The image of the charnel-house is, in various guises, a commonplace of the German war literature.[142] That of the madhouse is less common, although it appears in a number of the anti-war novels, most effectively in Edlef Köppen's *Heeresbericht* (1930, translated as *Higher Command*, 1931). Theatrical analogies, on the other hand, are rather rare (unlike the British literature, where they are quite common). After his vision of the marching charnel-house, Clemens in despair finally calls Verdun a comedy ("Lustspiel"), no doubt a blackly ironic one. Unruh's involvement with the theater is apparent not only in that image, but also in the construction of the book. It consists of a series of vivid scenes, loosely tied together by theme and image. The scenes equally provide an opportunity for the exclamatory speeches so typical of expressionist writing.

The same episodic construction and declamatory style also characterizes the other major expressionist work about the war, Leonhard Frank's *Der Mensch ist Gut* (Man is Good, 1918). In Frank's work the utopian aspect of expressionism is at its most apparent. If ironic despair typifies Unruh, a vision of an ideal future infuses *Der Mensch is Gut*. The epigraph combines a warning from Matthew III with a dedication to the coming generation. Like *Opfergang*, it is organized in a series of loosely-connected episodes, each focused on a nameless representative generic figure. The action takes place in a German city rather than at the front, and shows first those who stayed at home: the father, the mother, and the war widow. Frank then moves to the couple, and finally to the war cripples.

The father of the opening section is a waiter. He has sacrificed everything for the son he adores and wants to make into a good German bourgeois. When the son is killed in 1915 "on the field of honor" as the official language has it, "a whole world was slain."[143] In his despair and distraction, he sells food for too little money and loses his job. In the simple, declamatory style typical of the book, he addresses a crowd that turns into a protest march. For him a lack of

---

[141]Unruh, *Opfergang*, 44.

[142]The image of the charnel-house reaches back to the Thirty Years' War and the poetry of Andreas Gryphius. In visual form, it is an important component of Otto Dix's war paintings, especially *Der Schützengraben* and the central panel of *Der Krieg*. See Otto Conzelmann, *Der andere Dix: Sein Bild vom Menschen und vom Krieg* (Stuttgart: Klett-Cotta, 1983) for a thorough analysis of Dix's war imagery.

[143]Leonhard Frank, *Der Mensch ist Gut* (1918, reprint Munich: Nymphenburger, 1953), 8. "Eine Welt war erschlagen."

love is the enemy and the root cause of all wars. "All Europe weeps because all Europe can no longer love. All Europe is mad because it can no longer love."[144]

The second section, "The War Widow," opens with her despair:

"How many women is it then? Two million perhaps who sit in their rooms and, like me, think of their dead husbands? Who look out the window and think of their dead husbands, who dust, wait for children, knit stockings, cook, go to work and think of their dead husbands, think of their dead husbands, think of their dead husbands. Who go to bed at night and think of their dead husbands."[145]

The reiteration of the single phrase interwoven with the catalogue of daily activities gives this passage surprising power and is a fine example of Frank's style at its best. The widow cannot imagine the "Altar of the Fatherland" on which her husband has been sacrificed. For her he has been sacrificed in the barbed wire of the Fatherland (22). The irony of the word "sacrifice" is worth noting here, and for the same reason as in Unruh. Like the father, the war widow joins the growing crowd of war protesters.

The third section, "The Mother," is essentially a continuation of the protest march in progress, but the mother provides a symbolic level of meaning. She has a vision of the trenches as an enormous wreath of graves ("ein Riesen-Kreis-Grab") — a funeral wreath — spanning a silent Europe (62). The scene shifts to the front where her son is obsessed by a man he saw die in the barbed wire (the war widow's husband, naturally). After his terrible experiences, he concludes that all the best people have to die because there are only two ways to tolerate the slaughter of the war: to grow accustomed to it, or to go mad (82–83). The section closes with the cry (Schrei) of the mother — the symbol of European humanity. A vision of Christ lowers itself into her arms, and two streams of people form a human cross with the mother and Christ at the center. Despite the expressionist's rebellion against traditional society, the Christian symbolism fits into the framework of Frank's utopian and humanitarian vision.

The fourth section, "The Couple," is largely given over to a rambling and confused philosophical discourse on the war, turning primarily on the idea that everything in Germany has been created by the war, and everyone who does not oppose it is also a part of it (101). This echoes the earlier theme of war-guilt introduced by the father and the war widow — a theme common to leftist writers throughout the Weimar period.

[144]Frank, 14–15. "Das Nichtvorhandensein der Liebe ist der Feind und die Ursache aller Kriege. Ganz Europa weint, weil ganz Europa nicht mehr lieben kann. Ganz Europa ist wahnsinnig, weil es nicht lieben kann."

[145]Frank, 21. "Ja wieviel Frauen sind's dann? Zwei Millionen vielleicht, die in ihrem Zimmer sitzen und, wie ich, an ihren toten Mann denken? Zum Fenster hinaus sehen und an ihren toten Mann denken, Staub wischen, Kinder warten, Strümpfe stricken, kochen, auf die Arbeit gehen und an ihren toten Mann denken, an ihren toten Mann denken, toten Mann denken. Sich abends ins Bett legen und an ihren toten Mann denken."

The final section, "The War Cripples," centers on wounded and crippled veterans. Frank dwells on the horrors of a forward surgical unit, which he calls a butcher's kitchen (120), before shifting to the hospital train returning the wounded to Germany. They realize that all cripples are comrades (152). The book ends in the city with a festival of cripples who join the protesters. The cries of suffering are transformed into songs of love in an ecstasy of brotherhood and peace. At the end, militarism is banished from the world: "The uniform disappears. Disappears out of the world"(171).

I have examined the work of Unruh and Frank at some length because, along with Latzko's 1918 book, *Menschen im Krieg* (translated as *Men in Battle*) they represent the earliest fictional responses to the war. Leaving aside for the moment predictable pacifist propaganda and the attempts of eminent writers (such as Thomas Mann) to come to terms with the war, these works share a number of characteristics. First, they were all written during the war, and they possess, for better or worse, an emotional immediacy that later works rarely demonstrate. Secondly, they all expound pacifistic views. There are a number of reasons for the pacifism of wartime works. In some cases, such as that of Latzko, the writers were, before the war, already pacifists by conviction. Latzko was at the center of an important pacifist group in Switzerland throughout the war. Others, like Unruh and Frank, became pacifists through their experience of the war. Fritz von Unruh presents a particularly interesting case. Descended from a Prussian noble family of strong military traditions, he had spent his youth in cadet schools and as the companion of two of the Kaiser's younger sons. He rejected the army in favor of the bohemian theatrical life of Berlin, but when the war broke out he returned immediately and voluntarily to the army, where he spent the remainder of the hostilities as an officer in the trenches, including service at Verdun, which led him to write *Opfergang*.

The decline of expressionism after the war is linked to its espousal of pacifism during the war. Even late in 1917 and 1918, pacifism represented a radical revolt against established authority and the general tenor of public opinion. That was particularly true when the pacifism was of the international humanitarian variety found in Frank and Unruh. Utopian visions of universal brotherhood and peace which characterized the leftist-internationalist-pacifist world view ran entirely contrary to the nationalism and conservatism common to German thought. In the wake of the defeat, pacifist writers were not perceived as seers who had predicted the suffering of war, but as betrayers who had undermined the German will to fight.[146] The innate conservatism of German readers also militated against experimental form as well as against pacifist and

---

[146]For sources on the history of German pacifism, see chapter 6, notes 80 and 81. The influence of pacifism in France, on the other hand, was especially pervasive among veterans, although it was not usually of the internationalist sort. See Antoine Prost, *Les Anciens combattants et la société française, 1914–1939*, 3 vols. (Paris: Presses de la Fondation nationale des sciences politiques, 1977), 3:35–119.

internationalist content. The brief flash of expressionist sound and fury was followed, with a couple of exceptions, by a long literary silence about the war that was scarcely broken until 1928.

The silence was broken by the unprecedented success of the classic liberal (to borrow Leed's term) war novel, Remarque's *All Quiet on the Western Front*. Remarque's pacifism, unlike that of the expressionists, emerges from a realistic depiction of the horrors of trench warfare.[147] *All Quiet* and its 1931 sequel *Der Weg zurück* (translated as *The Road Back*, 1931) provide the best-known examination of the liberal experience of the war. The other major liberal texts are Ludwig Renn's *War* and *Afterwar* (*Krieg*, 1928; *Nachkrieg*, 1930), and Arnold Zweig's tetralogy *The Great War of the White Men* (Der Grosse Krieg der weissen Manner).[148] Leaving aside Zweig's attempt at a panoramic historical account of the war, Remarque and Renn are particularly pertinent to an analysis of the uses of the war experience, as both authors follow their characters into postwar Germany. In both cases, despite feelings of hopelessness and loss, there is a driving need to make some sense of the war, and to find some use for all of the horror. It is precisely on the last point that the German liberal experience seems to differ from the British experience of the war. The German writers, however pacifistic, seem unable to accept the war as meaningless loss, or their experience of it as useless. The German belief in experience as formative and creative prevents even terrible experiences from being viewed as purely destructive.

The final chapter of *All Quiet*, set in the autumn of 1918, mirrors the hopelessness of the troops. Paul Bäumer has lost all of his friends, and is the last of the seven volunteers from his class. Had the soldiers returned home in 1916, he thinks, "out of the suffering and the strength of our experiences we might have unleashed a storm. Now if we go back we will be weary, broken, burnt out, rootless and without hope. We will not be able to find our way anymore."[149] The utter exhaustion and despair of men trapped in a seemingly endless war appear consistently in writing about the last months of the war. Even Schauwecker, who stands at the opposite philosophical pole, speaks of the soldiers as

---

[147]Sontheimer, *Antidemokratisches Denken*, 119. Remarque's view of the war is not unlike that of a number of French memoirists, especially Roland Dorgelès in *Les croix de bois*, which may help to account for the enthusiastic reception for the French translation of Remarque's novel.

[148]The tetralogy includes *Junge Frau von 1914* (1931, *Young Woman of 1914*), *Erziehung vor Verdun* (1935, *Education before Verdun*), *Der Streit um den Sergeanten Grisha* (1927,*The Case of Sergeant Grisha*), and *Die Versetzung eines Konigs* (1938, *The Crowning of a King*). All of the published translations are by Eric Sutton.

[149]Remarque, *All Quiet*, 371–318. " . . . wir hätten aus dem Schmerz und der Stärke unserer Erlebnisse einen Sturm entfesselt. Wenn wir jetzt zurückkehren, sind wir müde, zerfallen, ausgebrannt, wurzellos und ohne Hoffnung. Wir werden uns nicht mehr zurechtfinden können" (261–262).

"victims of fate" and of the "vanity of human plans, of human thought."[150] Remarque's use of the word *wurzellos* (rootless) is especially appropriate here, as it reinforces the alienation and superfluity that Remarque treats at length in *The Road Back*. Bäumer's meditation ends with the quiet conviction that he has lost everything that it is possible to lose, his ideals, his friends, the chance for a happy, productive life, so "let the months and years come, they can take nothing from me, they can take nothing more. I am so alone, and so without hope that I can confront them without fear."[151] In the famous conclusion, Bäumer dies on a day in October 1918 so quiet that the army report is the single sentence which serves as the book's title. When found, his face is calm "as though almost glad the end has come."[152] The irony here, and Remarque is one of the rare German writers to employ irony in the English manner, is twofold: Bäumer's death just before the armistice, and the implication that even had he survived to the end, the war would not be over for him. The only escape from war is death. The irony is more pointed in the culminating image of Lewis Milestone's 1930 film of *All Quiet*. Although it does not appear in the book, the image of Paul Bäumer's hand reaching out of the trench for a butterfly and thereby exposing himself to a sniper remains one of the most evocative images of the First World War, embodying, as it does, the ironic contrast between the beauty and fragility of life and the universality of death in war.

The sense of profound loss that shapes *All Quiet* continues through *The Road Back*, published two years later in 1931. Again the title is ironic. The soldiers may have come back from the front, but the return is purely physical. Any attempt to return to a pre-war life or to realize a dream of "home" is doomed to futility. The abiding effect of the war on the combatants appears in several guises, often elaborations on earlier themes and scenes. Most evident is the unbridgeable gap between soldiers and civilians, and by extension between the life of the soldier and that of the civilian to which they are attempting to adjust. To take one example among many, Ernst, the protagonist, having just been demobilized, is invited to a party by his wealthy uncle and aunt.[153] He's somewhat reluctant to go, but is persuaded by his mother, who feels indebted to Uncle Karl for gifts of food during the war. Remarque slyly implies that Uncle Karl, who passed a safe war as a senior paymaster, had not been overly generous. In any event, Ernst goes to the party, is greeted first by a pompous butler, then by

---

[150]Schauwecker, *The Furnace*, 270. "Sie waren dem Schicksal verfallen . . . Die Vergeblichkeit menschlichen Planens und Deutens war ihnen hart und undurchdringlich beschlossen" (307).

[151]Remarque, *All Quiet*, 319. "Mögen die Monate und Jahre kommen, sie nehmen mir nichts mehr, sie können mir nichts mehr nehmen. Ich bin so allein und so ohne Erwartung, daß ich ihnen entgegensehen kann ohne Furcht" (262–263).

[152]Remarque, *All Quiet*, 320. " . . . als wäre er beinahe zufrieden damit, daß es so gekommen war" (263).

[153]Remarque, *Road Back*, 111–117.

his uncle, resplendent in full uniform, including spurs. Ernst, noting the spurs, makes a bad joke about having roast horse for dinner, which only annoys his uncle. At one point before dinner he uneasily scratches his back and his aunt stops in the middle of a conversation to ask him what he's doing. He calmly responds that it's probably a louse, as it takes a while to get rid of them all. As she steps back in horror, he reassures her that lice don't jump like fleas, so she is quite safe. She exclaims and signals him to be quiet, as if he had said something stupid. That, Ernst concludes, is the way these people are. "We are supposed to be heroes, so they don't want to know anything about lice."[154] He completes his disgrace by eating his food (real pork chops fried in real fat) with his hands. His embarrassment quickly turns to rage against all those people who "go on living their trivial lives as a matter of course, as if the monstrous years had never been, when only one thing existed: death or life and nothing else."[155] I have detailed this incident at some length because it represents a classic postwar confrontation. Essentially, it is an exacerbated version of the earlier confrontations on home leave. But in this case, the veteran, who ought to be seen as a heroic figure, is instead treated as a social outcast by the very society that he has suffered to protect. What is worse, he has been permanently altered by the war; the smug, self-satisfied civilians seem entirely untouched by it. Renn, for example, is astonished by showily dressed women in a café — he didn't know that such elegance *still* existed (my emphasis).[156] Disenchantment with the race of civilians is by no means the exclusive province of the liberal novelists. The gap between front and rear cuts across the entire literary corpus. At the opposite end of the philosophical spectrum, Bucher gives a different twist to the common feeling of betrayal and suspicion. Toward the end of *In the Line* he presents the most overtly political formulation of the theme. After the failure of the 1918 offensive, "the arguments of the pacifist conspiracy had begun insidiously to destroy our will to fight on,"[157] and then lashes out at the homeland's betrayal of their sacrifice with references to the desperation of the last battles, the enormity of the human losses, and the insinuations that the soldiers were prolonging the war (quoted earlier).

Bucher's formulation, however extreme, cannot be discounted. Even if one ignores the usual conservative clichés — the pacifist agitators from a weak homeland, the glorification of German will, the melodramatic invocation of

---

[154]Remarque, *Road Back,* 113. "Helden sollen wir sein, doch von Läusen wollen sie nichts wissen" (126).

[155]Remarque, *Road Back,* 116–117. " . . . die so selbstverständlich mit ihrem Kleinkram dahinlebt, als waren die ungeheuren Jahre niemals gewesen, in denen es doch nur eins gab: Tod oder Leben und nichts sonst" (129).

[156]Renn, *After War,* 30.

[157]Bucher, *In the Line,* 270. "An unserem Willen beginnen die Hetzreden unsichtbarer Verschwörer zu wüten" (314).

fallen comrades — the passage still reeks of genuine bitterness, betrayal and suffering, and there is little doubt that Bucher and others (Wehner, Hoffmann) spoke for the thousands who joined conservative veterans' organizations such as the Stahlhelm after the war. The majority of those who mouthed conservative platitudes were probably more bewildered than truly spiteful. They had, they felt, done their duty, and more than their duty. If the war was lost, the blame must lie elsewhere.

For the returning soldier, the loss of his comrades and his belief in his countrymen was augmented by yet another loss: loss of his ideals. Unlike the theme of civilian betrayal, or at the very least willful civilian ignorance, the theme of loss of ideals is mostly limited to the liberal novel. Where it exists in the conservative novel, loss of belief is of a special limited type, to which I shall return. Disillusionment, particularly about war, is, on the other hand, a broadly-based and inevitable phenomenon. Given the standard German patriotic education and the nature of the First World War, disillusionment with "Hurrah-patriotism," "the spirit of 1914," and similar notions of traditional combat was entirely predictable.

Fussell's remark that pre-war Britain was a world in which "the certainties were still intact"[158] is, in a different philosophical context, just as accurate for Germany. The whole framework of German idealism and nationalism must, in the heady days of August 1914, have appeared unshakable. That was particularly true for the German bourgeoisie with its devotion to spiritual values and traditional culture. The loss was, therefore, particularly striking among the bourgeois student-soldiers who exchanged the classroom for the trenches. As noted above, the growing meaninglessness of traditional culture for Paul Baümer appears clearly during his home leave in *All Quiet*.

The loss of that link to the past is even starker in *The Road Back*, particularly when the young men return to school. They had volunteered before taking their final exams, and after the war must finish their studies. Returning to the old school building, Ernst remarks that before they were soldiers "these buildings enclosed our world. Then it was the trenches. Now we are here again. But this is no longer our world. The trenches were stronger."[159] The situation deteriorates when the school director greets the soldiers with a patriotic speech, which they shout down with demands for separate, practical courses; their demands reduce the methodical director to bewildered silence. Later, as the men try to plan a curriculum to present to the education authorities, they can scarcely believe that any of it had been of value to them (141–142).

---

[158]Fussell, *Great War*, 21.

[159]Remarque, *Road Back*, 118. "Ehe wir Soldaten wurden, umfaßten diese Gebäude unsere Welt. Dann wurden es die Schützengräben. Jetzt sind wir wieder hier. Aber dies ist nicht mehr unsere Welt. Die Gräben waren stärker" (131).

Not only are *Bildung* and traditional learning no longer of value, the spiritual values have been replaced by material ones. The war-profiteer is the most obvious example of that change, but it appears among the soldiers as well. Karl Bröger, who before the war had been a voracious book collector, sells all his books with the words "a centimeter of business knowledge is worth more than a kilometer of Bildung."[160] Schauwecker's diatribe against percentages is only a more radical version of this use of units of measure to suggest the relative importance of spiritual and material values. The triumph of materialism is a constant theme in the liberal novels, as its opposite is in the conservative ones (for example, those of Schauwecker, Wehner, Zöberlein). Throughout his tetralogy on the war Arnold Zweig paints scathing portraits of self-centered, materialistic officers and men, most notably of the scheming and cowardly Sgt. Niggl of *Education before Verdun* and of General Schieffenzahn (the name means "crooked tooth") in the last two volumes, the incarnation of the modern, middle-class, technologically-adept general officer, said to be a portrait of Ludendorff. In Zweig's books, it is the Schieffenzahns of the world who triumph.

But for Remarque, the most terrible loss is the loss of his comrades and of comradeship itself, which he regarded as the only positive thing to come out of the war. He becomes aware of the change at the first regimental reunion after the end of the war (194-203). Most of the men have continued to wear their old uniforms as daily attire, but in honor of the reunion they all appear in civilian clothes for the first time. The pre-war social distinctions instantly reappear in their suits, causing some embarrassment. Tjaden accuses Kosole of having bought his suit from the rag man, making Kosole suddenly aware that some of the others are wearing much better suits. Men who were excellent soldiers and were in positions of responsibility at the front wear pre-war clothes and are patronized by worse soldiers who have returned to good jobs or made quick money on the black market. The world of comradeship that Ernst had known is suddenly topsy-turvy. These men are, he concludes, "still our comrades, and yet not any more; that's what makes it so sad. Everything else was destroyed in the war, but we had believed in comradeship. And now we see: What death has not brought to an end, life has. It separates us."[161] The resurgence of civilian society shatters the fragile community of the trenches, which depended upon the uniqueness of the situation. When the war ends, the community collapses. Renn likewise complains of the loss of comradeship in terms of loss of love.[162]

---

[160]Remarque, *Road Back*, 167. "Ein Zentimeter Handel ist besser als ein Kilometer Bildung . . ." (182).

[161]Remarque, *Road Back*, 200. "Es sind noch unsere Kameraden, und sie sind es doch nicht mehr, das macht gerade so traurig. Alles andere ist kaputtgegangen im Kriege, aber an die Kameradschaft hatten wir geglaubt. Und jetzt sehen wir: Was der Tod nicht fertiggebracht hat, das gelingt dem Leben: es trennt uns" (217).

[162]Renn, *After War*, 211.

But it goes further than that. After the riot in the city, in which one group of soldiers fires upon another, Ernst concludes that, "We are at war again, but comradeship no longer exists."[163] The one thing that had sustained them through the war would not sustain them through the civil insurrections of post-war Germany. So, in the end, everything of value has been lost, except life itself. And for Ernst, what hope there is lies only in the fact that he is still alive and must make a way for himself in life. Interestingly enough, the language in which he couches his resolution recalls the language of *Bildung*. Life, he says,

> . . . is almost a task and a way. I will work on myself and be ready, I will use my hands and my thoughts, I will not make myself important and I will go forward, even when I sometimes want to stay still. There is a lot to be rebuilt, and almost everything to make good, things that were buried alive in the years of grenades and machine guns must be dug up. . . . Then the dead will be quiet, then the past will no longer pursue me, but help me.[164]

What Ernst is attempting is nothing less than the creation of a new personality that will integrate his war experience into productive life. Remarque emphasizes the transformation of character by referring to the war in terms of its mechanical destruction ("grenades and machine guns"), and by using the German verb *ausgraben*, to dig up, the antithesis of *eingraben*, to dig in, that is, to entrench — an emblematic verb of the war.

The essential characteristic of German First World War narratives, even novels as nihilistic as those of Remarque and Renn, is an attempt to endow the war with some meaning, be it personal, moral or historical; or, failing that, to derive from it some lesson or means by which a survivor can continue with his life. Remarque, clearly, is on the latter path. For him the war's only significance was its destruction, physical or mental, of a generation of German men. The men who survived appear to him to have gained nothing from the experience except survival itself. But even Remarque hints that there must be a use for the past, if only he can find his way to it.

---

[163]Remarque, *Road Back*, 277–278. "Es ist wieder Krieg; aber die Kameradschaft ist nicht mehr" (303).

[164]Remarque, *Road Back*, 342. "Das ist beinahe eine Aufgabe und ein Weg. Ich will an mir arbeiten und bereit sein, ich will meine Hände rühren und meine Gedanken, ich will mich nicht wichtig nehmen und weitergehen, auch wenn ich manchmal bleiben möchte. Es gibt vieles aufzubauen und fast alles wieder gutzumachen, es gibt zu arbeiten und ausgraben, was verschüttet worden ist in den Jahren der Granaten und der Maschinengewehre. . . . Dann werden die Toten schweigen, und die Vergangenheit wird mich nicht mehr verfolgen, sondern mir helfen" (366–367).

The Search for Meaning

In his discussion of British Great War narratives and their contribution to the making of the British myth of the war, Samuel Hynes argues that "they are all disjunctive memoirs for a disjunctive time, parts of the myth of disruption and fragmentation that is the Myth of the War."[165] I should like to argue that the German narratives create a German myth of the war, which though equally mythical, embodies not historical disjunction and fragmentation, but coherence and wholeness. I am not arguing that Germans saw the world as unchanged, but that they saw the staggering personal and national changes brought by the war as part of a natural and inevitable historical continuum characterized by cycles of destruction and regeneration. While some writers sought a private significance for the war, an important majority defined the war in historical and national terms. In most of the German narratives, the meaning of the war to an individual soldier was inextricably bound up in its import for the community. The model of comradeship privileges the communal over the personal. The confluence of Romantic nationalism and the organic model of history produced, first, a paradigm that incorporated parallel development on individual, communal and national planes. That, in turn, established a coherent philosophical framework in which the events of German history, and the individual's part in those events, could be regarded as stages in the natural and inexorable development of the nation. Terrible events, even destruction, could serve as instruments of national testing and purification, and thus as a prelude to regeneration. The pervasiveness of the word *Schicksal* (fate) confirms the predominance of a natural historical order incorporating a belief in cyclical providence. Bucher concludes *In the Line* with a superb example:

> Avalanches may roll, winds of fury rage, unchained powers hold mastery for a time. As with nature, so is it in the life of the individual, of the masses, of a nation: one hour passes, another follows and with it the sun may shine again.[166]

Even the diction is organic.

The persistence of the organic model of human and national history conditioned the German writers to order their experience of war within its parameters. Faced with what appeared to be random events, they consistently attempted to see those events in a philosophical and even historical context. The urge to make sense of their experience leads most writers to echo the desperate

---

[165]Hynes, *A War Imagined*, 436.

[166]Bucher, *In the Line*, 325. "Mögen auch Lawinen rollen, mögen Furienwinde wehen, entfesselte Gewalten die Stunde beherrschen. Wie in der Natur, so ist es im Leben des Menschen, der Maße, des Volkes: eine Stunde verebbt, ihr folgt die andere. Diese neue kann schon wieder Sonne mit sich bringen" (390).

cry of one of Beumelburg's characters: "But it must have some meaning."[167]
The meanings that they created fall into three loose groupings, with much
overlapping. First, the war was a German spiritual victory, even if the physical
victory had been unjustly snatched from them. Secondly, the war functions as
the catalyst in the spiritual transformation of the front soldier, refining and purifying him into a future leader of his people. In this guise, the war serves as a
test of the spiritual mettle of individual and nation. Finally, the war itself is a
ritual of purification that will ensure the rebirth of the nation.

The theme of spiritual victory, or at least of spiritual survival, is one of the
most common in the corpus of Great War narratives. In contrast to the spiritual
destruction catalogued by Remarque, conservative writers felt a need to assert
the continuance of the individual and collective spirit. The theme tends to occur
in conjunction with that of transformation, and is particularly apparent in works
that focus on the *Materialschlacht*. Considering the anti-materialistic bias of
German philosophy, and the traditional suspicion of urban, democratic culture,
the soldiers' resentment of the enormous quantities of Allied materiel amassed
to destroy them is scarcely surprising. Add to that the genuine suffering of
German troops and civilians from a lack of essential commodities, and multiply
the equation by the German sense of spiritual and military superiority, and the
result is a witches' brew of loathing for the fat, well-supplied barbarians who
have used their material wealth to unjustly overcome a spiritually superior enemy.

Predictably, references to the incarnation of materialism, the American
army, abound. And indeed, the contrast between the fresh, well-supplied
Americans and the exhausted, tattered Germans in the final stages of the war
must have been devastating to German morale. Remarque describes an encounter with American troops during the retreat following the armistice. They
are all, he says, "big, powerful people, and one immediately saw that they had
always had enough to eat."[168] He also notes the contrast between the American
soldiers, who are all of normal military age, and the Germans, some of whom
are very old or very young, conscription having long since been expanded in order to put every available man into uniform. "They are wearing new uniforms
and new overcoats; their shoes are watertight and fit exactly; their weapons are
good and their pockets full of ammunition. All of them are fresh and not exhausted."[169] By comparison, the Germans look like "a band of robbers" (27) in
their filthy, tattered uniforms. The Americans subsequently trade cigarettes,

[167]Beumelburg, *Gruppe Bosemüller*, 126. "Aber es muß doch einen Sinn haben . . . ."

[168]Remarque, *Road Back*, 27. " . . . lauter große, kräftige Leute, denen man gleich ansieht, daß
sie immer satt zu essen gehabt haben" (31).

[169]Remarque, *Road Back*, 27. "Sie tragen neue Uniformen und neue Mäntel; ihre Schuhe sind
wasserdicht und passen genau; ihre Waffen sind gut und ihre Taschen voller Munition. Alle
sind frisch und unverbraucht" (32).

chocolate and soap for German insignia, and a generous quantity of real bandages for the German paper bandages (31-32). Remarque's treatment of the American troops is, despite his focus on their material well-being, quite generous. While they are made to look rather ridiculous with their mania for souvenirs, there is much understanding and fellow-feeling evident throughout the encounter. More conservative writers are significantly less generous, seeing the Americans as the embodiment of the Western materialism they have been fighting against.

The sense of spiritual triumph over the *Materialschlacht* is largely predicated upon having survived it. Key verbs such as *durchgehen, durchleben, überleben, durchhalten* (to get through, to live through, to hold out) appear with increasing frequency. Physical and nervous exhaustion are the common denominators of experience near the end of the war. Dreysse writes that he is spiritually broken ("seelisch ganz kaputt") and "tired to death — but we must hold out; we're protecting the homeland."[170] The letter of Johannes Philippson quoted above emphasizes not individual survival, but devotion to duty, to the fatherland, and to one's comrades, living and dead.

For Ernst Jünger it is man's power of resistance that makes him the victor in the battle against materiel. War is not only a question of materiel; higher values are in play: " . . . the war is more to us [the combatants] than a proud and gallant memory. It is a spiritual experience, too; and a realization of a strength of soul of which otherwise we should have had no knowledge."[171] The insistence upon the spiritual dimension of the war is characteristic not only of Jünger, but of the whole German attitude. The conviction that the war had to "mean" something beyond its material facts, especially the fact of defeat after so much suffering, is nearly universal among the German writers. Schauwecker's "there must be a reason,"[172] echoed by virtually every conservative writer, reveals the German conviction that only when an event has been fitted into its proper philosophical framework does it demonstrate its true significance. The idea of random discontinuous experience was intolerable. The conservative and National Socialist literary critics of the late twenties and early thirties criticized the liberal novels of Remarque, Renn and Köppen on precisely the grounds that the authors had failed to perceive the spiritual significance of the war experience, and therefore only whined about material and individual destruction.[173]

---

[170]Dreysse, *Langemarck*, 72; 67. "Todmüde — aber wir müßen durchhalten: wir decken ja die Heimat!" (67).

[171]Ernst Jünger, *Das Wäldchen 125* (Berlin: Mittler, 1929). Tr. by Basil Creighton as *Copse 125* (London: Chatto, 1930) x. The passage appears only in the 1929 edition; Jünger edited it out of the collected works.

[172]Schauwecker, *The Furnace*, 343.

[173]See Hermann Pongs, "Krieg als Volkschicksal im deutschen Schriftum," *Dichtung und Volkstum* 35 (1934): 40–86; 182–219. Also by the same author, "Neue Kriegs-und Nach-

Writing in 1927, Otto Baumgarten takes his countrymen severely to task for their weak grasp of reality and their obsession with idealism, which he calls the "greatest enemy" in the area of practical and political action.[174] He further inquires if the war has cured the Germans of this "ideological delusion," as it has so clearly done for the English, but regretfully concludes that

> . . . in us lived a stubborn belief in the idea even in the face of brutal reality. In the normal German way, it was therefore unthinkable that the Reich, which had become a world power through the victories of 1854, 1855 and 1870 could be brought down by mere numerical superiority. So these frightening thoughts . . . were pushed back into the unconscious mind. And what was unthinkable, inconceivable, could not be true.[175]

So the bad news, as Baumgarten scathingly comments, was transformed into such phrases as "'the will is always victorious,' 'it is the spirit that builds matter.'"[176]

The wishful thinking vivisected by Baumgarten was governed by a yearning for three qualities in national life: order, hierarchy, and wholeness.[177] The consequent privileging of the spiritual experience of the war permits German writers to place that experience in its full, orderly, individual and national context, a context that is spiritual rather than material. The Allied equation

$$\text{Superior manpower} + \text{superior materiel} = \text{victory}$$

was regarded in Germany as an inaccurate equation or, worse, as mere mathematics, smacking of the counting house (cf. Troeltsch and Schauwecker), because the spiritual strength of the German army was missing from the equation. The German spirit, individual and collective, was not destroyed by the experience of modern warfare; it survived the worst the *Materialschlacht* could do, and was transformed by that test into something stronger and more vital. Lest one should regard such convictions as the domain of intellectuals and self-justifying former combatants, even popular magazines such as the *Illustrierte Zeitung* em-

kriegsbücher," *Dichtung und Volkstum* 37 (1936): 219–235, and "Weltkrieg und Dichtung," *Dichtung und Volkstum* 39 (1938): 193–212. See also Helmut Hoffmann, *Mensch und Volk im Kriegserlebnis* (Berlin: Ebering, 1937), and Lutz, *Gemeinschaftserlebnis*.

[174]Baumgarten, *Geistige und sittliche Wirkungen des Krieges*, 6.

[175]Baumgarten, 9. "In uns lebte der Trotz der Idee gegen die brutale Wirklichkeit. Es war doch für normale deutsche Art undenkbar, daß das durch die Siege von 1864, 1866, 1870 zur Weltmacht aufgestiegene Reich der bloßen numerischen Übermacht unterliegen würde! Auch der furchtbare Gedanke an die Folgen des verloren Krieges für deutsche Macht, Ehre und Kulture trieb alle Vorahnungen dieses Ausgangs in das Unterbewußtsein zurück. Und was undenkbar, unausdenkbar, das konnte nicht wirklich werden."

[176]Baumgarten, 9. "'Der Wille siegt,' 'es ist der Geist, der sich den Körper baut'. . . ."

[177]I have borrowed George Mosse's terminology from *The Nationalization of the Masses*. Any political activity attempting to gain a following by tapping into the rich and emotional sources of national myth must, he says, display these three qualities.

phasized the survival and transformation of the German spirit in those issues that appeared just after the Armistice.

"Changed Men"

Whatever their other differences, the German writers of the First World War were in accord on one point: the authentic experience of the war was a spiritual experience, primarily an experience of spiritual testing, growth and metamorphosis — a special kind of *Bildung*. It is the sole theme that appears, almost without exception, in all the war books. Jünger compares soldiers to divers who threw themselves into experience and returned as changed men, a striking echo of Rupert Brooke's early war sonnet.[178] Precisely what was meant by an authentic spiritual war experience came to depend upon one's political and cultural alignment, but its centrality is unquestioned. In his discussion of the structure of war experience, Leed remarks on the consistent claim of combatants that their character had been altered.[179] In the case of the Germans, one expectation of war — that it would transform them individually and collectively — was never destroyed.[180] As I have noted earlier, the expectation of spiritual transformation is rooted in Romantic organicism, and in its intellectual parallel, *Bildung*. For the young soldiers, especially volunteers, the "spirit of August" was chiefly a rejection of the materialistic bourgeois ethos of an industrialized, urban Germany, and a corresponding reaffirmation of an abiding belief in the spiritual transformation of the individual and the nation through the cataclysmic experience of war. The experience of war, even of a war as disillusioning as the First World War, when set into this ideological framework, served not to disembarrass the combatants of their idealism, but rather to reinforce it, and eventually to convince them that only they had been true to the fundamental beliefs and values of German culture.

Since the experience of transformation is so widespread, it would be both tedious and repetitive to examine more than a few representative instances. Although the concept of change is virtually universal, the nature of the change differs. For some writers, the experience of death is so pervasive that even the survivors feel alienated from the world of the living. This is a more extreme variation on the theme of the front soldier's alienation from those who have not shared his experience, but in this case the severance from life is so strong that the men feel that they belong to the realm of the dead. *Reinhold oder die Verwandelten* (1932, translated as *Changed Men*, 1932) Paul Alverdez's collection of short stories, focuses on the spiritual changes brought about by the human losses of the war. The characters believe that they belong with the dead, and

[178]Ernst Jünger, "Der Krieg als inneres Erlebnis," *Werke* (Stuttgart: Klett, 1960–1965), 7:13.

[179]Leed, *No Man's Land*, 2.

[180]Leed, 17.

many try to join them. In the final story of the collection, "Dead Man's Holiday," the protagonist dreams that he rides an enchanted horse to a ferry crossing
on a river. His name is checked off the list and he joins the dead for the crossing, but then is suddenly left behind on the bank with a lantern. The lantern
may be conventionally interpreted as hope for the future or as the means by
which the protagonist sees all the more clearly his severance from the comradeship of death. He is condemned to go on living. The theme of the survivor
as ghost is a common one, here made more evocative by the use of folk themes,
which are very common in war narratives.

   What I have called the comradeship of death is an extension of the soldiers'
comradeship in life. Many survivors were unable to resist their longing to join
their dead comrades. At the end of *The Road Back*, Georg Rahe returns to what
had been the front and commits suicide in the military cemetery there, with his
comrades, who were, like him, "betrayed."[181] Another extension of comradeship
is found in the frequent dedications to dead comrades: "To the dead of Germany" (Bucher, *In the Line*); "A memorial for my dead brothers" (Wehner,
Seven before Verdun); "Dedicated to the dead and their mothers, especially the
dead of Verdun and my comrades in the 235th Infantry Division" (R. Hoffmann, *Frontsoldaten*). The examples could be multiplied almost ad infinitum, as
could examples from French and British texts. In *Jedermann* (Everyman),
Wiechert's protagonist believes that he will eventually become "a ghost of
life . . . like all the gray millions, a ghost who haunts the garden of life."[182]
These ghosts in their field gray uniforms are not only the dead, but all the front
soldiers whose spirits have been so damaged that they will be forever unable to
return to life.

   Wiechert's gray ghosts may stand as the symbol for all the men so altered by
their experience of war that any real resumption of life was out of the question.
Few of the metamorphoses, however, were so destructive. The majority of the
writers, for the reasons discussed above, perceived the spiritual metamorphosis
of the war as positive and even necessary. There is, first of all, the essential
transformation of civilian into soldier. The soldiers themselves are frequently
astounded at what has become of them. Richard Hoffmann refers to one character's time in training as "his first personal development lessons" ("Bildungs-
unterricht").[183] Later, at Verdun, Heinz Höfer, the young doctoral candidate
who is the author's porte parole, meditates on what has happened to him: "Who
is Heinz Höfer? — If you mean the fluently patriotic corps-student of the mo-

---

[181]Remarque, *Road Back*, 328–332.

[182]Wiechert, 440. " . . . ein Gespenst des Lebens werde ich wieder sein wie all die grauen Millionen, ein Gespenst, das umgeht im Garten des Lebens . . . ."

[183]Richard Hoffmann, *Frontsoldaten* (Hamburg: Fackelreiter, 1928), 60.

bilization, that doesn't fit anymore. . . . He had come through life. . . . So what was Heinz Höfer? — The commonest trench soldier. . . ."[184]

The initial development of the soldier is augmented by combat, and particularly by shelling. The effect of shelling on the human mind is only too evident from the use of the word "shell shock" to describe the mental disorder that would be called "battle fatigue" in the Second World War and "Delayed Traumatic Stress Syndrome" in our own time. Several authors compare that experience to a return to childhood. In Beumelburg's *Gruppe Bosemüller*, the company, after three months at Verdun, has buried two comrades in a pine forest, and mounted a guard to prevent their tribute of geraniums from being stolen a second time. While on guard, Siewers meditates on what they've just been through, and concludes first that they must live as children live — in the moment. For them, life has no past and no future. Then he concludes, "Death didn't leave Esser [one of their dead comrades] any time to complete the development that leads through the knowledge of horror to, finally, a new childhood, a higher childhood. . . . 'unless you become as a little child' — 'become,' the emphasis lies there, and what is meant by that is a development."[185] The elevated childlike state (there is no adequate English equivalent to the German *Kindsein*) described by Beumelburg clearly refers to a condition of heightened simplicity and reliance on one's innate qualities of spirit. His use of the biblical quotation also suggests that he sees this development as a rebirth of the soul into a state of greater wisdom. "For now," says Siewers, "I am a wise man and then I was a fool."[186] Both references emphasize the rebirth of the spirit into wisdom through the agency of experience.

A similar use of the dual themes of transformation and childhood occurs in Wiechert's *Jedermann*. The passage, though lengthy, is worth detailed examination, as it encapsulates in Wiechert's fine prose a plenitude of common themes. The scene is the eastern front, on the occasion of the first bombardment suffered by Johannes and his friend Klaus:

> They had not yet grasped, and probably would never grasp that the sky could change so much, that the home of birds, clouds and wind could suddenly become the home of death, and with that change they felt most irresistibly the

[184]R. Hoffmann, 110. "Was heißt Heinz Höfer? — Wenn der floße vaterlandsbegeisterte Korpstudent der Mobilmachung damit gemeint sollte, so stimmte das ganz nicht. Er war durch das Leben gekommen. . . .Was war Heinz Höfer sonst? — Ein Grabensoldat höherer Gemeinheit . . . ."

[185]Beumelburg, *Gruppe Bosemüller*, 207. "Dem Esser hat der Tod keine Zeit gelassen, jene Entwicklung durchzumachen, die durch die Erkenntnis des Schrecklichen zu seiner Überwindung führt und schließlich zu einem neuen Kindsein, einem höheren Kindsein. . . . 'Wenn ihr nicht werdet wie die Kindlein,' — 'werdet,' darauf liegt der Ton, es ist also eine Entwicklung gemeint."

[186]Beumelburg, *Gruppe Bosemüller*, 262. "Denn jetzt bin ich ein Wissender, und damals war ich ein Tor."

change of their lives. . . . They felt fear, a gray, formless, hitherto unknown
fear, something that split them into two beings, one who was strangling and
one struggling against strangulation, and they also felt that they would be
weighed in the balance in this split so that the emptiness of the words "duty"
and "spirit" and "discipline" now filled up with contents like a beaker that they
held in trembling hands, and that they must not spill if they did not want to
fall forever into shame.[187]

After they have survived the first shelling without breaking and running, Johannes compares their return to rest billets to coming home after the first day of
school: ". . . and so they walked next to each other, two small, innocent warriors, out of the chaos of the world and their first battlefield into the permanence
and protection of their little peace."[188]

The theme of change is the first to appear in these passages. The sudden
transformation of the peaceful sky — the realm of life and spirit — into the
realm of death heralds the equally sudden change in the men's lives. The second
part concentrates on the transformation of the soldiers through fear. The previously empty words now mean something: that they have to stay where they are
and not succumb to the animal instinct to run away. Wiechert, who frequently
employs biblical symbolism, is obviously referring to Christ's prayer to let the
cup pass (Matt. 26:42). It is also a wonderfully concrete metaphor — typical of
Wiechert — in which the abstract concepts take on the reality of a full cup in
the hands of a man in the last extremity of terror. But the strength of the spirit
overcomes the terror of the body — duty and discipline are not poured away —
and the men thereafter are warriors (*Krieger*). Here, Wiechert differs from
Beumelburg. The men are turned into warriors by the experience, but that is
only half of a dual nature. The final synthesis of the divided personality occurs
only after the war, at the end of the novel.

Another kind of metamorphosis lies in the realization that the life of the
front is the "true" life and that anything positive in the future will come out of
that experience and the recognition of its value. One of the most effective expressions of this form of transformation is found in Goltz's *Der Baum von Cléry*.

---

[187]Wiechert, *Jedermann*, 382; 384. "Sie haben es noch nicht begriffen und werden es auch wohl
nie begreifen, daß der Himmel sich so verändern kann, daß die Heimat von Vögeln, Wolken
und Winden plötzlich zu einer Heimat des Todes geworden ist, und an dieser Veränderung
ermessen sie am unwiderstehlichsten die Veränderung ihres Lebens. . . . Sie fühlen, daß sie
Angst haben, eine graue, gestaltlose, nie gekannte Angst, etwas, das sie in zwei Wesen zerspal-
tet, ein würgendes und eines, das sich gegen die Erwürgung wehrt, und sie fühlen auch, daß sie
in dieser Spaltung gemessen und gewogen werden, daß die Leerheit der Worte 'Pflicht' und
'Geist' und 'Diziplin' sich nun mit einem Inhalt füllt wie ein Becher, den sie in zitternden Hän-
den halten und den sie nicht verschütten dürfen, wenn sie nicht für ewig in die Schande stürzen
wollen."

[188]Wiechert, 390. ". . . und so gehen sie nebeneinander, zwei kleine, unschuldige Krieger, aus
der Wirrnis der Welt und ihres ersten Schlachtfeldes, in das Bleibende und Schützende ihres
kleinen Friedens."

The protagonist, Siebenreut, deeply depressed by the senselessness of the war, is heading into the line. He passes the wounded going back and thinks how fortunate they are to be out of it, but then,

> No, Siebenreut thought, you couldn't leave all that behind you so easily, it went with you and never let you go. What you had experienced out here would always accompany you, even at home. — And while he plodded with tired step over the pocked pavement a thought came to him that invigorated him and streamed through him with warm joy; here in the trenches and lousy shellholes, in filth and fear of death was genuine life. Out here was the soil into which everything rotten was plowed, and out of their experience a new crop had to grow! Who ever did not glorify that and take it into himself — the death and the destruction which considered no values — he did not count as one of them and he would be passed over![189]

Most of the essentials of the war experience are condensed into this passage: the inescapability of the front experience, the recognition of its centrality and authenticity, the organic diction, and the overriding conviction that the value of the front experience lay in its quality as the seedbed of the future. The permanent psychological scars left by the experience of combat need no further comment. What is interesting here is the insistence that the soldier not only cannot, but must not, try to "put the war behind him," because in that experience, however horrible, lies the only possibility for rebirth. Thus war is seen as an essential destructive phase in the organic process. In Goltz's metaphor, the battlefield — a place of death — becomes the plowed field, well-fertilized by rotting flesh, apparently barren, but ready to bring forth a new crop. Schauwecker uses a similar image when he says that his soul is like the plowed-up earth of the battlefield of Verdun, in which nothing can grow at first.[190] The metaphor serves two related purposes. First, it places the experience of war within the framework of the natural order. Secondly, the organic model also insists upon the necessary sequence of that development. Death and destruction are an essential phase of the organic process, and by extension, of the process of human development. Finally, it is the imperative duty of those who participated in the war to see their experience as a part of the natural process and to use it to benefit the future. True hope lies in using the past, not in forgetting it.

---

[189]Goltz, *Der Baum von Cléry*, 170. "Siebenreut dachte: nein, so leicht konnte man das alles nicht hinter sich lassen, es ging mit einem und ließ einen nimmer los. Was man hier draußen erlebte, würde einen immer begleiten, auch in der Heimat. — Und während er so mit müden Schritten über das löcherige Pflaster stapfte, kam ihm ein Gedanke, der ihn belebte und mit heißer Freude durchströmte: hier in den Gräben und verlausten Löchern, in Dreck und Todesangst war das wahre Leben, hier draußen war der Acker, in dem alles Faulende Verwesende untergepflügt wurde, und aus ihrem Erleben heraus mußte eine neue Saat aufgehen! Wer das nicht bejahte und in sich aufnahm — den Tod und die Zerstörung, die nach keinen Werten fragte — der zählte nicht mit und über den ging es hinweg!"

[190]Schauwecker, *The Furnace*, 202.

Both the organic metaphor and the hope it entails are fulfilled in an incident near the end of Goltz's book. Siebenreut is talking to his friend Karl about a tree he saw in Champagne:

> ... on the slope on the other side of the hollow there was a small tree, the only one far and wide. It was twisted and scratched by explosions. It was just good enough to serve as a telephone post. Suddenly, overnight, it bloomed and was an apple tree. It seemed to say: I can be struck dead at any moment, just like you, and see how I have bedecked myself! — Then the spring came in all its glory![191]

The analogy between the organic form — in this case the war-torn tree of the title that suddenly bursts into bloom — and the men who are equally vulnerable to destruction is obvious. The last sentence functions on both literal and figurative levels as a traditional symbol of rebirth. For readers steeped in the British tradition, the absence of an ironic twist to the symbolism is striking. A comparison with Edward Thomas's "The Cherry Trees," Sorley's "All the hills and vales along," or even American poet Alan Seeger's "Rendezvous" will quickly illuminate the essentially ironic use of natural symbolism in the British tradition. Since the experience of war in the German context is a positive transformative experience, the cheerful image of life returning with the spring can be used without irony. At the end of Goltz's book, we see Siebenreut, still hopeful and enduring despite the death of all his friends, digging shelters in a new firing position as the sun rises.

"The Front Is a Crucible..."

The belief in individual and collective transformation manifests itself most significantly in those conservative war novels that concentrate on the metamorphosis of the nation through war. Rooted in the idea of organic historical development, novelists such as Schauwecker, Wehner and Zöberlein depicted the war as an essential phase of national development. They, and many other writers, were inclined to see the war as a test of the nations involved, but particularly as a test of the German spirit. Ernst Jünger, a conservative, but one with his eyes open, also regarded the war as a test, but one which the Germans failed. Victory or defeat, he says, is always deserved, and always the fault of the people as a whole.[192] But even Jünger sees a bright future and uses an organic metaphor to express it: "Our hour will come; and then at last we shall see that

---

[191]Goltz, 269. "Auf dem Hang jenseits der Mulde stand ein Bäumchen, das einzige weit und breit, krumm war's und von einem Sprengstück angekratzt, es war grad noch gut, um als Telephonstange zu dienen. Auf einmal, über Nacht, war es erblüht und war ein Apfelbäumchen! Es schien zu sagen: ich kann jedem Augenblick erschlagen sein, wie ihr, und seht, ich habe mich doch geschmückt! — Und dann kam der Frühling mit Macht!"

[192]Jünger, *Copse 125*, 181. Both this passage and the next were removed from later editions.

the loss of this war brought us to our full height. Hard timber is of slow growth" (184). That future lies, for Jünger, as for so many others, in the strength of the German spirit and the German willingness to serve an ideal.

The classic formulation is found, predictably, in Schauwecker, who, more than anyone else, functions as the conservative spokesman. The passage that follows occurs early in *The Fiery Way*:

> This war, I feel, is a journey we have to make as individuals and as a community, a journey like the way of the cross, a journey on which souls are parted and transfigured, on which they must triumph or go to earth. It is more than an experience, it is catastrophe and chaos, it is life, it is trial by fire of one's innermost worth, it is Golgotha and triumphal throne in one, it breaks through all doors into the most secret chambers of the heart. There is no shirking it: everyone has to face it and make something of it. Whoever falters before it — whether through cowardice or inaptitude, righteousness or stupidity — war has done with him in a moment: it passes him by. These are the hours in which we meet new challenges, and battle with ourselves. It is no battle with enemies; it is the wrestling of Jacob with the angel: "I will not let thee go, except thou bless me."[193]

In its overblown, quasi-religious rhetoric, this passage embodies the nationalist view of the war. The first matter of significance is the depiction of war as a test of, and battle with, the individual spirit. Schauwecker begins with the words "I feel" and goes on to speak of "innermost worth" and the "most secret chambers of the heart," indicating that the real battle is not with the enemy, but with oneself. He concludes with the story of Jacob wrestling with the angel, which is clearly meant to symbolize the victory of the human spirit over a superhuman power. The biblical language is characteristic of Schauwecker and of many other conservative writers. The references to Golgotha and the way of the cross are especially significant. The analogy with Golgotha — the place of skulls — would have been too obvious to be ignored by well-educated young Christians. The motif of the journey, particularly the symbolic journey of the soul, often emerges in the war narratives as the way of the cross. Hans Zöberlein in *Der Glaube an Deutschland* (Belief in Germany, 1931), for example, compares the

---

[193]Schauwecker, *Fiery Way*, 21–22. "Das fühle ich deutlich: dieser Krieg ist ein Erlebnis aller und jedes einzelnen zugleich, ein Erlebnis wie ein Kreuzweg, an dem sich die Geister scheiden und wandeln, wachsen oder zugrunde gehen. Er ist mehr als Erlebnis: er ist Katastrophe und Chaos, Ereignis und Feuerprobe des innersten Wertes, Schädelstätte und Triumphthron, und er dringt torsprengend in die geheimsten Herzkammern. An ihm vorbei kam keiner, und jeder hat mit ihm fertig zu werden und irgend etwas mit ihm abzumachen. Wer dem ausweicht — feige oder untüchtig, korrekt oder dumm — mit dem wird der Krieg fertig, indem er über ihn wegschreitet. Die Stunden der Besinnung, das sind Stunden des Kampfes gegen die neuen Forderungen und gegen sich selbst. Das ist kein Kampf von Feinden, es ist der Kampf, den Jakob gegen den Engel rang, sei er ein Seraph oder Michael mit Schild und Schwert: ich lasse dich nicht, du segnest mich denn" (16).

road to Douaumont to the "way of the cross of the German soldier."[194] In these and similar references, the way of the cross symbolizes a journey of suffering leading to a sacrificial (usually symbolic) death and resurrection. Thus the Passion of Christ serves as a symbol for the spirit's journey of transformation through the war, with the emphasis not only on the severity of the test, but overwhelmingly on the death and transfiguration of the spirit. It is nevertheless possible to fail the test. Schauwecker implies that failure stems mostly from not facing the test, that is, from not recognizing that it is a test and that one must "make something of it." For those who do not, the experience of war can be nothing but a physical experience that destroys them.

The second significant point is the extrapolation of individual experience to the communal and national. The test of war was obviously shared by the community of comrades. The transformation of individual civilians, first into soldiers, then into comrades, created a natural community of leaders and followers, perceived by its members to be superior to civilian society in its freedom from superficial social distinctions, the warmth of its emotions and the naturalness of its hierarchy. The surviving combatants saw themselves as members of a model society which had transformed their way of life, and which they would use as the basis for a new Germany. They were the caretakers of the front spirit, which, in time, would transform the nation as it had transformed them, and which was their most precious inheritance. Beumelburg provides the most complete formulation of the regenerative power of comradeship:

> Perhaps comradeship is only the small, visible part of the whole that we are capable of grasping. Because, so I tell myself, if it's like this for us, it must be the same for the others, for the whole army, only we can't see it. But later, when we come home, we will see it, and then all the small circles will become the great circle that encompasses the whole. So we must start from the beginning, from the little circle, from man to man, so that later we can grasp the whole, the great circle.[195]

In addition to the theme of comradeship as social paradigm, Beumelburg's repeated references to "the whole" and his use of the image of the circle are significant. The value placed on "man to man" personal contact is likewise a reflection of the emotional completeness of comradeship.

In *The Fiery Way*, Schauwecker apotheosizes the soldier as the representative German on whom the future of the nation depends. The xenophobic spleen

---

[194]Hans Zöberlein, *Der Glaube an Deutschland* (Munich: Nachfolger, 1931), 58.

[195]Beumelburg, *Gruppe Bosemüller*, 261. "Vielleicht ist die Kameradschaft nur der kleine, sichtbare, für uns faßbare Teil des Ganzen. Denn, so sage ich mir, wie es bei uns ist, so ist es gewiß auch bei den andern, beim ganzen Heer, wir können es nur nicht sehen. Später aber, wenn wir zurückkommen, so werden wir einander gewiß sehen, und dann wird aus den vielen kleinen Kreisen der große Kreis, der das Ganze umfaßt. So ist es wohl, wir müßen von vorn anfangen, vom kleinen Kreis, von Mensch zu Mensch, damit wir nachher das Ganze begreifen können, den grossen Kreis."

is integral to the glorification of the soldier as savior of the nation, especially since the site of battle has been shifted to a postwar defeated nation:

> ... it is not in vain that we [Germans] are burdened with it all, with lies, slander, hatred, contempt, the thirst for vengeance, the superior strength of our enemies, the blockade, the annihilation of non-combatants at home, the inactive watching of the neutrals. It is not senseless that we should have to step naked before God, whipped by all the flames of Hell, pierced by the iron of the cold, kiln-dried and molten, one foot in a stinking common grave, the other on broken and swaying earth. It is not in vain that our heart and bowels are laid bare, and it only depends on us to see that it shall not be in vain.[196]

Whatever its obvious literary weaknesses, this passage is instructive on several points. Although a full analysis of German conservative political views would be inappropriate in the current context, Schauwecker's venomous diatribe is symptomatic of general nationalist concerns, and therefore requires some comment. It is, first, a catalogue of German national grievances against the Allies during and after the First World War. In the interwar period the nationalists and even some liberals consistently accused their once and future enemies of, in effect, not having "played fair" in the conduct of the war. The tone of aggrieved righteousness couched in quasi-biblical or apocalyptic imagery is characteristic of such perorations. Schauwecker was no voice crying in the wilderness.

Secondly, the matter of language merits an additional comment. John Brophy, in his introduction to the 1929 English translation of *The Fiery Way*, calls the style "... too adjectival and exclamatory for perfect art.... "[197] Questions of art aside, it is essential to distinguish between those linguistic qualities that are specific to a given language, and those elaborated by the author. In its nationalistic mode, the exclamatory style, it should be noted, has a long history, going back at least to Fichte's *Reden*. In addition, German tolerates a greater degree of emphasis than does English. Anyone who has attempted to translate a speech of Hitler's — or a paragraph of Schauwecker — will comprehend the difficulty. Furthermore, phrases that sound hopelessly pompous in English are perfectly acceptable in the language of German nationalism. In short, Schauwecker's emphatic and elevated style is not atypical of the German nationalist tradition of writing. It also demonstrates that the high rhetorical style of German nationalism was not undermined by the war. A truism of the British war

---

[196]Schauwecker, *Fiery Way*, 113–114. "... es ist nicht umsonst, daß wir mit allem beladen sind, mit Lüge, Verleumdung, Haß, Verachtung, Rachsucht, Übermacht der Feinde, Blockade, Vernichtung der Wehrlosen daheim, tatlosem Zusehen der Neutralen. Es ist nicht sinnlos, daß wir nackt vor den Gott hintreten müssen, halb von allen Flammen der Hölle gepeitscht, halb vom Stahl der Kälte durchbohrt, ausgedörrt und zerschmolzen, einen Fuß in einem stinkenden Massengrab, den andern auf zerborstenem, schwankendem Erdreich. Es ist nicht umsonst, daß uns Herz und Eingeweide bloßgelegt werden, und es ist nur an uns, daß es nicht vergeblich sei" (88–89).

[197]John Brophy, introduction to Schauwecker, *Fiery Way*, v.

literature is the loss of the high rhetorical mode, a loss that left the language as damaged as the men.[198] That linguistic decapitation did not occur in German until 1945, as National Socialism arrogated the Wilhelmine patriotic diction that had been preserved and elaborated by the conservative war writers.

Finally, there is no doubt that the burden of the suffering and, above all, the task of seeing that the suffering was not in vain, that is, meaningless, fell on the soldiers themselves. As I noted earlier, it was imperative to most of the combatants that the war be endowed with meaning, ideally through the use that the veterans made of their experience. The noblest use of that experience, according to the nationalists, was to create a new nation to replace the one destroyed by the war. But it is important to recognize that the nationalist credo insisted that the destruction had been material; the national spirit, embodied in its combat veterans, had survived the test of war. Baumgarten's model of transforming material loss into spiritual victory reaches its apogee in the nationalist war narratives, especially in Joseph Magnus Wehner's *Sieben vor Verdun* (Seven before Verdun, 1930). In the culminating scene of the novel, the German soldiers have been forced to evacuate Fort Vaux on All Saint's Day. But their evacuation is only physical in Wehner's vision, for the German dead occupy the burning fort and repel the French until November 3. The victory is that of "the invisible German Reich, which had its roots in their wounds. And they know that this Reich is deathless among dying troops." [199]

Wehner's poetic vision of a greater, spiritual Reich rooted (a *völkisch* word) in the wounds of the soldiers is intended to offset the factual loss of Fort Vaux and transform it into a spiritual victory for the Germans.

The notion of a deathless German Reich not only served as consolation for the actual loss of the second Reich but also provided conservatives with a foundation on which to build a new nation. The pattern of individual destruction and resurrection also became the national pattern. This is Schauwecker's version:

> We have always been destroyed from top to bottom. Only a spark, a breath, a flicker left for us to revive. Ever and again we have been faced with a new chaos, and every time we have raised — and herein is our belief, our hope, our future — a new Germany.[200]

[198]See Hynes, *A War Imagined*, 353, and Fussell, *Great War*, 21–23.

[199]Joseph Magnus Wehner, *Sieben vor Verdun* (Munich: Langen/ Muller, 1930; reprint Hamburg: Deutsche Hausbücherei, 1930, 307. " . . . vom unsichtbaren deutschen Reiche, das seine Wurzeln hat in ihren Wunden. Und sie wissen, daß dieses Reich unsterblich ist mitten unter sterbenden Völkern."

[200]Schauwecker, *Fiery Way*, 44. "Wir wurden immer von Grund aus bis ins Mark zerstört. Nur ein Funke, ein Hauch, ein Zucken blieb uns zur Erneuerung. Wir standen immer wieder vor einem neuen Chaos, und wir gebaren immer wieder — und das ist Glaube, Hoffnung und Zukunft — eine neue Gestalt des Deutschen" (34).

Schauwecker's conviction that Germans, especially the front soldiers, can raise a new nation out of the spiritual spark remaining is echoed in Bucher's conclusion quoted above. Both draw a parallel between the individual, nature, and the nation, and fit the possibility of rebirth into the organic framework, emphasizing its "rightness" in what they perceive to be the natural scheme of things.

In his foreword to Zöberlein's *Der Glaube an Deutschland*, Adolf Hitler wrote of

> The western front . . . where the belief in the old Reich was shattered on barbed wire and in drum-fire — and where, out of the crater fields in blood and fire, in hunger and death, the new belief in a better Germany was born.[201]

Like the others, Hitler insists that the new belief came out of the sufferings of the war, specifically the sufferings of the front line troops. Their suffering has vouchsafed the veterans a vision of what the new Germany must be, and the right to realize that vision. The new nation must, first of all, be created by the returning front soldiers. For Schauwecker, the troops are the nation, and the nation exists only at the front: "Here they stood alone, they stood for the nation that was to come, the nation that must not fall into the unclean hands of those behind the lines."[202] The front soldier's distrust and disdain of the rear echelons and the home front appears with singular viciousness in Bucher's *In the Line*. He states categorically that the soldiers were not to blame for the defeat (309), and has nothing but contempt for the civilian delegates to Versailles, who "were to gain nothing for us except unconditional surrender. That was to be our reward for enduring four years in the hell of the western front."[203]

If the despised *Etappenschweine* and profiteers could not be trusted to build a new nation, then only fellow front soldiers could be relied on to form a new state true to the authentic spirit of Germany: the spirit of the front soldiers. The so-called front spirit (*Frontgeist*) assumed increasing importance in the late twenties, because it represented everything that the Weimar government was not — at least in the eyes of conservative Germans. Through his character Lt. Wynfrith, Hein presents a representative spokesman. In Wynfrith's last speech to his men near the end of the war, he tells them that they must hope and work for a better peace,

[201] Adolf Hitler, forward to *Der Glaube an Deutschland*, 9. "Die Westfront . . . wo der Glaube an das alte Reich an Drahtverhauen und im Trommelfeuern zerbrach — und aus Trichterfeldern in Blut und Feuer, bei Hunger und Tod der neue Glaube an ein besseres Deutschland geboren wurde."

[202] Schauwecker, *The Furnace*, 201. "Sie standen hier für sich allein da und für die kommende Nation, die nicht jenen da hinten in die unreinen Hände fallen durfte!" (225).

[203] Bucher, *In the Line*, 308. " . . . diese Parlamentäre werden nichts erreichen können als bedingungslose Unterwerfung. Für diese sollen wir vier Jahre lang in der Westfronthölle gestanden sein?" (366). Bucher scathingly refers to the civilians who negotiated the treaty as "parliamentarians."

" . . . a peace without futile, petty trickery and haggling. Honesty and truth are the only real victors. . . . All shoving and wrangling must be utterly hateful to us — and all played-out flag-waving and hysterical hurrah-patriotism. Forget the bad time you've had up the line as quickly as you can, but not all the good that has come of it — the genuineness, the self-respect, the comradeship! Those we will take with us into a free, peaceful, better life . . . . What was in us was the finest and greatest thing I have ever experienced."[204]

Wynfrith's catalogue of onerous political activities coincides precisely with the democratic give and take of Weimar party politics. Genuine comradeship, on the contrary, with its honesty, true emotion, and "natural" hierarchy of leaders and followers serves as the model for an ideal society. Hein's 1937 book, *Das kleine Buch vom grossen Krieg* (The Little Book about the Great War) is intended to indoctrinate children into the Nazi interpretation of the First World War, but it is worth noting here that he focuses on the *Frontgeist* as the model on which the National Socialist state was built, and the thesis of the book is little more than an expanded version of the previous quotation.

Finally, the most famous exposition of the conservative position, and justifiably so, occurs at the end of Schauwecker's *The Furnace*. It became the rallying cry of the radical right because it encapsulates the major themes of nationalist war literature: the desperate search for meaning and coherence in a national-historical context, the belief in the survival of the German spirit, and the rebirth of that spirit through the crucible of a lost war.

---

[204]Hein, 361. " . . . daß danach ein besserer Friede kommt — ohne kleinliches eitles Gekünstel und Geschacher. Das Gerade und das Wahre allein, ihm gehört der Sieg. . . . Alles Streberhafte, alles Schieberische sei uns in tiefster Seele verhaßt. Und alles fadenscheinige Fahnenschwenken und alles hysterische Hurra-schreien. Vergeßt das Böse da vorn, so schnell ihr könnt, aber nicht, was dennoch in der Wüste aus uns wuchs: das Echte, das Menschenwürdige, das Kameradschaftliche, ja, das vor allem, die Kameradschaft! wollen wir in die ganze Welt tragen. Aus dieser Qual heraus in ein friedliches freies besseres Leben. . . . was in uns war dort vorn, das war für mich das Schönste und Größte, was ich erlebt — Kameraden — " (322).

I don't believe that a great calamity like this is without meaning and without result. There must be a reason and a consequence of our loss of this war. . . . But now we can at last begin anew and set free what is buried but still lives, aye, and that which has the will to life but is not yet born. . . . We had to lose the war to win the nation.[205]

[205] Schauwecker, *The Furnace*, 243–244. "Ich glaube nicht, daß ein großes Unheil ohne Sinn und ohne Schuld ist. Es hat gewiß seinen Sinn und seine Berechtigung, daß wir diesen Krieg verloren haben. . . . Aber jetzt können wir endlich von vorn anfangen und das freimachen, was verschüttet ist, aber noch lebt — jawohl — und das, was zum Leben will, aber noch nicht geboren ist! . . . Wir mußten den Krieg verlieren, um die Nation zu gewinnen" (402–403).

Poster for German war bonds. Fritz Ehrler, 1917.
Courtesy of Hoover Institute.

4: Narrating the War Experience

The structure of First World War narratives has, until recently, garnered very little critical attention. Evelyn Cobley has studied their narrative form and the ideological implications of that form from a post-structuralist point of view, but her reliance on the British myth of the war effectively limits the validity of her conclusions to the Anglo-American literature and a few similarly constructed French and German books.[1] The greater part of the German literature, on the contrary, plays out a rightist, nationalist war myth fundamentally at odds with the liberal myth of meaningless slaughter and pointless suffering in defense of a "botched civilization." An examination of the role of narrative structure in the literary creation of meaning must begin with the nature of the war experience itself, the impetus to translate that experience into narrative, and the audience for whom the narratives were intended.

War, by definition, lies at the extremity of human experience, and all the more so for young men raised during the forty-year peace that followed the war of 1870. The experience of the western front, by any earlier standards, was so excessive in its unexpected horror that it was virtually inexpressible. The recourses of traditional language and style must have seemed unequal to the task of expressing such monstrous otherness. A combatant writer faced three problems: how could he convey even a notion of the experience of war; whom did he wish to reach; and what effect did he hope to have on his reader? Such questions of purpose, means and audience lead directly to the cluster of vexing problems that beset any study of war narratives — questions of testimony, truth and authenticity — all entangled with narrative intention and strategy.

Let us begin with the question of audience. For whom, then, did these men write and why? At the outset, many must have written for themselves, either to record personal experience (diaries were very common), or, later, to exorcise psychological demons. But when a writer expanded his compass to an external audience, that audience, as Elizabeth Marsland has correctly pointed out, could contain only two categories of potential readers: combatants and non-combatants.[2] Someone writing principally for other combatants is effectually reinforcing a vision of war already held. The writer and his audience form a

---

[1]Evelyn Cobley, *Representing War: Form and Ideology in First World War Narratives* (Toronto: Toronto UP, 1993). For criticism of her thesis, see my review of *Representing War* in *SubStance*, 78 (1995):126–130.

[2]Marsland, *The Nation's Cause*, 157–167. Marsland's remarks are à propos of the British protest poetry, but her observations are equally applicable to German narratives.

community of like-minded believers who are in a position to insist on their own version of the war as authentic and to dismiss as untrue any competing vision.

Richard Kröner provides an excellent example of this mechanism at work in his 1931 *Landser. Im Westen viel Neues. Das Buch des Frontsoldaten in vier Jahren Krieg* (Lancer. Not All Quiet on the Western Front. The Book of the Front Soldier during Four Years of War).[3] I have provided the full title because it immediately indicates the direction of Kröner's intention. By mentioning his own military title and four years of service he has claimed the authenticity of his own experience. The second phrase of the title, a parody of Remarque's novel, correspondingly dismisses Remarque's vision of war as inauthentic and untrue. In German, the parodic "viel Neues" also implies that, contrary to Remarque's vision, something both new and valuable has come out of the experience of the western front. Kröner pursues the question of authenticity in his introduction, where he asserts that he will show the "full life and activities" of the front soldier, and implies that Remarque's narrative is incomplete and therefore factually unreliable (6). He completes his discrediting of *All Quiet* in the next sentence: "Smilingly the widely-read book of the 'war' writer Remarque will be laid aside: no, that wasn't the war, that was pure fantasy, perhaps a story heard, but not personally experienced. It's the kind of story told and retold by armchair strategists at tavern tables, meant to make your hair rise. The main thing always seems to be the enumeration of many corpses, and fighting and casualties of the worst kind."[4] I have quoted this passage at length because it exemplifies a situation in which an undistinguished writer embodies a set of attitudes more completely than his eminent contemporaries. Kröner's scorn characterizes the conservative backlash against *All Quiet* and similar denunciations of the war experience. The damning accusations of fantasy (that is, falsehood) and lack of personal experience constitute a crucial argument for former combatants. Kröner raises the level of invective by suggesting that Remarque's narrative is the kind of story a civilian searching for an easy thrill would have told. What Kröner is challenging on all levels is the authenticity of Remarque's narrative, and he is doing it by suggesting that Remarque does not belong to the community of combatants. At the end of his introduction, Kröner invites his "liebe

---

[3]Richard Kröner, *Landser. Im Westen viel Neues. Das Buch des Frantsoldaten in vier Jahren Krieg* (Chemnitz: Pickenhahn, 1931).

[4]Kröner, 6. "Lächelnd wurde das vielgelesene Buch des 'Kriegs'-Schriftstellers Remarque aus der Hand gelegt: ja, das war der Krieg nicht, war reichliche Phantasie, vieleicht Gehörtes, aber wenig Selbsterlebtes. Was da manchmal an Biertischen von Heimstrategen erzählt wurde und noch erzählt wird, zieht einem die Haare zu Berge, die Hauptsache schien die Aufzählung recht vieler Toter, und die Kämpfe und Verluste waren immer schlimmster Art." My translation of the last sentence is loose, as the German syntax is virtually untranslatable.

Kameraden" (dear comrades) to read his book, in which they will find experiences to rejoice over and remember with a smile.[5]

Kröner's invocation of his comrades, although more elaborate than most dedications, is by no means unique. Most of the German war narratives are dedicated to former comrades, living and dead. Even *All Quiet* is dedicated to the destroyed generation of Remarque and his comrades. Such dedications fulfill a twofold function. First, they are emblems of authenticity; they proclaim that the author was there and so has the right to speak, and speak authoritatively, of the war. Secondly, they proclaim the community of experience that validates the author's vision, both for the community of comrades and for a large audience of non-combatants whose concurrence is being solicited. Narratives intended primarily for an audience of former combatants nevertheless display a consciousness of a non-combatant audience, which, in the cultural polarization of Weimar, needed to be won over to the author's view of the war.

The critical role of persuasion as a motivating purpose for war writers is yet another indication of the centrality of the war experience to national identity between the wars. The meaning of the war was the base on which decisions about the shape and direction of the nation rested, and the national debate about that meaning was largely carried out in the war literature. The need for a persuasive picture of authentic war experience ensures the privileging of narrative content over form, of the message over the medium. Recourse to experimental narrative form is rare even in liberal texts, and unheard of in conservative ones.[6] The stakes were simply too high to risk alienating an essentially conservative reading public with literary experimentation. There are two other reasons for the general avoidance of modernist style. First, many (probably most) of the authors of war narratives were novice writers. The war book was usually the author's first, and often his only book. In keeping with the importance of their testimony, even professional writers such as Arnold Zweig tended to retain traditional narrative techniques.

But the most important reason is that experimental narration accords ill with the literature of personal testimony. Narrative complexity could only distract and distance the reader from the authenticity of the personal narrative where the key issue is truth, not aesthetics. The author presents himself as a simple, honest soldier, a latter-day German Michael, telling his story in plain

---

[5]Kröner, 6. In *Soldier from the Wars Returning* (London: Hutchinson, 1965), Charles Carrington dismisses *All Quiet* on the same grounds. "The back-area accounts of soldiers at the base were true to life and sometimes powerfully depicted, but the nearer the characters came to the front, the more did critical readers doubt the author had ever been there" (264).

[6]The obvious experimental examples are Unruh's *Opfergang*, Frank's *Der Mensch ist Gut* and especially Köppen's *Heeresbericht*, which fulfills many of the requirements for a modernist text. See Cobley 183–188. Her remarks about Jones's *In Parenthesis* largely apply to Köppen's structure, although Köppen is uninvolved with linguistic complexity.

language and straightforward chronology.[7] The personal narrative thus assumes the position of representative narrative, a vision of war elevated to national myth. It is therefore unimportant that the story be well or interestingly told, or that it be on the cutting edge of narrative experimentation; but it is crucial that it be authentic.

The perception of authenticity raises another problem bearing on the present discussion. As discussed earlier, Jean Norton Cru recognized that the public regards war novels not as fictions, but as truthful "depositions."[8] Although no friend to the war novel ("If all the war novels of the literati came to disappear, art would lose nothing and history would gain in force and influence"), Cru, who was attempting to thoroughly document combat experience, still sees some value in fictional accounts.[9] He is willing to consider fictional accounts as documents, but only those in which "the fiction is only a thin veil through which one can distinguish the person of the author, his experience of the war, his units, the sectors he occupied, in a word, the actual facts of his own campaign."[10] He continues, "there are very few war novels, and these novels are only scarcely disguised personal memories."[11] Despite his antagonism toward war fiction, Cru clearly delineates the troublesome blurring of generic and fictional lines characteristic of it. On the first level the blurring occurs between genres. An examination of the texts makes it immediately apparent that it is impossible to distinguish between a fictionalized autobiography and an autobiographical novel. The traditional generic lines vanish into a series of gradations. In categorizing such works as confessions Northrop Frye has recognized their two essential qualities: personal testimony and what he calls "an integrated pattern."[12] The creation of a representative pattern of personal experience links the war narratives together no matter what their political positions, because it is the foundation of the claim to authenticity.

On a deeper level, the blurring of fiction and non-fiction produces a second, more complex ambiguity. If war fiction, as Cru suggests, is regarded as truth, does that constitute a new criterion for literary judgment? Is the "good" war

[7]See Cobley, *Representing War*, 29–54 for a discussion of documentary narratives. See also Jean Norton Cru, *Témoins* (Paris: Les Étincelles, 1929), 10–11 for his view of the centrality of the documentary account.

[8]Cru, *Témoins*, 50. See chapter 3, note 10 for the French text.

[9]Cru, *Témoins*, 50. "Si tous les romans guerriers des littérateurs venaient à disparaître, l'art n'y perdrait rien et l'histoire gagnerait en force et en influence."

[10]Cru, *Témoins*, 10–11. " . . . les récits fictifs, mais seulement lorsque la fiction n'est qu'un voile léger sous lequel on peut distinguer la personne de l'auteur, son expérience de la guerre, son unité, les secteurs qu'il a occupés, en un mot les faits réels de sa propre campagne."

[11]Cru, *Témoins*, 11. " . . . il y a fort peu de romans de guerre, et ces romans ne sont que des souvenirs personnels à peine déguisés."

[12]Northrop Frye, *Anatomy of Criticism* (Princeton: Princeton UP, 1957), 307.

novel one that is deemed to be "truthful"? In Germany between the wars, the answer to those questions is a resounding "yes." The meaning of the war had become a national issue of such importance that aesthetics had to be subordinated to authenticity and multiplicity to a single representative experience.

Paradoxically, the privileging of individual experience in the war narratives contributes to the formation of national war myths because that experience is perceived by writer and reader as representative of the national experience.[13] The typical focus of many narratives, the infantry squad functions as a common denominator of experience, and is invariably composed of comrades from various parts of the Reich and from different classes. The squad serves as a microcosm of Germany and consequently as a paradigm of the national war experience.[14] In Germany, the representative war experience is not presented by way of a jumble of disconnected episodes in the picaresque mode, but by an integrated chronological narrative whose pattern and closure are fundamental to the significance of the experience.[15]

The structure of the German war narratives is primarily determined by the goal of telling an authentic story about what the war was like, a story that documents physical experience in realistic detail, but nevertheless privileges a spiritual development that leads to individual knowledge and to the integration of the war into the collective historico-cultural continuum. Obviously, not every German war narrative adheres to this paradigm, but it is the pattern of virtually all of the conservative narratives and even a few of the liberal ones (notably Remarque's *The Road Back* and Wiechert's *Jedermann*). The rest of the liberal novels are closer to the picaresque model, as Cobley has argued.[16] But the controlling paradigm remains that of the Bildungsroman and related forms.

In its traditional form, the Bildungsroman narrates the development of a representative young man through a chronological series of experiences from which he must learn. Two elements are essential. First, the protagonist's development is an inner, spiritual development — a psychological transformation. It is not merely the learning of a certain set of lessons, but the gradual, organic "becoming" of an individual character. In a word, the emphasis is on *Bildung*. This development is triggered by a series of external material experiences, but the development itself remains essentially spiritual. The experiences are often episodic, but the protagonist's growth is always progressive. The other fundamental characteristic of the Bildungsroman is its circular form — a form that includes a posi-

---

[13]See Cobley, *Representing War*, 72.

[14]The pattern is similar in the French *témoinage* literature, for example Barbusse's *Le Feu* and Dorgelès's *Les Croix de bois* among others. The tendency to create representative groups seems less marked in the British narratives.

[15]It is here that I depart radically from Cobley's argument, as she seems to have overlooked the effective use of the Bildungsroman form in the German rightist narratives.

[16]Cobley, 131–143.

tive conclusion. The protagonist moves from his own world into and through another, larger world, and then, his development complete, returns home. At the conclusion, he is able to integrate his new knowledge of himself and his understanding of life into his native social world.

Two important cultural influences lie behind the structure of the war narratives. As the pattern of choice, the Bildungsroman represents the eighteenth- and nineteenth-century flowering of a much older formal structure. The irreducible narrative pattern is one of "there and back again," a movement from home into an alien otherworld, and back home again. The paradigm implies a journey undertaken for a purpose — in folklore, often the acquisition of knowledge or magic essential to the survival of the protagonist's people. This pattern is, of course, characteristic of folkloric journeys and of quest literature,[17] and shapes the Romantic *Kunstmärchen* from Novalis to E. T. A. Hoffmann. As noted earlier, medieval, Romantic and folk literature were in high favor in the secondary schools of prewar Germany, and even more influential among the members of the youth movements, especially the Wandervogel. Such influences were reinforced by an abiding confidence in cyclical historical patterns predicated on organic models.

For young German men searching for a way to chronicle their experience, especially their spiritual experience of the First World War, the Bildungsroman offered a nearly irresistible narrative format.[18] It responded, first, to the cultural value of *Bildung* in German society, in spite of, or perhaps because of, the damage done to that intellectual goal by the war.

Martin Swales provides a pivotal definition of *Bildung*. It is, he states,

> ... the whole man unfolding organically in all his complexity and richness. *Bildung* becomes, then, a total growth process, a diffused *Werden*, or becoming, involving something more intangible than the acquirement of a finite number of lessons. Such a concern is the expression of a certain kind of bourgeois humanism, one that retains a special (albeit problematic) hold over the German imagination.[19]

Swales accurately focuses on the centrality of organic *development* (not material *progress*), the yearning for wholeness and the conviction that *Bildung* is not attained through intellectual training or the amassing of knowledge, however much those may assist in the general process of development, but through *Erlebnis*, human experience of life. The roots of *Bildung* in bourgeois humanism

---

[17]Stith Thompson, *Motif-Index of Folk Literature* (Bloomington: Indiana UP, 1975), 3:F0-F199 and H1250–1299, "Otherworld Journeys."

[18]An examination of the innovative current criticism of the Bildungsroman lies beyond the scope of this study. Although that criticism is illuminating, my concern is limited to perceptions of the Bildungsroman in the early part of this century.

[19]Martin Swales, *The German Bildungsroman from Wieland to Hesse* (Princeton: Princeton UP, 1978), 14–15.

are particularly pertinent to the First World War writers, since most of them were sons of the bourgeoisie, raised in the atmosphere of *Bildungsburgertum* with its persistent celebration of spiritual culture.[20]

Despite the collapse of some of the peripheral values of *Bildung* in the course of the war — notably cultural learning — the fundamental worldview embodied in the concept retained its hold on the combatants. Without a seminal belief in the organic development of the spirit through experience, it would have been impossible for them to see the war as a means to individual and collective spiritual transformation and regeneration. While superficial illusions concerning the glory of war and other civilian patriotic values perished in the *Materialschlacht*, the fundamental belief in the primacy and potential development of spirit and will did not, with far-reaching consequences for the shape of the German war narrative and of the German nation.

Attempting to explain why German war writers preferred the form of the Bildungsroman for their narratives tends to trap the critic in a chicken-and-egg argument. Did the writer's intention come first, or did the form impose itself? Although the question is unanswerable, it may be useful to examine a few pertinent factors. To begin with, both the class and national origins of the form are significant. I have already noted that the Bildungsroman emerged out of and is associated with the bourgeois world.[21] Just as important for the generation of men who became the war writers was their perception of the Bildungsroman as a specifically *German* form in origin and practice. The inward orientation of the genre reflects both aspects of that view. Most recent criticism of the Bildungsroman has emphasized its existence in most European cultures — in short, its identity as a Western literary form rather than a specifically national one.[22] That was not the view in the early part of the century. Most German criticism from the early twentieth century either overtly claimed the Bildungsroman as a German narrative form, or at least strongly suggested that it had reached its highest level of development in Germany. In her 1926 study, for example, Melitta Gerhard regards the entire history of the Bildungsroman as a reflection of the essential human problem of bringing the individual into unity with "German

[20]See Fritz Stern, "The Political Consequences of the Unpolitical German," in *The Failure of Illiberalism: Essays on the Political Culture of Modern Germany* (New York: Knopf, 1972), 3–25.

[21]In addition to Swales, see Franco Moretti, *The Way of the World: The Bildungsroman in European Culture* (London: Verso, 1987); Rolf Selbmann, *Der deutsche Bildungsroman* (Stuttgart: Metzlersche Verlag, 1984); Randolph P. Schaffner, *The Apprenticeship Novel* (New York: Lang, 1984), Melitta Gerhard; *Der deutsche Entwicklungsroman bis zu Goethes Wilhelm Meister* (Halle/Saale: Niemeyer, 1926), and Helga Esselborn-Krumbiegel, *Der "Held" im Roman: Formen des deutschen Entwicklungsromans im frühen 20. Jahrhundert* (Darmstadt: Wissenschaftliche Buchgesellschaft, 1983).

[22]See especially Moretti, *The Way of the World*, and Susan Ashley Gohlman, *Starting over: The Task of the Protagonist in the Contemporary Bildungsroman* (New York: Garland, 1990).

cultural and spiritual life."[23] The entry on the Bildungsroman from the 1925–1926 *Reallexikon der Deutschen Literaturgeschichte*, running to nearly eight columns, doesn't define the genre as German, but cites almost exclusively German examples, and concludes with the statement that the Bildungsroman is one of the genres most beloved by Germans, and that other nations possess far fewer works of the type.[24] Such assertions of the "germanness" of the Bildungsroman were current at the turn of the century and surely informed middle-class education, where young men would have acquired that knowledge as part of their patriotic upbringing.

The germanness of the Bildungsroman would have exerted a strong appeal on certain of the conservative authors, to whom I shall shortly return, but it can scarcely account for the wide distribution of the form in the German war literature. What characteristics, then, made the form so appealing? On a strictly narrative level, the Bildungsroman offered mostly inexperienced writers a flexible and adaptable format within an essentially chronological if episodic framework. The chronological and biographical structure of the form coincides with the experiential nature of the soldier's life.[25]

The plot outline of a "classic" German war novel takes the following course: an idealistic schoolboy, swept up in the patriotic fervor of August 1914 (or later) volunteers for service. After a period of training in barracks, during which he learns the fundamentals of soldiering and grasps that he is entering an alien world, he crosses Germany by troop train on the way to the front. His feelings of comradeship, already awakened in the caserne, become stronger and are reinforced by a surge of patriotism, particularly if the goal is the western front and the train crosses the Rhine, the "German river." After a long, grueling march to the front, the new soldier is initiated into war by his first combat. He feels some combination of fear (of death, wounds, or cowardice), horror and disgust at the human carnage, and anxiety that his spirit won't be strong enough to get him through. The action then follows the course of the stalemated war: periods of action and bombardment at the front alternate with intervals of rest and even amusement behind the lines. There is at least one home leave, during which he comprehends the bottomless chasm between the front soldiers and civilians, deepening his alienation from the homeland and strengthening his feelings of comradeship for his fellow soldiers, especially those in his company. From 1916

[23]Gerhard, *Der deutsche Entwicklungsroman*, 2. " . . . spiegelt sie die verschiedenen Studien, die die Stellung des Einzelnen zur Gesamtheit im deutschen Kultur- und Geistesleben durchgemacht hat."

[24]Paul Merker and Wolfgang Stammler, eds., *Reallexikon der Deutschen Literaturgeschichte*, 5 vols. (Berlin: de Gruyter, 1925–1926), 1:141–145.

[25]On chronological and biographical structure, see Selbman, *Der deutsche Bildungsroman*, 9; Esselborn-Krumbiegel, *Der "Held" im Roman*, 20–21, and Swales, *The German Bildungsroman*, 19.

onward, he is gradually exhausted physically and mentally by the *Materialsch-lacht* and the consequent loss of his comrades to death or disabling wounds. At his physical and psychological nadir, he realizes that his experience of war has transformed him into a better, stronger man. By the end, he sees his future path clearly before him, or at least knows what significance the war has for him and what he as an individual and as a member of the community must do in peace.

That, in its essentials, is the plot of a German First World War narrative. The flexibility of the biographical narrative permits wide variations within the basic framework. Some narratives start later in the war to coincide with the narrator's age; some terminate before the end of the war. Some take place on both fronts, or even in Serbia or with the fleet. A few begin and end *in medias res*; a few are spread over two volumes (Remarque and Renn) or even three or four (Zweig and Dwinger). But the easily managed chronological format accommodates all circumstances and organizes the chaos of war experience into a recognizable, even familiar form. The familiarity of the Bildungsroman was no small part of its appeal.

The familiar order that the Bildungsroman could impose on the representative scenario described above extends to the individuality and representativeness of the characters. Gohlman and Moretti have both remarked that the hero of a Bildungsroman is a representative or symbolic youth.[26] The youth of the protagonist is an essential precondition; it allows for development. In the case of the war narratives, it is also obviously mimetic, since the vast majority of soldiers were young. The protagonist's status as a representative German soldier, the exemplar of his generation, is likewise essential for ideological reasons that have already been enumerated. The strength of the Bildungsroman as narrative structure in this context is that it allows the creation of a protagonist who is simultaneously unique and representative. The protagonist's spiritual odyssey through the experience of war is both biography (or autobiography) and model journey.

The typical focus on the interior development of the protagonist has significant ramifications for the treatment of other characters. Subsidiary characters in the war narratives often function as contrasting or parallel figures.[27] Although I would not imply that all figures other than the protagonist are colorless ciphers of social or ideological stereotypes, stereotypical characters preponderate. The reader repeatedly encounters the same types. The hero is usually a bourgeois student-soldier (often called the student, the scholar, or the philosopher by the other men); his comrades form a collection of geographically and professionally diverse types. A typical selection includes a farmer, an urban socialist, a clerk, and a man from the eastern reaches of the German empire. In most cases, they are differentiated superficially through manners, accents, political views and so-

[26]Gohlman, *Starting Over*, 16–20; Moretti, *The Way of the World*, 5.

[27]Esselborn-Krumbiegel, *Der "Held" im Roman*, 17.

cial attitudes. They provide the hero with new experiences and ideas that expand his understanding and encourage his development. As the war wears on, the initial types are often replaced by a new set specific to the war: the fatherly old hand, often a sergeant, the raw recruit, the clever scavenger, the shell-shocked soldier and the dedicated combat officer. The last is particularly important because, as we have seen, the officer often serves as an example of true leadership, the natural leadership that would become the conservative ideological model between the wars. These company commanders additionally function as a secondary *porte parole* for the author, particularly where political statements are concerned. Beumelburg's and Hein's officers (the latter's final speech has already been quoted) are noteworthy examples.

On the other hand, one does find some well-developed characters, although they may simultaneously fit the preceding types. The most obvious example is Kat in *All Quiet*, the scavenger par excellence, but Arnold Zweig likewise provides a whole range of well-drawn characters, many of whom are symbolic. The cowardly and sneaking Sergeant Niggl of *Education before Verdun* is unforgettable as an individual and as a military type, as is Bertin's beloved Lenore, probably the most complete and moving female character in the German war literature. It is worth noting again that Zweig was a well-established writer before the war, while many of the others were novices. Literary inexperience may have had something to do with underdeveloped characters; nevertheless the fact that they are representative types who affect and are affected by the protagonist links them to the tradition of the Bildungsroman.

The dynamism of the spiritual transformation in the war narratives contrasts forcefully with the stasis of the war. The endless, unchanging reality of stalemated, mechanized trench warfare throws the spiritual growth of the characters into high relief, and reflects the antithesis of the mechanical and the human typical of German thought on the *Materialschlacht*. Selbman suggests that the renaissance of interest in the Bildungsroman in the twentieth century is attributable to the German hatred of industrial technology and the dehumanization that followed in its wake.[28] Significantly, in the war narratives, it is the soul-wrecking technology of death that provides the essential stimulus for the protagonist's survival and development as a spiritual being. The fear of imminent annihilation triggers the growth of human impulses, above all the spiritual bond of comradeship. The growth of the individual soldier into the community of comrades thematically mirrors the narrative movement of the traditional Bildungsroman.

If the overriding theme of the Bildungsroman is the inner development of the hero in response to external stimuli, then the structure of the plot must take into account the relationship of the individual to the outer world. The organization of the traditional Bildungsroman displays a pattern of movement from

---

[28]Selbman, *Der deutsche Bildungsroman*, 153.

the inner world of the spirit into the outer world of society. Gerhard suggests that the pattern is tripartite, consisting of " . . . the gradual turning of the gaze from the outer world to one's own inner world, and the reawakening will to turn from self-contemplation back to the world . . . . "[29] That scheme corresponds very closely to the common structure of the German war narrative. Most begin in the social world of the homeland — the rigid, materialistic world of the Wilhelmine bourgeoisie. As noted earlier, the success of the Wandervogel in the pre-war years suggests the extent of the younger generation's rebellion against their parents' world, and explains the joy with which they welcomed the onset of war. For the young soldiers, the "spirit of August" included the expectation of spiritual transformation and regeneration.[30] The war assumed the role of character-forming experience, and the journey through the war a journey of the spirit.[31] The incidents of home leave in many books reinforce rather than negate the pattern, because the soldier's temporary return to the world is invariably a failure. His alienation from his *Heimat* reflects his incomplete development. He has not yet learned all the lessons of war and is as yet unprepared to return to the world.

Once he feels himself to be a "changed man," he is ready to return to the social world, which, incidentally, has not undergone a corresponding transformation. The goal of his development is to give to the world what he has learned from the war. Esselborn-Krumbiegel states that " . . . the goal of the novel is reached when the hero, in his search for an order, . . . enters into a life situation that makes both personal development and integration [with society] possible for him. . . . "[32] Her definition is particularly applicable to the conservative narratives, where the transformation of the hero and his understanding of the spirit of the front form the necessary foundation for the construction of a new nation.[33] Even in narratives that are largely apolitical, such as Wiechert's *Jedermann*, the hero's development culminates with his return home and discovery that he can use his experience of the war creatively rather than letting it destroy him. For example, Johannes discovers that he can love his widowed mother

[29]Gerhard, *Der deutsche Entwicklungsroman*, 167. " . . . die allmähliche Abkehr des Blickes von der Außenwelt ins eigene Innere, und der wiedererwachende Wille, sich von der Selbstbetrachtung hinweg der Welt zuzuwenden . . . ."

[30]Leed, *No Man's Land*, 17.

[31]Hermann Glaser, *Literatur des 20. Jahrhunderts in Motiven* (Munich: Beck, 1979), 2:80.

[32]Esselborn-Krumbiegel, *Der "Held" im Roman*, 23. "Das Ziel des Romans ist erreicht, sobald der Held auf seiner Suche nach einer Ordnung, der er sich zubilden und in die er sich hineinbilden kann, in einen Lebenszusammenhang tritt, der ihm Selbstverwirklichung und Integration ermöglicht . . . " (23). See also Gohlman's discussion of the practical values of the Bildungsroman in *Starting Over*, 3–4.

[33]Todd Kontje remarks in his *Private Lives in the Public Sphere: The German Bildungsroman as Metafiction* (University Park: Pennsylvania State UP, 1992) that the ideology of *Bildung* is easily (and dangerously) transferred from the individual to the state (14).

enough to give her permission to marry the crippled schoolmaster, and that he can regenerate his own life through farming. The same pattern is apparent in Renn's *War* and *Afterwar*. The changes wrought by the war render the protagonist unable to tolerate the situation in Germany after the armistice. He is convinced that the older generation is " . . . already on the pounce to set up all this authority again."[34] His yearning, not for love or for a return to his life before the war, but for an active political party in which to believe leads him gradually to the communists (211).

Paul Fussell has suggested that the literate and literary British soldiers of the First World War saw their experience in terms of the British literary canon.[35] Although I would not pose the argument quite so categorically for the relationship between the German soldier and the canonical form of the Bildungsroman, I would propose that the Bildungsroman presented on several levels an appealing narrative equivalent to the soldiers' *Weltanschauung*. Even Cobley admits that among men desperate to find some justification for their terrible experiences, the meaningfulness conferred by the narrative structure of the Bildungsroman was nearly irresistible.[36] On a practical level, the chronological recounting of a spiritual autobiography paralleled the soldiers' sequential *Kriegserlebnis* and their focus on individual spiritual development into the community of comrades. It further provided a paradigm of spiritual transformation through which a series of horrific experiences could be perceived as productive and meaningful in both individual and social contexts. In short, the Bildungsroman permits a positive conclusion. At a deeper level, the Bildungsroman provided a paradigm of closure and meaning that corresponded to the historical German commitment to a cyclical model of human history, while simultaneously responding to the concerns of a defeated and seemingly chaotic nation. Moretti has argued that the classical Bildungsroman "allows for *one* meaning only, one truth: and obviously, their contrary: error."[37] Moretti's absolutist paradigm accords precisely with the representative experience of the war and the equally representative judgment of its significance found in most of the German war narratives. As I have noted earlier, in a defeated Germany, the national stakes of the meaning of the war were simply too high to tolerate a diversity of

---

[34]Renn, *After War*, 176. See chapter 2, note 72.

[35]Fussell, *Great War*, 155–174.

[36]Cobley, *Representing War*, 125–27, 143–45.

[37]Moretti, *The Way of the World*, 61.

"meanings." National regeneration required a unified, even monolithic national war experience. And that experience could be best conveyed in the complete, harmonious German form of the Bildungsroman. In spite of the horrific reality of war depicted in the narratives, the authors' commitment to the philosophical and formal expression of *Bildung* places them within the continuity of German culture.

5: Imagining War

The First World War is the first European war for which we have large numbers of visual images that have significantly shaped our perception of the war. This is due to the growing dominance of the photograph and its offshoot, the motion picture.[1] Nineteenth-century European wars had been grandly depicted in drawings and paintings, the latter, in particular, focusing on stirring battle scenes and triumphant generals. Both the battle scenes and the portraits are part of the Romantic heritage of the battle paintings of David, Delacroix and Géricault. The persistence of heroic subjects (cavalry charges, "last stands" and the like) continued throughout the nineteenth century, as did the unwritten prohibitions against showing particularly bloody or dismembered corpses.

The survival of traditional battle painting was prolonged by the huge success of the popular illustrated papers that emerged in the middle of the century. *Die Illustrierte Zeitung*, *L'Illustration* and the *London Illustrated News* fed the voracious public appetite for pictures, among them pictures of wars European, foreign and colonial. The tradition lasted well into the First World War. An examination of issues published during the last months of 1914 reveals a preponderance of conventional and thoroughly sanitized battle scenes. In most cases, altering the uniforms and flags would replicate scenes from 1870 or earlier. Some images were irresistibly romantic: an early drawing from *L'Illustration* showing an artillery man galloping a caisson was copied by both the German and English magazines. In September of 1914 the war still seemed romantic to the non-combatant populations, and such drawings responded to the tradition of glamorizing and glorifying war. These conventional images yielded only slowly to the grittier realism of photographs, the proportion of photos to drawings gradually increasing over the course of the war, although illustrations were still favored for covers. In spite of official and editorial censorship, photos and illustrations revealed, if not the full extent of the devastation, at least some idea of what the front looked like. The taboo against showing badly mangled corpses largely remained in effect. The horrifying photos, along with the paintings of Nevinson, Nash, Dix and even Leroux did not appear until after the war.[2]

[1] The American Civil War marks the origin of battlefield photography.

[2] Beyond official censorship, many publications practiced self-censorship to avoid difficulties with the authorities, which often produced late issues and unsightly pages that had been censored after typesetting. The editor of *L'Illustration*, for example, was very proud that his magazine had been censored only three times during the war. See Jean-Noël Marchandiau, *L'Illustration 1843/1944: Vie et mort d'un journal*, (Toulouse: Privat, 1987), 207–229. Some of Leroux's paintings appeared in *L'Illustration* toward the end of the war. Hynes provides a good

The flood of visual images of the war was accompanied by an equally copious flood of literary images, mostly in the form of lyric poetry.[3] The heavy reliance on figurative language typical of poetry diminishes significantly in the narratives, where such language is interlocked with the process of description. Cobley has correctly signaled the dominance of the descriptive in these narratives, and with it the pervasiveness of descriptions of life in the battle zone — in short, descriptions of the indescribable.[4] The general dearth of figurative language in the narratives coincides with their mimetic goal. In an essentially testimonial and persuasive literature, the factuality of the witness carries more weight than complex metaphorical constructions. The preference for crisp, realistic narration and description cuts across the philosophical boundaries, and is particularly characteristic of the younger writers. Established writers, naturally, tended to retain their earlier style, for example Carossa and Arnold Zweig. In spite of its fundamentally mimetic style, the testimonial literature also seeks to convince, and it is primarily out of that persuasive intention that evocative metaphorical language emerges. Through the allusive patterning of descriptive detail, the authors are able to draw on a limited but emotionally evocative range of cultural sources.

What were those sources? The Bible is an obvious source, as is Goethe's *Faust*, especially the *Walpurgisnacht* scene, which coincides with the battle zone as a sinister otherworld. One might expect a reasonable level of familiarity with classical authors, given the infamous rigors of the classical *Gymnasia*, but classical references are remarkably few. References to Dante (the *Inferno*), on the other hand, abound. Given the realities of secondary education, one can assume on the part of educated soldiers a good knowledge of German literature, especially of folklore and of the classical and Romantic periods. But there is astonishingly little evidence of what German troops read. Few sources mention any books at all, and in those that do, only three titles are consistently cited. Georg von der Vring maintained that every pack contained the Bible, *Faust* and Nietzsche's *Also sprach Zarathustra*.[5] Goltz's Siebenreut finds *Faust* and *Zarathustra* in the pack of a dead comrade, and later in the exhaustion of the

general overview of the problems of depicting the battlefield and the limitations imposed by censorship and the public sense of the acceptable in chapter 9 of *A War Imagined*. For an excellent analysis of Dix's war art, see Otto Conzelmann, *Der andere Dix: Sein Bild vom Menschen und vom Krieg* (Stuttgart: Klett, 1983). Matthias Eberle, *World War I and the Weimar Artists* (New Haven: Yale UP, 1985) also contains useful material.

[3] Although tangential to this inquiry, the German lyric poetry of the war is very rich. The best study is Patrick Bridgewater's *German Poets of the First World War*, but see also the anthology and commentary of Anz and Vogl in *Die Dichter und der Krieg*, and Marsland, *The Nation's Cause* on the patriotic lyric.

[4] Evelyn Cobley, *Representing War: Form and Ideology in First World War Narratives* (Toronto: Toronto UP, 1993), 29–70.

[5] Vring, *Soldat Suhren*, 202.

Materialschalacht remarks that even those leave him cold, "it is as if the written word had lost its power."[6] The popularity of *Zarathustra* is difficult to gauge, although it is clearly the model for Glavina's poem in Carossa's *Rumanian Diary*, and one critic notes that the publisher produced a special edition for the troops, bound in field gray and containing an introduction with Nietzsche's sayings for war and peace.[7] The tendency of many conservative writers to end their books with a homily on the meaning of the war, couched in elevated, rhapsodic prose, suggests that the influence of *Zarathustra* was both wide and deep.[8]

In addition to the specifically literary sources, the metaphors of the war narratives are underlain by a less obvious but enormously important stratum of folklore and folksong, particularly where nature metaphors are concerned. As I have argued elsewhere, the sinister natural world of the *Kunstmärchen* and the *Volksmärchen* is never far away and colors the use of natural metaphor, making it quite different from the negated arcadias of British war literature.[9] The wildness of nature equally appears in the storm metaphors preferred by many authors. Jünger's *Storm of Steel* and the stormy conclusion of Bucher's *In the Line* are only the most obvious examples. The persistence of the organic paradigm and the concomitant tendency to view the war as a natural force are also apparent in such references.[10]

Whatever their sources, the German literary images of the war fall into three broad categories: images centering on the soldier's life and role in the war, on the landscape of the war and the battles that created it, and on the war itself, viewed as a separate entity.

"Anything," wrote Ernst Jünger of his feelings at the outbreak of war, "rather than stay at home."[11] His cry was echoed by young men all over Europe as they set out on what they envisioned as a journey into the greatest event, even

---

[6]Joachim von der Goltz, *Der Baum von Cléry* (Berlin: Gutenberg, 1934), 80. " . . . selbst Nietzsche und Faust lassen mich kalt, es ist als ob alles Geschriebene seine Macht verloren hätte."

[7]W. H. Bruford, *The German Tradition of Self-cultivation: "Bildung" from Humbolt to Thomas Mann* (Cambridge: Cambridge UP, 1975), 185.

[8]Karl Prümm, "Tendenzen des deutschen Kriegsromans nach 1918," in Klaus Vondung, ed., *Kriegserlebnis* (Göttingen: Vandenhoeck, 1980), 217.

[9]Ann P. Linder, "The Landscape of the Battlefield in British and German Literature of the First World War," *Comparative Literature Studies* 31:4 (1994), 351–369.

[10]Karl Prümm, *Die Literatur des soldatischen Nationalismus der 20er Jahre (1918–1933)* (Kronberg: Scriptor, 1974), 40. See also Otto Dix's description of the war as "eine Naturerscheinung," quoted in Ranier Beck, ed. *Otto Dix, 1891–1969*, Exibition catalogue from Museum Villa Stuck, Munich, 23 August to 27 October 1985, 13.

[11]Ernst Jünger, *In Stahlgewittern: Aus dem Tagebuch eines Stoßtruppführers* (Berlin: Mittler, 1922), 1. Tr. by Basil Creighton as *The Storm of Steel* (New York: Fertig, 1929), 1. " . . . nur nicht zu Hause bleiben . . . ."

the greatest adventure, of their times. Young German men, even more than those of the other combatant nations, had been conditioned through the idea of *Bildung* to conceptualize life as a journey through experience toward a meaningful goal. Prewar youth literature abounded with memoirs of young soldiers, fictional or otherwise, and this encouraged young men to perceive their lives in the format of a Bildungsroman.[12] The ramblings of the prewar Wandervogel and other youth groups reinforced the paradigm of a collective journey devoted to the ideals of national community. In those sources two ideas are paramount. First, the journey is away from home into a different world, and is thus a journey of discovery and development. Second, it is a journey toward a goal, one so important that the entire group is prepared to sacrifice itself in the attempt to reach it.

The actualities of induction and military training, and especially of the mobilization of 1914, further reinforced the mental pattern of a journey. Initial training took place in casernes, often in the soldier's home town, but that was followed by the slow railway journey west or east, and the equally slow march to the front. In our own days of mechanized and aerial transport that can deliver troops directly to the scene of an engagement we tend to forget that in the first modern technological war troops still reached the front on foot. Once beyond the railheads, troops were required to march to their objectives. The situation was exacerbated on the Russian front by the distances involved. Russian railroads used a different gauge, so German transport effectively ended at the eastern frontier of Prussia, forcing troops to march across Russia. Jungnickel's *Brennende Sense* (Burning Scythe, 1928), a novel filled with striking images, repeatedly evokes the limitlessness of the Russian plain that the troops had to traverse — and eventually retreat across.

The discomfort and even suffering occasioned by a long march was particularly acute in August of 1914. In the west the month was unusually warm and sunny and the troops — in woolen uniforms and fully-loaded packs weighing nearly a hundred pounds — marched down Belgian and French roads, sweating and singing. Many writers speak of blisters from new boots, shoulders deeply indented by pack straps, and skulls that felt near bursting from the constriction of the helmet with its field cover. When they weren't marching in the burning sun, they were marching in the dark, in total ignorance of location and destination.

The genuine suffering involved in long marches carrying a heavy load quickly merged with Christian tradition to provide the metaphor of the way of the cross, symbolizing a physical and spiritual journey. By implication, the soldier assumes the identity of the suffering Christ — a willing sacrificial victim for the resurrection of the nation. The way of the cross is by far the most common

---

[12]Marieluise Christadler, *Kriegserziehung im Jugendbuch: Literarische Mobilmachung in Deutschland und Frankreich vor 1914* (Frankfurt am Main: Haag und Herchen, 1978), 70.

of the images of Christian derivation in the war novels. Its elements — a physical and spiritual odyssey passing through suffering and despair and culminating in self-sacrifice and redemption — exerted a powerful hold on the largely Christian troops. Fritz von Unruh's 1916 *Opfergang* (Way of Sacrifice) is clearly modeled, however ironically, on the way of the cross. As the war progressed into the *Materialschlacht*, especially at Verdun, the image appears with increasing frequency. Even Zöberlein, who is otherwise little inclined to a Christian view of life, employs an explicit parallel: the way to Douaumont becomes the German soldier's way of the cross.[13]

The soldiers' tendency to see their existence as a way of the cross was encouraged by the extensive presence of roadside calvaries in Belgium and France. Although calvaries were familiar to the Catholic Bavarians and Rhinelanders, they were alien to the Protestant north Germans, which may have made them more noticeable and symbolically significant, particularly when the calvary had been damaged by the war. Johannsen provides a good description of one in northern France:

> At the entrance of the village is a shattered cement pedestal and upon it a cross of iron. The cross-tree is broken; there, shockingly mutilated by shell-splinters, hangs the Savior by one arm. The white chalk of the ground, the light of the flares, or the firing of the guns makes it visible even on a starless night as you draw near. There it towers, a symbol, accusing.[14]

The symbol of the crucified Christ further mutilated by the war provided soldiers German and English with an evocative emotional correlative to their own situation, and simultaneously endowed their sacrifice with a level of significance that it might not otherwise have possessed.[15]

The soldier as a Christ figure carries other implications. The most important of these is the separation of the soldiers from the people at home. A man who has traveled the way of the cross is permanently altered and cut off from those who have not shared his experience. That is what Wiechert means when, near the end of *Jedermann*, Johannes says that the people at home will never un-

---

[13] Hans Zöberlein, *Der Glaube an Deutschland* (Munich: Nachfolger, 1931), 58.

[14] Ernst Johannsen, *Vier von der Infanterie: Ihre letzten Tage an der Westfront 1918* (Hamburg: Fackelreiter, 1929). Tr. by A. W. Wheen as *Four Infantrymen on the Western Front, 1918* (London: Methuen, 1930), 75. "An seinem Eingang [das Dorf] steht ein zerschlagener Zementsokkel und darauf ein eisernes Kreuz. Der Querbalken ist zerfetzt und Gottes Sohn hängt, von den Granatsplittern elend verstümmelt, nur noch mit einem Arm da oben. Der weiße Kalkboden und die Leuchtkugeln, oder das Aufblitzen der Geschütze lassen es zu, daß du, wenn du nahe herantrittst, es auch in der sternlosen Nacht betrachten kannst. Wie ein Symbol ragt es anklagend seltsam empor" (50).

[15] Paul Fussell, *The Great War and Modern Memory* (New York: Oxford UP, 1975), 117–120.

derstand that the soldiers have been crucified.[16] Wiechert's "nameless, faceless, homeless" Johannes, the symbolic soldier, is transformed into the emblem of suffering through the medieval figure of *Jedermann* (Everyman).[17] The erasure of an individual identity and the assumption of a symbolic one accords with the general movement of the narratives toward the representative and even symbolic, a movement equally evident in the depiction of landscape.

The Landscape of Hell

It is a truism of First World War narratives that the front is an otherworld with its own apparently indestructible existence and its own grotesque landscape. The distinction between front and home existed from the beginning of the war; that between front and rear followed shortly after it. Linguistic differentiation appears in many texts. Soldiers on home leave speak of having been "out there." One of Unruh's characters, questioned by a young male civilian in a railway station, says, "Ich komme daher!" (I come from out there!).[18] Texts also abound with such prepositions as *vor* and *hinter*. The paired epithets *Frontschwein* and *Etappenschwein* draw a similar antithesis. Significantly, the epithet *Frontschwein* is a term of belonging, even of endearment, denoting membership in the fraternity of those with direct experience of the front. *Etappenschwein*, on the other hand, is entirely pejorative, used by the true *Frontschwein* to denigrate those who spent the war in the safety and comparative comfort of headquarters. The otherworld of the front appears most significantly in its embodiment as the sinister otherworld of folk tales. Wiechert, expressing the despair of exhausted troops standing in freezing rain, sighs that "Perhaps they will still be standing so ten years hence, turned to stone, as in some dark fairy tale."[19] Wehner calls the front at Verdun an in-between realm (*Zwischenreich*), lying between life and death, the real and the imaginary, partaking of both. In a Kafkaesque scene, a young NCO with burned hands goes searching for water, finds a dying man whose feet have been shot off, and becomes aware of many voices begging for help that will never come, for " . . . they were already fettered by the demonic power of this in-between realm."[20] Moving on, he finds a man with a wounded hip who has been lying out for days, for the worms are already at home in the

[16]Ernst Wiechert, *Jedermann: Geschichte eines Namenlosen* (1931); in *Sämtliche Werke* (Vienna: Desch, 1957), 3:422.

[17]Wiechert, 3:421. " . . . kein Zuhause, keinen Namen und kein Gesicht. . . ."

[18]Unruh, *Opfergang*, 201.

[19]Wiechert, 3:419. "Vieleicht werden sie nach zehn Jahren noch so stehen, versteint wie in einem dunklen Märchen . . . ."

[20]Josef Magnus Wehner, *Sieben vor Verdun* (Munich Langen/ Muller, 1930; reprint Hamburg: Deutsche Hausbücherei, 1930), 222. "Aber der unterweltliche Zauber dieses Zwischenreiches hatte ihn schon gefesselt."

wound. The NCO is finally hit by shrapnel and falls into a water-filled shell hole, where, unable to crawl out, he too slowly succumbs to the demonic power of the *Zwischenreich*.[21]

The otherworld of the front, as seen through the German narratives, is both brutally real and grotesquely fantastic. Realistic descriptions of the battlefield are most often tinged with the grotesque or the fantastic, as in Remarque's much-discussed accounts of the shelling of the cemetery and the dismembered corpses in the mortared forest.[22] The German way of seeing and rendering nature, so very different from the British and French traditions, becomes especially apparent in the images of the front. The choice of descriptive elements mirrors the German Romantic vision of nature and its function.

Landscape and Nature

For the soldier in the trenches, the major component of his personal landscape was the earth itself. Trenches were dug into the soggy soil of Flanders, the chalky soil of the champagne, and the frozen earth of Russia. They were the front soldier's home and only protection from enemy fire. A number of British writers have commented on the superior engineering and cleanliness of the German trenches when compared to their own, or worse, to the French trenches, but neither the German descriptions nor photographs bear this out. With the single exception of the well-documented deep bunkers along the Somme, the German trenches were likely to be just as wet and nasty as anyone else's. In sectors that were particularly wet (Flanders) or where the shelling was particularly heavy (Verdun), any sort of trench, however well-structured, tended to disintegrate. In such areas it was rare for soldiers to be able to stand up and walk about. The combination of abasement and entrapment inherent in having to crouch in the earth appears in one of the titles from Ford Madox Ford's tetralogy *A Man Could Stand Up*. It takes on a more forceful significance when one of Hein's characters says, "I'd like to stand erect as quiet as a wood — not crouch in shell-craters."[23] The oblique reference evokes the German love of forests, but also the need to escape from the cratered landscape of the front.

The most famous metaphor for the trench system, and by extension the stalemated war in which everyone was trapped, was that of the labyrinth. The significance of the labyrinth as a locus of entrapment, betrayal, bewilderment

---

[21]Wehner, 214–230.

[22]Remarque, *All Quiet*, 76–77, 227–228; *Im Westen nichts Neues*, 69–70, 207–208.

[23]Alfred Hein, *Eine Kompagnie Soldaten in der Hölle von Verdun* (Minden i. W.: Kohler, 1930). Tr. by F. H. Lyon as *In the Hell of Verdun* (London: Cassell, 1930), 331. "Wie Wald so still möchte ich ragen. Sich nicht ducken im Höllenkratern" (296).

and death has been discussed at length by Leed.[24] It is worth noting, however, that the symbol of the labyrinth is far less widespread in the German literature than in the English, although its suggestions of being both lost and trapped are picked up in other metaphors. Goltz's Sergeant John, for example, dreams that he is imprisoned in the earth, but is then lifted to a festively lighted room filled with well-dressed women — a classically antithetical model of entrapment and escape.[25] The terror of entrapment becomes real for the men of Bröger's *Bunker 17*; they die trapped inside when a heavy shell buries the entrance. Vring does use the metaphor in its full sense when he states that no one who has not been in the "labyrinth of this time" can understand it.[26]

A more common metaphor in the German texts is that of the earth as womb. It implies, first, the protection that a mother's womb provides her un-born child, with, of course, resonances of Mother Earth. Both Schauwecker and Remarque use the metaphor in that sense. Schauwecker compares his dugout to the protective womb of Mother Earth,[27] while Remarque delves into the earth for protection during heavy shelling.[28] Secondly, the metaphor suggests a return to life at its simplest level. In the German Romantic context digging into the soil represents a search for the origins of life, for the roots of existence. The in-terest (almost amounting to obsession) in mining among many Romantics (notably Novalis) finds its oblique continuance in Schauwecker's "foundations of life" and "womb of Mother Earth."[29] The grave of the trench is likewise the womb — a place of death but also, in the course of nature, of rebirth.[30] The same paradox of death and birth is at work in the metaphors of plowed fields, particularly, as we shall see, in the work of Jungnickel. The image of the earth as a protective womb stands in significant contrast to the clearly threatening image of the labyrinth as it appears in the British literature. The frequency of its ap-pearance reinforces the conviction that the German soldier carried with him into war a perception of nature different from that of his English opposite num-ber. The ironic contrast between the pastoral ideal and the reality of a devastated landscape typical of the English experience of the war is largely absent from the German war literature. When it does occur, it tends to be in isolated fragments rather than as part of a controlling ironic vision.

[24]Eric J. Leed, *No Man's Land: Combat and Identity in World War I* (Cambridge: Cambridge UP, 1979), 77–80.

[25]Goltz, *Der Baum von Cléry*, 17.

[26]Georg von der Vring, *Der Goldhelm* (Oldenburg i.O.: Stalling, 1938), 226.

[27]Schauwecker, *The Furnace*, 45, 188.

[28]Remarque, *All Quiet*, 64–65.

[29]Schauwecker, *The Furnace*, 91, quoted above.

[30]It is a quirk of German not lost on the soldiers that the root of trench "der Schützengraben" is "das Grab," the grave.

For example, those staples of the English war literature, larks and poppies, occur in only a few German works in a similar form. Sulzbach provides a classic example of the contrast between the beauties of nature and imminence of death when he speaks of enjoying the month of May with "a million Deaths" sitting next door.[31] Jungnickel notes a lark singing during a bombardment, and later invokes an even more poetic bird — the nightingale. The Germans have burned a Russian village and are sleeping in a nearby field. The wind blows the smoke toward them. "It smells like charred wood and burned flesh. But the nightingale sings ever more beautifully. Perhaps she is glorifying the recently fallen, who go into the shadows."[32] But Jungnickel, like most of the other German writers, makes an ironic point only in passing. The real significance lies elsewhere. The passage above concludes with the narrator's dream (another important Romantic legacy) of a Russian farmer plowing everything into the earth, including the dead, to the song of the nightingale. Here the nightingale functions not so much as the embodiment of lost beauty, but as the eulogist of the dead whose return to the earth at least implies the possibility of resurrection.

Two other texts bear close examination in this context. Sulzbach speaks of birds again in an entry from May of 1917:

> Once more I make the beautiful and comforting discovery that birds do not worry about all this large-scale dying — they sing and twitter whether the barrage is raining shells or not, and give great pleasure to us, who are now hardly men at all.[33]

Here, despite a perfect opening, the ironic contrast is deliberately avoided. Instead of aggravating the men's bitterness over their own dehumanization, the singing of the birds is consolatory.

Jünger, immune to sentimentality and choosing to avoid irony, makes the point even more sharply:

> During the last spell a light streak behind us in the eastern sky heralds the new day. The contours of the trench show up more sharply, and the impression made by the dawning light is one of unspeakable desolation. A lark soars up. I feel that its trills underline the situation too obtrusively, and I am annoyed.[34]

---

[31]Herbert Sulzbach, *Zwei lebende Mauern: 50 Monate Westfront* (Berlin: Bernard und Graefe, 1935). Tr. by Richard Thonger as *With the German Guns* (Hamden: Archeon, 1981), 80.

[32]Max Jungnickel, *Brennende Sense* (Bad Pyrmont: Schnelle, 1928), 105. "Es riecht nach verkohltem Holz und verbranntem Fleisch. Aber die Nachtigall singt immer schöner. Vielleicht besingt sie die Gefallenen von vorhin, die jetzt zu den Schatten gehen."

[33]Sulzbach, 112. "Wieder mache ich die schöne und wohltuende Wahrnehmung, daß die Vögel sich nicht um das große Sterben kümmern — sie singen und zwitschern, ob's trommelt oder nicht, und erfreuen uns, die wir kaum noch Menschen sind" (108). In the last clause, the German word *Menschen* means human beings.

[34]Jünger, *Storm*, 41. "Während der letzten Wacht kündet ein heller Strich hinter uns am östlichen Himmel den neuen Tag. Die Umrisse des Grabens werden schärfer; er macht im grauen

Jünger's avoidance of the irony, or more accurately, his refusal to underscore it, is illuminating.

The red field poppy, an inescapable motif in the English war literature, is also rare in German. There are, however, three interesting loci, only one of which carries the full load of ironic meaning that one would expect in an English text. Two are in novels by Georg van der Vring. The hero of *Soldat Suhren* (1928; translated as *Private Suhren*, 1929), a soldier of the same name, is a painter. At one point he complains that his platoon suffers from a divided spirit. A dozen of them believe that they are fighting to bring the German spirit to the world. The rest "would rather go home today than tomorrow."[35] Suhren attempts to convince the latter group of their error and of the importance of unity by drawing an analogy to a flower that he might paint. It would be a red aster, all the petals the same size and radiating alike from the yellow center. The center, he says, is God. Or, his opponent responds, gold, by which he means money, playing on the similarity in German of *Gott*, *Geld*, and *Gold*. "It is God," Suhren insists, "The deep red petals are the peoples [*Völker*]. They radiate from God in a beautiful color." "In the color of flowing blood," comes the retort.[36] In this case the flower is not a poppy, but functions in the same way. Suhren's chauvinistic argument is undercut by his comrade's pointed reference to blood.

In Vring's other war novel, *Der Goldhelm* (The Gold Helmet, 1938), the reference is specifically to poppies. The novel takes place in a Swiss internment camp at the end of the war. Thrown together in a single barracks are two Germans, a Hungarian, and a Frenchman, all front soldiers. The book deals with their attempt to come to terms with their experiences and to arrive at an understanding of the war and of each other. When the German sergeant tells of one of his experiences, he describes a shell hole full of poppies: "The petals stirred in the moonlight like black drops of blood."[37] This — to the modern ear — clichéd comparison has more than a hint of expressionism about it, and reminds one of Otto Dix's macabre war drawings of flower-filled shell holes. The poppies reappear forcefully in Thor Goote's little-known novel *Wir fahren den Tod* (We drive Death, 1930) about drivers of munitions wagons. The scene, mentioned earlier, is the young narrator's first train journey west to the front. He sees a field of poppies and responds to them with a single word, "Schön" (Beautiful!). His traveling companion, a hardened veteran, shakes his head and

Frühlicht einen Eindruck unsäglicher Öde. Eine Lerche steigt hoch; ich empfinde ihr Getriller als aufdringlichen Kontrast, es irritiert mich" (28).

[35] Georg von der Vring, *Soldat Suhren* (Berlin: Spaeth, 1928). Tr. by Fred Hall as *Private Suhren* (London: Methuen, 1929), 106–107. "Die anderen gingen lieber heute als morgen nach Hause" (133).

[36] Vring, *Suhren*, 106–107. "Er ist Gott. Die purpurroten Blätter sind die Völker. Sie strahlen rund um Gott in einer schönen Farbe." "In der Farbe des fließenden Blutes." (133).

[37] Vring, *Der Goldhelm*, 197. "Die Blüten bewegten sich im Mondlicht wie schwartze Blutstropfen."

says, "Blut" (Blood).[38] The ironic contrast between beauty and death is effectively condensed into two words and comes close to the English symbolism of the poppy.

As is readily apparent from the preceding discussion, the ironic vision typical of the English reaction to the war is largely missing in the German literature. The sharp juxtapositions of opposites that characterize the work of Sassoon, Blunden, and Graves, for example, are in short supply, as is the irony they engender. It is scarcely surprising then that the classic First World War metaphors — poppies and birds — receive so little play in German writing. The vision of the German writers is of a different order, and their metaphors are likewise of a different nature, particularly those centering on flora and fauna. German references to nature are rarely an invocation of a pastoral ideal destroyed by war. On the contrary, as Germany lacks a vital pastoral tradition, and has instead a Romantic one, the battlefield becomes, metaphorically, a bizarre, deadly garden, the descendant of the weird, dangerous landscapes of the Romantic *Kunstmärchen*.

This characteristic is most obvious in the metaphoric descriptions of battle. The central problem for a writer wanting to describe a modern battle scene, particularly something like heavy shelling, is finding a way to describe the indescribable, to find some way to literarily render the monstrous destructiveness of the scene. One possible solution is a resort to conventional literary references, to which I shall later return. The other tactic — less common but more interesting — is to use some sort of natural metaphor. The widespread German conviction that the war was an integral stage in an organic historical development creates a mental disposition to see nature and war as part of a whole, rather than as positive and negative poles. It is not, moreover, a prettified, pastoral nature, but "nature red in tooth and claw" — the elemental, menacing natural forces neatly pinpointed by Gordon Craig in his discussion of Romanticism.[39] Craig identifies the forest in its beauty and menace as the central German locus. Although the heavy shelling on the western front destroyed most wooded areas along the front, the forest still echoes in the German narratives. The reference in Hein's *Verdun* has already been noted. Ernst Jünger finds the woods of *Copse 125* menacing at night.[40] The heavily wooded hills around Verdun provided Arnold Zweig with a means of evoking both the reality of the war and the Romantic past. Werner Bertin, Zweig's protagonist, and his wife are walking across a meadow toward a "rich and verdant forest" in the summer of 1919. Bertin can see the meadow and woods only in terms of how to defend the terrain in a battle.

[38]Thor Goote, *Wir fahren den Tod* (Gütersloh: Bertalsmann, 1930), 23.

[39]Gordon Craig, *The Germans* (New York: Putnam, 1982), 193–197.

[40]Jünger, *Copse 125*, 44–45.

"Yes," said Werner Bertin, . . . "the woods by Verdun looked like that, only much thicker, when we got there." "I wish you could forget those woods," said Lenore tenderly. Secretly she feared it would be long before this man of hers found his way back out of those magic woods into the present — into real life.[41]

In this case, the magical power lies in Bertin's inability to forget the woods of Verdun or to think of a forest in any context except war. The menace of the forest remains vivid to the former front soldier.[42]

Like the enchanted forests of German folklore, the apparent beauty and benignity of gardens belie their true sinister and even deadly nature. Using both actual (usually destroyed) gardens and metaphoric ones, the authors of the German narratives create an inverted paradigm of beauty and fecundity in which the garden becomes the garden of the dead, as it quite literally does in Bröger's poem "Die Gärten des Todes." Jünger uses the metaphor repeatedly in *Copse 125*. The clump of woods becomes a "garden of ghostly flora" when lit by Verey lights (flares).[43]

The trees are inverted into spectral flowers, mimicking the transformation of men into specters by the shelling that flares usually heralded. Later, the ruined villages near the front become gardens of death and evil, the metaphorical equivalents of the graveyard:

> The moonlight, silent and metallic, lay on them as in some enchanted garden of evil, and the shot-up bushes of the neglected gardens stood ghostly, as in huge cemeteries. . . . Over this legendary landscape of death the odor of corpses hung heavily.[44]

Schauwecker employs similar metaphors, although unfortunately without Jünger's subtlety. In *The Furnace* the shells and flares look like "hothouse or-

---

[41]Arnold Zweig, *Erziehung vor Verdun* (Amsterdam: Querido, 1935). Tr. by Eric Sutton as *Education before Verdun* (New York: Viking, 1936), 447. "'So,' sagt Werner Bertin . . . 'ganz so, nur viel dichter sahen die Wälder vor Verdun aus, als wir hinkamen.' — 'Wenn du nur zurückgekommen bist aus diesen Wäldern,' entgegnet Lenore zartlich. Heimlich fürchtet sie, es werde noch lange dauern, bis der Freund und Mann aus jenen Zauberwäldern und Gestrüppen in die Gegenwart zurückfindet, ins wirkliche Leben" (370).

[42]It is illuminating to compare Zweig's passage with thematically similar material in Robert Graves's *Goodbye to All That* (New York: Blue Ribbon, 1930), 340, and Siegfried Sassoon's *Complete Memoirs of George Sherston* (London: Faber, 1937), 322. In both cases the nature evoked is benign and pastoral.

[43]Jünger, *Copse 125*, 56.

[44]Jünger, *Werke*, 1:317. "Schweigend und metallisch, wie auf Zaubergärten des Bösen, liegt das Mondlicht darauf, und die emporgeschoßenen Büsche der verwilderten Gärten stehen gespenstisch wie auf großen Friedhöfen. . . . Über dieser sagenhaften Landschaft des Todes lastet ein schwerer und dichter Leichengeruch."

chids" in "overrich" soil.[45] They later become the souls of fallen soldiers that can't escape and fall back to earth (179). In this image, the fin de siècle taste for exotic hothouse flowers is transposed into a symbol of death. The soil, overrich from the millions of dead buried in it, metaphorically produces flowers that kill (the shells), and even death brings no escape.

Organicism also encouraged the use of figurative language derived from storms and stormy seas. Herf correctly associates such natural imagery with Jünger's transformation of trench warfare into aesthetic experience, but the tendency to apply the terminology of *Lebensphilosophie* (vitalism) to the war is more broadly distributed than he suggests.[46] Schauwecker, for example, compares the soldiers to Germans in exile "ploughing through the flaming seas of war."[47] In his famous graveyard scene, Remarque describes the fields under fire as "a surging sea, daggers of flame from the explosions leap up like fountains."[48] He earlier attempts to suggest the noise of the battlefield through a brief description in which the darkness "heaves and raves" (76). Hein draws not only on raging nature for his battlefield descriptions, but also calls on the reader's sense of revulsion by his choice of animal metaphors.

> Yes, homelessness, devilishly cold, cruelly gray, was the presiding genius of crater land. Vulture-flocks of howling shells, insect-swarms of rifle bullets, huge lizards of trench mortar bombs had raged over it and made it their home, seeking their nests in the peaceful earth with terrific explosions and swift hurricanes of torn-up soil.[49]

Only aggressive nature appears in the alien desolation of the battlefield. The earth itself may have been peaceful, but its peace has long since been shattered.

"War is Hell"

With apologies to William Tecumseh Sherman, the equation of war with hell counts as a conventional image. In the case of the German war narratives, literary and biblical allusions dominate the traditional descriptions of the battle zone. As noted earlier, one can assume that educated soldiers were familiar with

---

[45] Schauwecker, *The Furnace*, 168.

[46] Jeffrey Herf, *Reactionary Modernism* (Cambridge: Cambridge UP, 1984), 72–73.

[47] Schauwecker, *Fiery Way*, 57. " . . . ausgewandertes Deutschland, . . . durch die flammenden Meere des Krieges pflügend" (43).

[48] Remarque, *All Quiet*, 76. "Sie sind ein aufgewühltes Meer, die Stichflammen der Geschoße springen wie Fontänen heraus" (64).

[49] Hein, *Verdun*, 221. "Ja, ein teuflisch kalte, grausiggraue Heimatlosigkeit geisterte über das Trichterland. Geiervölker von heulenden Granaten, Insektenschwärme von Gewehrschüßen, Molche von schweren Minen tobten und nisteten sich ein, mit riesigen Explosionen in jähem Aufschleudern ihr mörderisches Nest in der friedlichen Erde suchend" (197).

the Bible, *Faust*, the *Inferno* and, to a lesser extent, Nietzsche's *Zarathustra*. The literary images of the battlefield are concentrated on two central metaphors: the biblical and Dantesque visions of hell, and the German and Goethean tradition of the witches' sabbath (*Walpurgisnacht*). There are some additional interesting, although less frequent, images associated with the apocalypse and with German medieval art.

The most common analogy, by far, is also the most obvious — the front is hell. The reference originates in general Christian belief, although some writers employ more specific references to Dante's *Inferno*. A handful of examples from the many instances will suffice. Verdun is more frequently characterized as the locus of hell than any other area of the front. That coincides with the onset of the *Materialschlacht* and the German belief, common long after the war, that Verdun was the key to German victory and "the moral heart of the front."[50] Schauwecker describes Verdun as a hell in which the soldiers are lost souls,[51] and as Golgotha.[52] The allusion to Golgotha coalesces with that of the way of the cross and the soldier as sacrificial victim. Alfred Hein makes the most extensive use of the "war is hell" metaphor, emphasizing the particularly hellish nature of Verdun. He uses it first in the title of his book and repeatedly thereafter: "No previous war was ever such hell as this one, and in this war there's been no other place so hellish as Verdun."[53] Then later, at the beginning of an attack, he remarks "around them hell was unchained . . . . "[54] Hein, who employs a wide range of literary references in *Verdun*, and has an unfortunate tendency to mix them, maintains that Goethe and Lilienkron are unequal to describing the situation at the front. Only Dante will do (96). Nevertheless, the only specific reference to the *Inferno* is to the Malebolge, which he compares to the battlefield at Verdun and calls a "place of murder"(320). The allusion, though evocative, is inaccurate, as the Malebolge is the eighth circle of Dante's hell, the circle of the fraudulent. The violent are higher up, in the seventh circle. Hein's reference was most likely influenced by the characteristics Dante attributes to the physical geography of the Malebolge. As Dante describes it, the eighth circle is of iron-colored stone and is divided into ten concentric valleys with ridges of rock between them. A man familiar with the passage could not have missed the similarities between concentric valleys and parallel lines of trenches, nor between iron-colored stone and iron-filled earth, nor the filth, stench, and boiling pitch

---

[50]Wehner, *Sieben vor Verdun*, 21.

[51]Schauwecker, *The Furnace*, 163.

[52]Schauwecker, *Fiery Way*, 21–22.

[53]Hein, *Verdun*, 59. "Denn noch nie war solche Hölle aufgetan in früheren Kriegen wie in diesem, und niemals in diesem Kriege so doll wie vor Verdun" (55).

[54]Hein, *Verdun*, 306. "Ringsum war die Hölle los . . . " (272).

in Dante's catalogue of eternal punishment. The reference is less to the sinners than to the geography.

In another set of references, Hein creates an imaginative geographical confluence of the New Testament and the *Inferno*. He compares a return to the front to climbing Golgotha and entering Malebolge (262-263). Although jarring to a purist, the anomaly of mixing metaphors from different sources can be seen as an attempt to suggest the spiritual geography of a return to the front. But there is a less disconcerting reference to Golgotha that coincides with the spiritual journey of the way of the cross. One of the soldiers, Lutz, collapses during heavy shelling, praying for the cup to pass: " . . . what was Golgotha compared to Hill 304?"[55]

Unlike Hein's geographical vision, Schauwecker focuses on the fires of hell in his references. In his vision, the front is "a crucible amid the darting flames of the shells and the fires of affliction."[56] The image of the crucible evokes not only fire, but refining fire, the purging away of inferior matter. That transformation through the fires of hell parallels the spiritual transformation of the soldier via the way of the cross, suggested by the book's title—*The Fiery Way*—and by other references.

Allusions to what is probably the single most famous scene in German literature, the *Walpurgisnacht* on the Brocken in Goethe's *Faust*, are scarcely more consistent, either in Hein or in other writers. The motif of the *Walpurgisnacht* has its origins in folklore, but as Goethe's version would have been the most familiar to the writers under consideration, I have chosen to discuss the references here. Most general references invoke the *Walpurgisnacht* directly, as in Hein's "it was the rage and hate of the human heart that had unloosed these iron demons to celebrate a Walpurgis night of massacre."[57] But most allusions focus on two central motifs: the witches' cauldron and the witches' dance.

The many references to a cauldron (*Kessel*) range from those that refer specifically to a witches' cauldron to more generalized boiling and seething cauldrons. It is also pertinent that the noun *Kessel* can mean a pocket of troops, and in the combination *Kesselschlacht* refers to an encircling battle. The diction was still current a generation later, in the Second World War, when the Germans called the British defense of Oosterbeek during Operation Market Garden "*der Hexenkessel.*" To the fundamental association with the demonic and with the boiling and seething movement of the contents, the cauldron adds implications of encirclement and entrapment which were singularly appropriate to the situation of the trench-bound troops. Schauwecker, with his consistent use of meta-

[55]Hein, *Verdun*, 225. "Golgotha, was war das gegen die Höhe 304?" (201).

[56]Schauwecker, *Fiery Way*, 208. "Die Front ist ein Schmelztiegel über den Stichflammen der Granaten und allen Feuern der Qual" (164).

[57]Hein, *Verdun*, 221. " . . . die Wut und der Haß des menschlichen Herzens entfesselten diese eisernen Höllengeschöpfe zu einer Walpurgisnacht blutigen Zerfleischens" (197).

phors of fire, calls the front "a flaming melting-pot."[58] On his march to the front, Wiechert's Johannes feels that he is marching into a boiling kettle.[59] Bucher specifically calls the front a witches' cauldron.[60]

The other common reference is to the witches' dance. The wild cavorting of the witches on the Brocken plays a major role in Goethe's version of the *Walpurgisnacht*, because the witches draw Faust into their dance and thus ever deeper into the demonic world. The essential components of the *Walpurgisnacht* — the witches' dance, the noise, the fires — generate a variety of metaphoric references. Beumelburg, for example, provides the following description of a spot on Louvemont hill during the campaign for Verdun: "There the devil dances all night with his grandmother and his other kinsmen. The goings-on are truly infernal."[61] Beumelburg's image of the devil dancing with his grandmother recalls Goethe's old witches, who are particularly powerful. It also suggests the infernal nature of high-explosive shells. A similar, but less specific reference occurs in Jünger's essay "Der Krieg als inneres Erlebnis." In the section on horrors he calls the front "this hellish dance hall of death," thus retaining the suggestion of a demonic *Totentanz*, but modernizing and de-mythologizing the locale.[62] Latzko modernizes further in his collection of anti-war stories, *Menschen im Krieg* (1918; translated as *Men in Battle,* 1918). There he speaks of the battlefield as "a dancing floor on which two worlds had fought for a loose woman."[63] Here, the battlefield has degenerated to a shabby dance floor and a competition for sexual favors, which are, traditionally, demonic and even deadly.

Other than references to the Bible and to *Faust*, there is little in the way of literary allusion in the German narratives. Those books that are most traditionally literary, such as Carossa's *Rumanian Diary* (with its key pseudo-Nietzschean passages) consistently employ the most literary reference.[64] In the front narratives, the references tend to be scattered and unconnected. There is, however, one interesting exception that warrants a brief examination. Max Jungnickel's little-known novel *Brennende Sense* (Burning Scythe, 1928) comes close to having a controlling metaphor. That metaphor is, of course, the scythe, specifically the scythe of death. Represented by a skeleton clutching a scythe,

[58]Schauwecker, *The Furnace*, 213. " . . . in diesen zerbrennenden Schmelzöfen . . . " (240).

[59]Wiechert, *Jedermann*, 376.

[60]Bucher, *In the Line*, 20.

[61]Beumelburg, *Gruppe Bosemüller*, 105. "Dort tanzt der Teufel allnächtlich mit seiner Großmutter und seinen übrigen Anverwandten. Es geht dabei wahrhaft infernalisch zu."

[62]Jünger, *Werke*, 5:23. " . . . dieser höllische Tanzplatz des Todes . . ."

[63]Andreas Latzko, *Menschen im Krieg* (Zurich: Rascher 1918). Tr. by Adele N. Seltzer as *Men in Battle* (London: Cassell, 1918), 75. " . . . wie einen Tanzboden, auf dem zwei Welten um eine Dirn' gerauft" (66).

[64]The German lyric poetry naturally employs far more literary allusion, most notably to the apocalypse.

Death leading great and common alike in the *Totentanz* was a familiar image in the art and literature of the late Middle Ages, and was particularly abundant in German art of the fifteenth and sixteenth centuries. Jungnickel associates another specifically German image with it: Dürer's engraving *Knight, Death and Devil*. Near the beginning of the book he declares that "Knight, Death and Devil hunt across the earth."[65] Jungnickel consistently employs the verbs "jagen," to hunt or pursue game, and "mähen," to mow or cut grain. The metaphor of the hunt refers not only to the Dürer engraving, but reaches back to evoke the Horsemen of the Apocalypse and the wild hunt of Odin's horsemen.

The image of the scythe and the mowing down of grain — and men — is particularly effective in Jungnickel's novel because the action of the book follows the progress of the German army deep into Russia and chronicles the burning of villages and crops. The scythe, with its simultaneous suggestions of pastoral rural occupations and the figure of death, is singularly appropriate. A brief review of the most significant references shows the completeness of Jungnickel's vision. After the first episode of village-burning, he calls death "freigiebig" (generous). "He [death] dogs our steps. His scythe mows."[66] A little later he speaks of a machine gun mowing soldiers down (237). One should note that the same phrase exists in English, but has become clichéd. In Jungnickel's case, the image is a part of his overall vision, and as such carries the full force of metaphor. In the central incident of the book, the narrator sees a burning barn as a scythe with a burning blade:

> Perhaps this burning scythe is a symbol for this year out here. . . . For days, weeks and months this sharp, burning scythe has stormed along with us. It alters the appearance of all things and all people. . . . It makes us different, the burning scythe; different from the time when it lay on the creaking harvest wagon. The burning scythe — it hunts us down, it cuts us down. It comes from the other side and goes back to the other side. Always the same scythe. It mows on our side. It mows on the other side. — Bind the sheaves! Bind the sheaves! The earth is the harvest wagon. The earth is the granary. Always mowing, always mowing; burning and sharp.[67]

At the core of Jungnickel's impassioned peroration (his ties to expressionism are obvious) lies the central image of the scythe which mows men, not grain, and

---

[65]Jungnickel, *Brennende Sense*, 10. " . . . Ritter, Tod und Teufel jagen über die Erde."

[66]Jungnickel, 122. "Auf Schritt und Tritt ist er hinter uns her. Seine Sense mäht."

[67]Jungnickel, 197. "Vielleicht ist die brennende Sense ein Symbol für dieses Jahr hier draußen, . . . Durch Tage, Wochen, und Monate stürmt diese brennende scharfe Sense mit uns. Sie verändert das Aussehen aller Dinge und aller Menschen. . . . Sie macht uns anders, die brennende Sense; anders als damals, da sie auf dem knarrenden Erntewagen lag. Die brennende Sense. — Sie jagt über uns, sie schlägt in uns hinein. Sie kommt von drüben; sie geht von uns nach drüben zurück. Immer dieselbe Sense. Sie mäht bei uns. Sie mäht dort drüben. — Garben! Garben! Die Erde ist der Erntewagen. Die Erde ist die Scheuer. Immer mähen, immer mähen; brennend und scharf."

stores them in the granary of the earth. The agricultural image parallels the earlier one of the Russian farmer plowing everything, including the dead, into the earth. Worth noting also is the affirmation of the changes brought about by the presence of death. The narrator yearns for a pastoral time when the scythe cut only grain, that is, a time before everything had been permanently altered by war and death. Later he tries to convince himself that the "breath of peace" can "extinguish and chill the burning scythe, so that it can once again mow corn, heavy golden corn."[68] But what power, he wonders, has the song of a bird (a symbol of peaceful, tranquil nature) against the "storm of the burning scythe?"[69] Unlike similar dichotomies drawn by British writers, Jungnickel's images have a macabre edge to them, largely created by the constant reminder of the medieval figure of death leading the *Totentanz*.

Jungnickel is unique among the German war novelists in his use of a single, dominant symbol to control the fabric of the novel. Furthermore, the symbol moves from being a mere literary allusion to being a symbol, more visual than literary, of the war itself. The grotesque and macabre are the characteristic qualities of the German symbols of the war, above all those of the latrine and the death mill.

The Latrine War

Remarque's novels were roundly castigated by his conservative critics for depicting a "latrine war," by which they meant both his concentration on bodily functions and his insistence on a naturalistic depiction of the war unmitigated by any high-minded concern for spiritual values. The scandalous (at the time) latrine scene that opens *All Quiet* was sufficient to ensure the disapprobation of the prudish, who found the discussion of defecation in literature shocking, and the nationalistic, who did not care to regard the war in such inglorious terms. Despite the criticism, latrine metaphors are widespread in the German war literature, appearing in novels of nationalistic as well as pacifistic slant. Their prevalence forces one to conclude that the criticism of such metaphors in Remarque's work is merely a part of a broader critical condemnation of the author's views. Their prevalence also suggests a cultural bias in the direction of scatological language and metaphor, a tendency that has been extensively investigated by Alan Dundes.[70] His contention that German culture harbors a strong bias for the scatological, and that it is closely associated with the firing of weapons, is

---

[68]Jungnickel, 210. "Es kann doch nicht unmöglich sein, daß der leichte Atem des Friedens die brennende Sense löscht und kalt macht damit sie wieder Korn mähen kann, schweres, gelbes Korn."

[69]Jungnickel, 213. "Aber was ist ein Vogellied im Sturm der brennenden Sense?"

[70]Alan Dundes, *Life is Like a Chicken Coop Ladder: A Portrait of German Culture through Folklore* (New York: Columbia UP, 1984).

borne out by the evidence in the First World War material. I am not speaking of merely scatological language, which is common in most war literature, but of the scatological raised to the level of metaphor and symbol.[71] Its significance in the war literature is reinforced by the widespread use of scatological images in German picture postcards produced during the war. Most of the available collections show a surprisingly large number of examples.[72]

Köppen provides a striking literary example in *Heeresbericht* (Higher Command). The protagonist, the volunteer Adolf Reisiger, has grown progressively disenchanted with the war. In 1918 he is suffering from a severe case of dysentery, but the doctor heartily assures him that he will soon be back in the line. "My dear doctor, shot to death or shit to death — it's all the same," Reisiger wearily replies.[73] The parallelism of the structure, even more effective in German, reduces the supposedly "honorable" death on the battlefield to the level of a "dishonorable" death from dysentery. Death is death, Köppen is suggesting, however it comes. Death in battle is no more glorious than a filthy death from dysentery.

Fear of dying an ignoble death in the latrine is a common denominator of many works. Its importance as a motif suggests that the men regarded the latrine as a place of singular physical and emotional vulnerability. While most soldiers may have casually accepted common latrines and bathing facilities (usually the nearest river) and the exposure involved, they are appalled by the idea of being killed in the act of defecation; killed, in effect, with their pants down. Such an event is therefore noted and commented upon, often ironically. Hein remarks on the death of two soldiers in the latrine, "that's death on the field of honor."[74] Again, the implication is that the circumstances of death, particularly on the western front, do not render one death more honorable than another.

In Beumelburg's *Gruppe Bosemüller* the latrine becomes an appropriate and ironic form of punishment. The lieutenant, annoyed with a soldier who has diarrhea before every attack, sends him to clean the divisional latrines (84). Widely regarded as the dirtiest and most insulting of jobs, the punishment is even more ironic in the light of an earlier comment. During the German attack on Hardoumont (Verdun) the lieutenant remarks to Wammsch that attacking

---

[71]Dundes, 132–135. For an interesting discussion of scatalogical thought in war literature, see the chapter provocatively entitled "Chicken shit, an Anatomy" in Paul Fussell, *Wartime* (Oxford: Oxford UP, 1989), 79–95.

[72]See Weigel, *Jeder Schuß ein Russ* for a good selection of examples. Scatological phrases are also common in German trench slang. The latrine is the usual source of false rumors, as in *Latrinengerücht* and *Scheißhausparole*. See Otto Mausser, *Deutsche Soldatensprache: Ihr Aufbau und ihre Probleme* (Strassburg: Trübner, 1917), 51–53.

[73]Köppen, *Higher Command*, 352. "Totgeschossen oder totgeschissen, lieber Doktor — es ist schon ganz egal" (380).

[74]Hein, *Verdun*, 79. " . . . das ist nun auf dem Felde der Ehre" (71).

is preferable to cleaning latrines. "Every job honors its master," Wammsch replies, exploiting a German proverb to place cleaning latrines on the same level as soldiering.[75] He finishes his comparison by stating that to him "here we are all in a big latrine."[76] The last metaphor, which initially seems very straightforward, reveals several layers of meaning on closer inspection. On its most obvious level, the latrine is the place of defecation. It is, in fact, the equivalent of excrement, and the metaphor implies that war is precisely that. On a deeper level the metaphor suggests other associations. First, war, like the latrine, is a necessity — disgusting and repellent perhaps — but a necessity nonetheless. The implication of "dirty necessity" accords well with the spirit of the war of attrition, especially with Verdun, which is the primary setting for *Gruppe Bosemüller*. It coincides also with the reduction of the soldiers to the lowest level of existence. Many writers comment on the debasement of a soldier's life to the absolute basics: eating, sleeping, and defecating. But being diminished to the lowest common denominator suggests a final reference — one to the commonality of the situation. The strong German sense of community, which appears in the war narratives as comradeship, here receives a slightly different emphasis. We are all stuck here in the shit, Beumelburg seems to be saying, but at least we are in it together, and from that community of situation it is possible to draw strength.

The Death Mill

That same community of misery permeates the second group of metaphors for the war. All of these share a single common trait: they are grounded in technological images, primarily those of machines and factories. In these metaphors Germany's notorious anti-technological bias merges with the destructiveness of the "circus of matter" to produce metaphors of mechanical annihilation.[77] From the nearly universal experience of the war of machines on the western front it is only a step to seeing the war itself as a machine. As we have seen, the inhumanity and ingloriousness of killing by machine, at a distance, is a particularly significant theme in the German literature. It is important to note that the anti-technological stance echoed by these metaphors was not universal, although it does span the ideological spectrum. The most important exception, in this as in so many other areas, is Ernst Jünger. He embraced the technology of war and glorified the soldier as machine in the form of the storm trooper. His later books would provide much of the intellectual groundwork for the absorption of technology into the previously anti-technological conservative movement.[78]

---

[75] Beumelburg, *Gruppe Bosemüller*, 39. "Jeder Handwerk ehrt seinen Meister. . . "

[76] Beumelburg, *Gruppe Bosemüller*, 39. "Mir scheint, wir sind hier alle in einer großen Latrine."

[77] Schauwecker, *Fiery Way*, 144. "Zirkusgallierienvorstellung von Material" (111–112).

[78] See Herf, *Reactionary Modernism*, 72–106 for an analysis of Jünger's contribution.

But in the mainstream of the German war literature, machine metaphors of war recur frequently. Köppen frames his metaphor within the machine-like predictability of the war:

> The war had become a machine, and an automatic one at that. First an infantry attack with a barrage, and then an artillery duel. And the latter always entailed losses. Not that the losses were not heavy enough even without a duel.[79]

The war mimics the machine in its predictable activities, a chain of action and reaction that is unalterable and leads with mechanical inevitability to the death and wounding of men. This last is the subsidiary theme of most of the mechanical metaphors. The machine destroys men. Latzko, in 1915, called the war "this wholesale cripple-and-corpse factory," raising the single machine to the level of production-line destruction.[80] Latzko, a leftist and pacifist, uses the capitalist symbol of the factory to insinuate the equivalence of the war with capitalist-bourgeois production. The depiction of mechanical cripples in the post-war drawings of Grosz and Dix — cripples whose suffering on the public streets of Berlin is ignored by the smug respectable bourgeois — belongs to the same *Weltanschauung*.

Oddly enough, one of the few machines found in the agricultural Germany of old, the mill, is the most common of the machine metaphors. The mill as a symbol for the war is significant for several reasons. First, mills were a fixture in the rural landscape, as familiar to the urban boys involved with the *Wandern* of the youth movement as to rural boys who lived alongside them. Secondly, the interlocking mill wheels suggest the circular movement of history and fate, the relentless and unavoidable turning of the wheels, and the position of man as a mere cog in a mechanism over which he has no control. Lastly, the mill's major functions — to grind grain, crush grapes and apples, pump water or beat cotton to a pulp for making paper — suggest a series of ironic metaphors of destruction. Wiechert invokes millstones when he says that death the leveler silently gropes after soldiers new to the front, "grasps them, and shoves them silently into the grinding mill-wheels."[81] An exhausted Schauwecker, mourning the loss of enthusiasm and heroism, concludes that "there is only a stamping and panting sweatmill, grinding life and bone."[82] In both cases, what is being ground is not the beneficial grain, but men.

---

[79]Köppen, *Higher Command*, 214. " . . . der Krieg ist zur Maschine geworden, zur automatischen Maschine. Infanterieangriff: Sperrfeuer. Artilleriekampf: Antwort. Und Antowrt heißt: Verluste. (Und noch das Schweigen heißt: Verluste)" (233).

[80]Latzko 160. " . . . diese Krüppel und Leichenfabrik mit Maschinenbetrieb. . ." (137).

[81]Wiechert, *Jedermann*, 471. "Die Gleichmachung des Todes tastete lautlos nach ihnen, ergriff sie und zog sie schweigend in das mahlende Räderwerk."

[82]Schauwecker, *Fiery Way*, 65. " . . . hier walkt nur eine stampfende, keuchende Schweißmühle auf Knochen und Fleisch" (49).

In other examples, the mill functions as a mechanism to squeeze and pump juices — but in this case the juice is blood. In Jungnickel's novel, the major has the face of someone damned, someone who "sits with other men in a blood-mill."[83] Similarly, Wehner's image for Verdun, "the famous blood-pump," echoes General Erich von Falkenhayn's remark that his attack on Verdun was intended to bleed the French army white.[84] What these metaphors have in common with each other and with the preceding ones is that the products of the war-mill are human food products. The implied comparison of men to food gives these images their edge of horror. Metaphorically, the war becomes a mill that traps, grinds and squeezes men, transforming them into a cannibalistic meal for a devouring god of war, often characterized as Moloch.

While some writers only suggest the comparison, others make it explicit. The transformation of men into food, even metaphorically, evokes a horrified response because it plays to the most deeply ingrained of western cultural taboos. These metaphors are not unlike the dead metaphor "cannon fodder," which comes to us from the First World War, but has lost most of its evocative meaning by overuse. In this case the entire metaphor is animalistic. The guns are animals — domestic ones at that — for whom the men are the fodder. In the German literature, one of the earliest references comes from Latzko, when he calls the front a place for "man-salad."[85] The visual image of the chopped-up ingredients of a salad is supplemented by the colloquial German expression "im Salat," (in the salad), which means to be in a mess. But the most effective metaphors of this category focus on the grinding and pulverizing effects of the heavy shelling on the western front. Beumelburg, for example, speaks of the men being "made into applesauce" by the shelling.[86] Such metaphors achieve their most extreme form in the references to the front or the war as a human sausage grinder or factory. The effectiveness of the symbol resides in its cluster of references: the grinding up of men, the element of mechanical production and, as the end product, a food so familiar and homey as sausage. Bertin in *Education before Verdun* dreams of the front as a human sausage machine and, in a fine jab at the notorious bureaucracy of the Imperial German Army, examines the new regulation about the use of human flesh "correctly posted on a door."[87] The image of a flesh or meat grinder penetrated even into German trench slang, where

---

[83]Jungnickel, *Brennende Sense*, 235. "Einer, der mit Menschen in einer Blutmühle sitzt."

[84]Wehner, *Sieben vor Verdun*, 21. " . . . der berühmpten Blutpumpe . . . "

[85]Latzko, *Men in Battle*, 165.

[86]Beumelburg, *Gruppe Bosemüller*, 113. " . . . dann wären wir jetzt vielleicht alle zu Apfelmus verwandelt!"

[87]Zweig, *Education before Verdun*, 175. "Ja, in den Kellern der Chambrettes-Ferme ging es munter zu. Da rasselten die Wurstmaschinen, da wurden Därme gedehnt, an der Tür hing die neue Verordnung über die Verwendung von Menschenfleisch, grauhäutigem Menschenfleisch . . . " (148).

one of the many names for a machine gun was *Fleischhackmaschine* (flesh chopping machine).[88] No similar slang terms seem to have existed in French or English.

Like the German battlefield landscapes, these images partake of the grotesque and macabre rather than of the ironic. In both cases, heroic images of war have been shattered and replaced by anti-heroic ones, but instead of the British anti-heroic irony based on dichotomous thinking, the German writers see death in the tradition of Grimmelshausen and Goethe's witches — as grotesque. For the Germans, the loss of the heroic mode of death leaves no imagistic recourse except the macabre and the grotesque.[89]

[88]Karl Bergmann, *Wie der Feldgraue spricht: Scherz und Ernst in der neusten Soldatensprache* (Giessen: Töpelmann, 1916), 17.

[89]Robert Weldon Whalen, *Bitter Wounds: German Victims of the Great War, 1914–1939* (Ithaca: Cornell UP, 1984), 44–47.

6: Weimar and the War Narrative

The Undefeated Army

On 11 December 1918, Friedrich Ebert, the president of the newly created German Republic, stood beneath the Brandenburg Gate, the historic symbol of German victory, and greeted German troops returning from the western front. Berlin had just emerged from the brief but bloody November Revolution of the Spartacists with order restored, but the chaos left by the collapse of the Second Reich was everywhere apparent. Nevertheless, Ebert, a lifelong Social Democrat, proclaimed to the soldiers, "I salute you who return unvanquished from the field of battle."[1] However fanciful Ebert's words may now appear, they were symptomatic of the German refusal to acknowledge defeat, military or otherwise, and of a willingness to clothe that defeat in any illusion that would blur its edges and conceal its harshness. The flight into illusion had detrimental consequences for the German Republic, both early and late, and its genesis is therefore worth examining.

The first pertinent fact, and one so obvious that its significance is frequently overlooked, is that the hostilities ended in an armistice, an agreement to cease fighting, not in the surrender of the German army. Although the army was unquestionably close to collapse, and the armistice terms dictated by the allies amounted to surrender, the German army never officially capitulated. It was spared that humiliation by the covert maneuvers of Hindenburg and Ludendorff, who had been the virtual rulers of Germany since mid-1916.[2] After the failure of the March offensive, Ludendorff announced to the Crown Council in August that the war could no longer be won in the field.[3] The eventual collapse of the exhausted army was inevitable. But thanks to Ludendorff's Zentralstelle für Werbe- und Aufklärungsarbeit (Central Office for Propaganda and Information), which carefully managed internal propaganda, neither the civilians at

[1]T. N. Dupuy, *A Genius for War: The German Army and General Staff, 1807–1945* (London: Macdonald, 1977), 185; John W. Wheeler-Bennett, *The Nemesis of Power: The German Army in Politics, 1918–1945* (London: Mcmillan, 1964), 31.

[2]Wheeler-Bennett, 14; Barry Leach, *The German General Staff* (New York: Ballantine, 1973), 24; Walter Goerlitz, *History of the German General Staff, 1657–1945* (Westport, Ct.: Greenwood, 1975), 200–203. Tr. Brian Battershaw.

[3]Lindley Fraser, *Germany between Two Wars: A Study of Propaganda and War-Guilt* (Oxford: Oxford UP, 1944), 7.

home nor the soldiers in the trenches knew the actual condition of the army and of the civilian population.[4] Interestingly, the memoirs and novels that cover this period emphasize two things: first, the exhaustion, deprivation and decimation of the troops, and secondly — especially in the conservative narratives — the determination of those troops to hold out to the end no matter what the cost, and to maintain good order and discipline. The maintenance of discipline was paramount for front line infantry and artillery units, who viewed the insurrections and formation of soldiers' councils in the rear areas as the ultimate betrayal of the despised *Etappenschweine*. After the Armistice, the conviction of having held the line to the end outside the frontiers of the Reich and of having marched home in order only widened the existing abyss between civilians and front line soldiers, who, despite their sacrifices, came home to unimaginable chaos and misery — who came home, in fact, to a nation in collapse and revolution. That situation provided fertile soil for the betrayal myths that sprang up immediately after the war.

The most pervasive and destructive of those legends was the "stab-in-the-back" (Dolchstoß von hinten), the essential corollary to the myth of the undefeated army. Through the autumn of 1918 Hindenburg and Ludendorff schemed and maneuvered to protect the German army from defeat, and more important yet, from blame for defeat. To that end, the generals first insisted in October that the government request an immediate armistice, then withdrew their demand, maintaining that the army would fight on. That ploy effectively placed the responsibility for peace or war precisely where the generals wanted it: in the hands of a civilian government, while giving the impression that the army wanted to go on fighting in the face of defeatist civilians. This became even more significant after the Kaiser's abdication, as the governments that carried through the armistice negotiations and eventually signed the Treaty of Versailles were not only civilian but republican. The generals' plans were ultimately successful; the army emerged from the war with its honor unbesmirched by defeat or invasion.[5] The civilians bore the onus of having given up, and thus of having "betrayed" a loyal and still effective army.

That, at least, is how it appeared to a majority of soldiers and to a large portion of the civilian population. The conviction of betrayal crystallized first into the stab-in-the-back legend. The phrase itself is evocative, with its use of the semi-archaic *Dolchstoß* (which literally means a stab with a dagger) and its undertones of the betrayal and murder of Siegfried. Its origins are unclear. Fraser

[4]Fritz Fischer, *Bündnis der Eliten: Zur Kontinuität der Machtstrukturen in Deutschland 1871–1945* (Düsseldorf: Droste, 1979), 56–57.

[5]Fraser, *Germany between Two Wars*, 7–15; Wheeler-Bennett, *Nemesis of Power*, 18–24; Hans Ernest Fried, *The Guilt of the German Army* (New York: Macmillan, 1942), 32–36. On the influence of the old General Staff on the writing of military history between the wars, see Reinhard Brühl, *Militärgeschichte und Kriegspolitik: Zur Militärgeschichtsschreibung des preußisch-deutschen Generalstabes 1816–1945* (Berlin: Militärverlag der DDR, 1973).

states that it originated in a remark of British General Sir Neill Malcolm, as a crystallization of Ludendorff's thought about the end of the war, which Ludendorff then appropriated and used widely.[6] If true, it is wonderfully ironic that a British general should have provided German conservatives with one of their most effective emotional weapons against Versailles. Fried suggests only that it may have originated with Hindenburg.[7] Whatever its origin, the stab-in-the-back legend became current immediately after the war and was extensively used by conservative groups as explanation and excuse for the defeat and the imposition of the Treaty of Versailles. The party or parties held responsible for wielding that dagger ranged from all civilians to the republican government, armchair strategists, speculators, food-hoarding farmers, black-marketeers, communists, and Jews. In common with most vital images, the stab-in-the-back legend embodied a resentment that was emotional in content and general in object.

The full shock of being a defeated nation broke upon Germany with the revelation of the punitive and humiliating terms of the Treaty of Versailles. Fritz Stern refers to the period between the armistice and the treaty as a "dreamland" full of hopes and utopian schemes.[8] Within Germany, the treaty was almost universally regarded as the final treachery: the unjust treatment of an undefeated nation as a vanquished one. Though the provisions of Versailles are familiar, it is worth reviewing the primary demands because of their effect on public opinion. Germany returned the territories of Alsace and Lorraine to France, along with the rights to the coal mines of the Saarland; territories in the east were lost through plebiscite and formation of the Polish Corridor. All her colonies were lost; the army was reduced to 100,000 men, the general staff abolished and any military air forces forbidden; the Rhineland was to be occupied for 15 years, and heavy reparations were levied based on the infamous "war guilt" clause, Article 231. There were additional humiliating special provisions regarding the return of French archives, trophies, and works of art taken in 1870, the return of the Koran of the Caliph Othman to the King of the Hedjaz, and the presentation to the British of the skull of the Sultan Mkwawa from German East Africa. To complete Germany's degradation, the treaty was signed on August 28, 1919, the fifth anniversary of the assassination at Sarajevo, in the Hall of Mirrors at Versailles, where the German Empire had been proclaimed in 1871.[9]

[6]Fraser, 16.

[7]Fried, 56–57.

[8]Fritz Stern, *The Politics of Cultural Despair: A Study in the Rise of the Germanic Ideology* (Berkeley: U of California P, 1961), 223.

[9]Of the enormous literature on the treaty, Alan Sharp, *The Versailles Settlement: Peacemaking in Paris, 1919* (New York: St. Martin's Press, 1991) provides a brief and readable overview of the conference and the settlement that emerged from it.

The provisions of Versailles, intended by its framers to extinguish the fires of German nationalism and transform Germany into a respectable, democratic "small" nation, had exactly the opposite effect. True to the traditions of German nationalism, Versailles only reinforced the Germans' feeling of "germanness" and their rejection of French *Zivilisation*, now symbolized by the treaty. The struggle against what was referred to in conservative terminology as the *Verrat* (betrayal) of Versailles coincided with the rejection of the West that had marked German nationalism since the Wars of Liberation. The treaty represented Western civilization, democracy, rationalism, internationalism, modernism and all the other "isms" unhappily flung about by German thinkers in the wake of the war. It was, in the German view, the unjust imposition of an alien way of life.

Hans Kohn, delineating the German state of mind in the first part of the century, enumerates its obsessions:

> ... a romantic interpretation of the past; a feeling of having been unjustly treated by history and of having suffered at the hands of inferior people; a conviction that Germany's great merits were not recognized by mankind; finally the expectation of a future in which the myths of the past would turn into realities and thereby German history and destiny find their fulfillment.[10]

At the root of these obsessions lies the incontrovertible truth that the Germans were not disillusioned by the war, or even by the defeat, in the same way as the peoples of the other combatant nations. Young German soldiers may have been disillusioned about the actualities of war, but unlike their British counterparts, they largely retained their ideals about the nation, especially their belief in the uniqueness of the German people and their sense of spiritual superiority over the putative "victors."[11] Embittered they certainly were, but not by the experience of war itself; rather they were embittered by the betrayal of that experience and what it meant to them.

The double treachery of the stab-in-the-back and the Versailles Treaty provided a rallying point for the existing anti-democratic forces in Germany. They were many.[12] Dahrendorf has correctly pointed out that pre-democratic and even feudal patterns of government and social organization had persisted into twentieth-century Germany, despite the rapid industrialization of the nineteenth century.[13] As both Fischer and Dahrendorf have amply demonstrated,

[10]Hans Kohn, *The Mind of Germany* (London: Macmillan, 1961), 14.

[11]Kohn, 305; Robert Weldon Whalen, *Bitter Wounds: German Victims of the Great War, 1914–1939* (Ithaca: Cornell UP, 1984), 30–32.

[12]See especially the first chapter of Kurt Sontheimer's *Antidemokratisches Denken in der Weimarer Republik* (Munich: Nymphenburg, 1962).

[13]Rolf Dahrendorf, *Society and Democracy in Germany* (London: Weidenfeld and Nicholson, 1968), 61, 381. See also Thorstein Veblen's classic analysis, *Imperial Germany and the Industrial Revolution* (1915; reprint Ann Arbor: U of Michigan P, 1966).

the German ruling elite, both professional and commercial, altered little between 1871 and 1945, with decisive change coming only in the latter year.[14]
Needless to say, the German aristocracy was opposed to any sort of mass rule.
The views of the academic establishment, as well, were prevailingly anti-
democratic. The faculties of history, law and German language and literature
represented the "staunchest bulwarks of the old order."[15] The old romantic nationalism and *völkisch* ideologies flourished unabated, strengthened by the constant irritation of a functioning republican government.

The army, in its turn, hated the Republic as a creation of the despised treaty
and hated the restrictions on army size, composition, and training imposed by
the treaty. Most war veterans, similarly, had few republican sympathies. The
many veterans' organizations, notably the Stahlhelm, were generally conservative in their political and cultural views. As the largest and most important of
the veterans' groups, Stahlhelm began as a self-help organization but became increasingly political in the course of the twenties. It was particularly with them
and even more radical rightist groups such as the National Socialists that the
belief in *Frontkameradschaft* as a basis for a new society appeared and grew.[16]

Fathered by the *Freikorps*, the explosive growth in size and militancy of
paramilitary organizations in the twenties has been ably chronicled elsewhere.[17]
In the context of this argument, only a few matters require comment. The first
is the extent of the influence of the front generation in such organizations and in
German society at large. Merkl discusses the gradual weakening of the leftist
and center paramilitary groups (especially the Communist and Social Democratic parties and the Reichsbanner) throughout the twenties, and the corresponding rise and radicalization of the rightist parties.[18] But how great was the
influence of the front generation in these groups? Obviously the *Freikorps* were

[14]Dahrendorf, 227. See also Fritz Fischer, *Bündnis der Eliten: Zur Kontinuität der Machtstrukturen in Deutschland 1971–1945* (Düsseldorf: Droste, 1979).

[15]Walter Laqueur, *Weimar: A Cultural History, 1918–1933* (New York: Putnam, 1974), 187.

[16]On the provisions of the Treaty of Versailles concerning the German armed forces, see
Sharp's *The Versailles Settlement* for a brief analysis. On the Stahlhelm, see Volker R. Berghahn,
Der Stahlhelm, Bund der Frontsoldaten (Düsseldorf: Droste, 1966), and Peter H. Merkl, *The
Making of a Stormtrooper* (Princeton: Princeton UP, 1980), 38–49. For a broader account of
paramilitary groups, see James M. Diehl, *Paramilitary Politics in Weimar Germany* (Bloomington: Indiana UP, 1977). Joachim Petzold, *Wegbereiter des deutschen Faschismus: Die Jungkonservativen in der Weimarer Republik* (Cologne: Pahl-Rugenstein, 1978) provides a useful overview
of the young conservative movement.

[17]On the Freikorps, see Nigel H. Jones, *Hitler's Heralds* (London: Murray, 1987), and Merkl,
16–159. See also Klaus Theweleit, *Männerphantasien* (Frankfurt am Main: Roter Stern, 1978)
and Waltraud Amberger, *Männer, Krieger, Abenteuer: Der Entwurf des "soldatischen Mannes" in
Kriegsromanen über den Ersten und Zweiten Weltkrieg* (Frankfurt am Main: Fischer, 1984) on the
psychology of paramilitary organizations.

[18]Merkl, 26–100.

composed largely of veterans, and the early veterans' organizations limited their membership (the Stahlhelm was founded exclusively to look after the concerns of First World War veterans).[19] Although one may question both the sources of his statistics and his manipulation of them, Merkl's analysis of the pre-1933 National Socialist party membership provides a valuable model for front generation involvement in paramilitary formations (107-113). Using the Abel collection of autobiographical statements of pre-1933 National Socialist party members (now in the Hoover Library at Stanford), and official party statistics, he concludes that the number of veterans in the party was about fifty percent, and made up about thirty-nine percent of the leadership of the SA and the SS (107-109), the majority of the latter groups, that is, the fighting wings of the party, being composed mainly of younger volunteers. Merkl further suggests that the prime function of the war generation was the transmission of "superpatriotic" beliefs to younger party members.[20] If Merkl's analysis is correct, then the front generation was present in significant numbers in even far right-wing organizations and played an important role in the dissemination of their own beliefs about the war and its meaning.

The precise nature of those beliefs forms the second matter for discussion. The one characteristic that most readily distinguishes the majority of German veterans from their counterparts in France and Britain is their refusal to relinquish their nationalist idealism. The experience of war did not destroy their belief in the nation; rather it reinforced it. The only worthy goal of that belief was the rebirth of the nation from the ashes of defeat, or, as John Keegan has succinctly phrased it, "among the victor nations the cost of winning the First World War had left the populations determined never to bear it again; in Germany the cost of losing the war seemed to be justified only if the result could be reversed."[21] The commitment to reversing the result flowed from their sense of betrayal and sprang from authentic personal experience. They knew *Gemeinschaft* existed; they had experienced it in the trenches. Their fundamental opposition to the *Gesellschaft* of the Weimar Republic was as absolute as it was authentic. This was not the Germany that they and their comrades had fought and suffered for.

Suffering was a particularly sensitive issue among conservative troops, especially where the suffering of wounded and crippled veterans was involved.

---

[19]Merkl, 42. On veterans' problems in general, see Whalen, *Bitter Wounds*. For a history of French veterans affairs, see Prost's superb *Les Anciens combattants et la société française, 1914–1939*.

[20]Merkl, 110. See also George Mosse, "Death, Time and History: Volkish Utopia and its Transcendence," in *Masses and Men* (New York: Fertig, 1980), 69–86. He argues that the "fallen" also transmit Germanism.

[21]John Keegan, *A History of Warfare* (New York: Knopf, 1993), 368. See also Nigel Jones, *Hitler's Heralds*, 105–112.

Rightist accounts of the post-armistice period abound with stories of civilian crowds (and individual civilians) verbally and physically abusing returning veterans, including wounded and crippled soldiers. Many of the accounts are highly suspect, and as many more are probably apocryphal, but their adherence to the typology of soldierly suffering in the face of civilian indifference and betrayal is characteristic of the conservative war mythology. The depictions of crippled soldiers as subhuman, mechanized automatons found in such artists as Dix and especially Grosz did little to endear avant-garde art to conservative veterans.

With such formidable opposition, one is left wondering how the Weimar Republic managed to survive even its brief thirteen years. Having come into existence as the "illegitimate child of defeat," the Weimar Republic suffered from a profound lack of public support.[22] As the Social Democrats and other democratic left-leaning parties had been instrumental in its founding, it had at least some support from the moderate urban proletariat. The radical leftists had been defeated in the November Revolution, and played no central role. Democratic governments in Europe traditionally have drawn their strongest support from the middle class. Unlike the French and English middle classes which had developed slowly, had benefited directly from industrialization, and had, in fact, driven the industrialization of those countries, the middle class in Germany was not in that position. German industrialization, as Veblen has argued in his *Imperial Germany and the Industrial Revolution*, was directed by the government, and largely controlled by the powerful banks and major industrialists. A strong class of small businessmen and entrepreneurs never developed. Early twentieth-century Germany was not a classic capitalist society; it merely appeared to be one. Thus Germany lacked the powerful, politically active bourgeoisie that backed the democratic governments in France and England, and the Weimar Republic suffered for it. Whatever tentative support the middle class vouchsafed at the outset was rapidly wiped out (along with their savings) by the hyperinflation of 1923. The inflation, combined with the traditional unpolitical stance of the German bourgeois, eroded what should have been Weimar's political mainstay.[23]

The collapse of the Empire, the November Revolution and the founding of the Weimar Republic had left a traditionally authoritarian nation with a power vacuum. After generations of government censorship the political left and the artistic avant-garde found their voices and the freedom to use them. The political polarities —conservative vs. liberal, right vs. left, national vs. international — spilled over into all facets of national life, particularly cultural life. As far back as the Romantic period, German political arguments have usually been couched in cultural and philosophical terms, and Weimar is surely the zenith of that tradi-

---

[22]Louis L. Snyder, *The Roots of German Nationalism* (Bloomington: Indiana UP, 1978), 157.

[23]See Fritz Stern, *The Failure of Illiberalism: Essays on the Political Culture of Modern Germany* (New York: Knopf, 1972), especially the introduction.

tion. Virtually the whole rhetoric of German nationalism from Fichte through the National Socialists is clothed in cultural rhetoric. By the time of the First World War Germans spoke of their "world civilizing mission" and their "superior spiritual strength" rather than of annexing territories or of possessing superior numbers and equipment, and despised as spiritually and morally base those who spoke in political or practical terms.[24] Writing nostalgically and somewhat disingenuously in 1925 about the "ideas of 1914," Ernst Troeltsch claimed that it was allied propaganda that had made the war a "Geistkrieg," a war of spirit.[25] The opponents of Weimar were particularly prone to attack, according to Martin Swales,

> . . . not in specific (institution) terms, not at the level of legislation, of policy or administrative programme, but rather in terms which asserted the cultural and spiritual unacceptability of republican government to the deepest instincts of the German soul.[26]

Swales goes on to remark that in Weimar Germany "cultural terms were the best political terms" (1–2) and to explain Thomas Mann's pro-republican essays as an attempt to give the republic "that sorely-needed cultural, spiritual, in a word *geistig* validation that alone could give it the cachet of respectability" (9). The relative importance of culture in Weimar Germany ensured that the political struggle would be fought not only on the political battlefield, but on the cultural one.

What, then, do we mean by the term "Weimar culture"? The commonly held vision of Weimar is a collage of Grosz, Dix, Benn, Bauhaus, the *Threepenny Opera* and bearded leftists arguing in coffee houses and sleazy cabarets, with an overlay of SA Brownshirts beating helpless Jews and tangling with communists in street fights. The trouble with this Isherwood-inspired vision is that it emphasizes, on the cultural side, the avant-garde, and on the political side, the ultra-conservative, (the Nazis) to the exclusion of everything else. That dangerously falsifies the cultural and political realities of the period by ignoring the diversity of philosophical and political persuasions and by implying that the free and humane avant-garde was overwhelmed by the inexplicable rise of the conservative right. Certainly the "conservative revolution" channeled powerful forces within German society, but alongside the growing power of conservatism through the twenties, there existed active and vocal communist and socialist

[24]See, for example, Werner Sombart's *Händler und Helden* (Munich: Duncker, 1915).

[25]Ernst Troeltsch, *Deutscher Geist und Westeuropa* (1925; reprint Aalen: Scientia, 1966), 32.

[26]Martin Swales, "In Defence of Weimar: T. Mann and the Politics of Republicanism," in Alan Bance, ed., *Weimar Germany* (Edinburgh: Scottish Academic Press, 1982) 1–13.

movements.[27] Indeed, if those movements had been less effective, they would not have posed such a threat to the conservative majority and eventually to the National Socialists. The avant-garde displays of the expressionists coexisted with the conservative bourgeois *Plüschära*, the "living room culture" that thrived in the overstuffed philistine comfort of the bourgeois home.[28] In 1934, Werner Sombart outlined his idyllic vision of conservative bourgeois life:

> A comfortable dwelling of one's own in a well-kept garden which is more than a pasteboard box or a cell in a honeycomb, with more rooms than are necessary for merely sleeping and cooking, in which the members of the family may also be separated; means to cultivate a decent conviviality: good wine, fine linen, old silverware for the table; festive baptisms and weddings in a circle of friendship; room and appreciation for old family portraits; a select library — all these things we regard as also having a cultural value which we would not deny, call it "bourgeois"if you will. It merely shows that the bourgeois class is in no sense destitute of culture.[29]

Those who valued family portraits and old silver were "irritated and confused" by the explosion of cultural experimentation that took place in the twenties.[30]

The conservative majority saw Weimar as "a period of cultural decay and moral bankruptcy."[31] The traditional bourgeois regarded the frankly internationalist avant-garde movement as "un-German" and probably decadent. Conservative literary historian Adolf Bartels, writing in 1921, proclaimed that

[27]See Keith Bullevant "The Conservative Revolution," in Anthony Phelan, ed., *The Weimar Dilemma: Intellectuals in the Weimar Republic* (Manchester: ManchesterUP, 1985), 47–70. See also Sontheimer, *Antidemokratisches Denken* and Petzold, *Wegbereiter des deutschen Faschismus* .

[28]Hermann Glaser, *The Cultural Roots of National Socialism* (Austin: U of Texas P, 1978), 51, 94.

[29]Quoted in Herman Lebovics, *Social Conservatism and the Middle Classes in Germany, 1914– 1933* (Princeton: Princeton UP, 1969), 75.

[30]Kohn, *The Mind of Germany*, 307. Of the plethora of books on Weimar culture, the following are particularly useful: Peter Gay, *Weimar Culture* (London: Secker, 1968) is an early classic that emphasizes the avant-garde. Laqueur's *Weimar* offers a more balanced view. John Willett's, *The New Sobriety, 1917–1933* (London: Thames, 1978) is a standard text, and his *The Weimar Years: A Culture Cut Short* (London: Thames, 1984) provides a good visual overview of primarily modernist expression. Of very recent vintage,Thomas W. Kniesche and Stephen Brockmann, eds., *Dancing on the Volcano: Essays on the Culture of the Weimar Republic* (Columbia, SC: Camden House, 1994) includes a variety of current critical views, while Gérard Raulet, *Weimar ou l'explosion de la modernité* (Paris: Anthropos, 1984) focuses on questions of modernism and modernity.

[31]Laqueur, *Weimar*, 36; see also J. M. Ritchie, *German Literature under National Socialism* (London: Helm 1983), 6–7. Although the cultural conservatism of the majority of the population is generally accepted by scholars, work remains to be done to establish the real quality and extent of that conservatism. See Lebovics's definition in his *Social Conservatism*, 3–48.

"sensationalism, advertising and Expressionism are not of German origin."[32] Bartels's indiscriminate amalgamation of journalism, business and avant-garde art for the purpose of moral condemnation on the grounds of perceived national character is typical of the cultural arguments of the right.

The extent of conservative distaste for modernist culture reveals itself not only in the appeal of traditional values and conventional art forms, including the conventional form of the nationalist war narratives. It is also evident in the wide influence of rightist political and cultural magazines and of the press in general.[33] As Lebovics has argued, the "middle-brow" publicists of the conservative magazines "purveyed the social and economic ideas which could be molded into clichés at the beer hall *Stammtisch*" and "at the innumerable meetings of the societies and clubs to which so many members of the middle class belonged...."[34] Rightist magazines such as *Die Tat* (to name only the most famous) rendered political thought accessible and acceptable to the bourgeois household and helped to create an "imagined community" (to borrow Benedict Anderson's phrase) of like-minded citizens.[35]

On a more popular level, the views of the conservative community can be gauged through the astonishing production of fantasy, science fiction, and futuristic novels in the twenties and early thirties. These novels are fundamentally visions of the future in which Germany's current problems are fictionally resolved in Germany's favor. In his fine study, Peter Fisher distinguishes the Weimar fantasies from Wilhelmine futuristic writing by defining them as attempts to compensate for defeat and its aftermath.[36] The rise of anxiety and irrationalism in the Weimar middle class created a fantasy-seeking public eager

---

[32]Adolf Bartels, *Die deutsche Dichtung der Gegenwart* (Leipzig: Haessel, 1921), 189. Bartels was one of the founders of the Heimatkunstbewegung (Homeland art movement) and became a member of the National Socialist party in his old age. See the biographical sketch in Ernst Loewy, *Literatur unterm Hakenkreuz: Das Dritte Reich und seine Dichtung* (Frankfurt am Main: Europäische Verlagsanstalt, 1966), 301–302.

[33]Despite the experience of wartime propaganda and censorship, Germans seemed to retain a faith in the authority of the press on factual and ideological matters that had disappeared in Britain and France. See Modris Eksteins, *The Limits of Reason: The German Democratic Press and the Collapse of Weimar Democracy* (Oxford: Oxford UP, 1975), 70–74. Most of the Weimar political parties had official organs which were supplemented by a wide range of non-affiliated newspapers and magazines expressing every shade of political thought.

[34]Lebovics, *Social Conservatism*, 179.

[35]Lebovics, 178–182. On *Die Tat* see Petzold, *Wegbereiter des deutschen Faschismus*, 273–294, and Sontheimer, "Der Tatkreis," *Vierteljahrshefte für Zeitgeschichte* 7:3 (1959), 229–260. For a catalogue of German cultural magazines, see Fritz Schlawe, *Literarische Zeitschriften, 1910–1933* (Stuttgart: Metzler, 1962).

[36]Peter S. Fisher, *Fantasy and Politics: Visions of the Future in the Weimar Republic* (Madison: U of Wisconsin P, 1991), 3.

for "visions of revenge and renewal."[37] Most of the radical rightist visionaries were former soldiers, and, as is the case with the conservative war narratives, there is a strong sense of the war not having ended in 1918.[38] The sacrifices of the fighting men having been betrayed by cowardly civilians, the battle for national rebirth shifts to the civilian, political field. The triad of betrayal, revenge and renewal forms the core of the rightist fantasies and the impetus behind the conservative war narratives.

The conservative obsession with betrayal, revenge and national renewal appears dramatically in German cinema of the twenties. Even if one harbors reservations concerning Paul Monaco's psychoanalytical argument, betrayal and revenge are clearly important themes in Weimar film, and in Weimar culture generally.[39] Betrayal, revenge and renewal, whether of the individual, the society or the nation is the insidious theme that snakes through conservative Weimar culture. Whether it takes form in the political, social and economic theories of Spengler and Sombart, in the fantasy novels, in the cinema or in the war narratives, it is essentially the same theme. It is no accident that, as Monaco maintains, forty of the sixty German films that can be documented as widely popular had themes of betrayal, nor that *Die Niebelungen* (1924) enjoyed an unprecedented success with German audiences.[40] Thea von Harbou's version of the tale, centered on Hagen's murder of Siegfried by a stab in the back (closer to the medieval sources than to Wagner's scenario) makes of it a quintessential national myth of betrayal and revenge, newly revitalized by the cinematic medium.

These expressions of conservative thought and feeling are but a few examples of a broad cultural resistance to the artistic avant-garde that runs counter to the popular, and sometimes even scholarly image of Weimar as a paradigm of artistic modernism.[41] Despite the aesthetic brilliance of the Weimar avant-garde, it is likely that their creations reached a narrow audience of urban cultural sophisticates and fellow travelers, while the mass audience, when not totally ignorant of those creations, was likely to be confused, incredulous, disgusted or

[37]Fisher, 6–12. Fisher notes that leftist fantasies were more grounded in realism and thus less successful.

[38]Fisher, 21–22.

[39]Paul Monaco, *Cinema and Society* (New York: Elsevier, 1976), 115–154.

[40]Monaco, 116. See also Johannes G. Pankau, "History as Myth: Historical Processes in Early German Film," in Gisela Brude-Firnau and Karin J. MacHardy, eds., *Fact and Fiction: German History and Literature, 1848–1924* (Tübingen: Francke, 1990), 197–208, and especially 201–202. See also Siegfried Kracauer, *From Caligari to Hitler* (Princeton: Princeton UP, 1947), 91–95, and on the problem of a "national" cinema, Thomas J. Saunders, "History in the Making: Weimar Cinema and National Identity," in Bruce A. Murray and Christopher J. Wickham, eds., *Framing the Past: The Historiography of German Cinema and Television* (Carbondale: Southern Illinois UP, 1992), 42–67.

[41]See Kniesche and Brockmann's introduction to *Dancing on the Volcano*, 1–18, for a succinct review of scholarship on Weimar.

appalled by them. Nor should one overlook the hostility evident in Bartels's re-mark, quoted earlier, that expressionism was not of German origin. The chasm between Sombart's idyllic bourgeois house and garden and Gropius's Bauhaus ideal — a house as a "machine for living" — was fundamentally unbridgeable. Hans Johst, the leading National Socialist dramatist, summed up the conserva-tive view of Weimar theater as nothing but "ladies' underwear, sex, drunkenness and mental illness. Drama was the most blatant seat of decadence, materialism and bias."[42] The distance between Bartels's remark at the beginning of the Weimar period and Johst's at the end of it (1933) is not very great, and argues for the continuity of conservative thought throughout the period. The residual cultural conservatism of the general population provided the artistic and literary bedrock that prepared the way for National Socialism, and eased its compre-hensive establishment once it had become a political actuality.[43] Despite Wei-mar's reputation for artistic innovation, the cultural attitudes of the majority of Germans in the Weimar Republic were clearly conservative. It is only in that light that one can understand the cultural appeal of the conservative vision and the influence of the German war narratives.

Not All Quiet on the Literary Front

War narratives occupy a peculiar historical niche between past and present. Combat narratives, for obvious reasons, cannot be contemporaneous with the combat itself, and are rarely even close to it; most are written years after the events they depict. Those written shortly after combat are immediately distin-guishable by their immediacy, concentration on the event, and general lack of contemplative and historical perspective. On the other hand, narratives written long after the fact, even when based on a contemporary diary or notes, are, as Hynes has observed, as much about the post-war period as about the war it-self.[44] This Janus-like stance is emphatically typical of the German war narra-tives. They narrate the experience of the war through the polarizing catastrophes of the post-war period.

The existing polarities of German society, radicalized by the collapse of the Empire, grew more extreme with each new political and economic crisis. The first wave of war narratives in 1928 and 1929 coincided with the advent of the Great Depression, which dealt a severe blow to a nation that had achieved only limited stability after 1923. In the abject misery of the Depression, the voices of the political and cultural extremes became ever more strident in demanding a

[42]Quoted in J. M. Ritchie, "Johst's 'Schlageter' and the End of the Weimar Republic," in Bance, *Weimar Germany*, 153–167.

[43]Ritchie, *German Literature under National Socialism*, 6.

[44]Samuel Hynes, *A War Imagined: The First World War and English Culture* (New York: Athen-aum, 1991), chapter 17 "Botched Civilization," and chapter 18, "Wars after the War."

solution to the nation's woes. That desperate search for explanation and solution triggered a re-examination of the state of the nation, focusing on what was universally regarded as the "key" to Germany's degradation: the war, the defeat and the noxious Treaty of Versailles. At a critical point in the history of the Weimar Republic, 1929–1933, the war narratives occupied a central position in Germany's national re-examination of its history, identity and future. The war narratives and their critical reception embody the complex relationship between the war and German society in the late twenties.

That uneasy relationship is most obvious in the reception accorded the war narratives when they began to appear. Several books had appeared just after the war, notably Unruh's *Opfergang* in 1919, Flex's *Wanderer* in 1917, and Ernst Jünger's *Storm of Steel* (1920). Jünger had the field to himself through the early twenties with "War as Inner Experience" (1922), *Feuer und Blut* (Fire and Blood, 1924) and *Copse 125* (1925). Otherwise, there was virtual silence until the end of 1928, except for the thirty-six volumes of a popular history series funded by the Reichsarchiv, *Schlachten des Weltkrieges* (Battles of the World War).[45] The appearance of Ludwig Renn's *War* in late 1928, and of Remarque's *All Quiet on the Western Front* in early 1929 brought the literary silence to a thunderous end and initiated a noisy political and cultural debate on the literary depiction of the war, the interpretations of the war experience, and the meaning of the war itself.[46] In the atmosphere of heightened political and social tensions, the war narratives were judged primarily on their content, that is, on their depiction of the war experience and its significance for German society and for the nation's future.[47] While one would expect such a critical orientation from the press of the nationalist right, in whose ideology the war experience already occupied a central position,[48] its centrality for the liberal and leftist press is surprising and suggests the extent to which the war experience, with the help of the military histories of the twenties, had permeated the thinking of Weimar society and attained a quasi-mythical status — a status that the war narratives would expand into a full-scale front mythology.

---

[45] Such was not the case in France, where the majority of the literature of *témoinage* appeared in the early twenties. See Maurice Rieuneau, *Guerre et révolution dans le roman français de 1919–1939* (Nancy: Klincksieck, 1974). See also Léon Riegel, *Guerre et littérature* (Nancy: Klincksieck, 1978), which is, despite its weaknesses, the only comparative study in the field. On the histories in Germany, see Reinhard Brühl, *Militärgeschichte und Kriegspolitik* (Berlin: Militärverlag der DDR, 1973), 275–280.

[46] Michael Gollbach, *Die Wiederkehr des Weltkrieges in der Literatur* (Kronberg/ Taunus: Scriptor, 1978), 43. See Gollbach and Hans-Harald Müller, *Der Krieg und die Schriftsteller: Der Kriegsroman der Weimarer Republik* (Stuttgart: Metzler, 1986) for detailed accounts of the critical reception of the most important war narratives, especially Remarque's *All Quiet*.

[47] Müller, 65.

[48] Müller, 71.

Most of the literary criticism of the period was published in a plethora of cultural magazines and newspapers, each of limited circulation, and each with its political attitudes and affiliations. From such liberal publications as *Die literarische Welt* and *Die neue Rundschau* , one could turn left to *Die Linkskurve* and *Die Aktion*, or right to *Die Deutsche Rundschau* and *Das Kunstwort*, or even further right to *Die Tat* and *Deutsches Volkstum*.[49] The cultural positions reached even to the choice of type face: liberal and leftist publications typically used Roman type; conservative ones stayed with traditional *Fraktur*.[50]

From all points on the political spectrum *All Quiet*, and the books that followed it, were greeted with a barrage of praise or blame. For the most part, the criticism is entirely predictable in content and style. *All Quiet* provides only a particularly well-researched example. The earliest reviews appeared in the liberal press, which received the book very favorably.[51] It was widely accepted as a true depiction of the war experience, one to which many veterans responded,[52] and as an anti-war, even pacifist novel.[53] The pacifist label did much to draw down the ire of the nationalist right onto Remarque's work.[54] While liberal journals praised the novel, and the leftist press dismissed Remarque's hero as a petty-bourgeois with no awareness of the class system,[55] the conservative criticism was uniformly venomous, ranging from Schauwecker's Nietzschean dismissal of Bäumer's vision as that of an *Untermensch* (a subhuman), to criticism of his projection of himself as the representative of his generation, to the following statement from critic Wilhelm Westecker, which serves as a model of conservative criticism:

> In a war that we have fought through with such great sacrifices, and from which we believe ourselves to have saved an essentially unbroken people, we wish to check the idea that there is nothing there but blind luck.[56]

Aside from the typically conservative diction, Westecker expresses the essence of the conservative view of the war: neither the war nor its results can be allowed to be seen as merely contingent, because that quality reduces the experience to meaninglessness. It must be seen as a part of the historical continuum, with a specific significance for the German nation. In short, the war must have a

---

[49]Gollbach, 277; Ecksteins, *The Limits of Reason*, 70–103.

[50]Gollbach, 276.

[51]Gollbach, 309–314; Müller, 72–79, 80–92.

[52]Gollbach, 343–345.

[53]See Müller, 80–85 for the pacifist reception of the novel.

[54]Müller, 71–72.

[55]Gollbach, 309–310.

[56]Quoted in Gollbach, 295. "Wir wehren uns dagegen, in einem Krieg, den wir mit so großer Opfern durchkämpft haben und aus dem wir ein zutiefst ungebrochenes Volk gerettet zu haben glauben, nichts als einen blinden Zufall zu sehen."

meaning on the national scale, without which no true presentation of the war is possible.

Thus we return to the ever-vexing problem of what the truth was. Virtually all the contemporary critics used truth — by which they mean the authenticity of the war experience —as the most important criterion for judgment. The authenticity of any given experience was naturally gauged according to the critic's own ideological perspective. Remarque presented his own experience as authentic and representative (and always maintained that the incidents in the book were true and mostly from his own experience).[57] Much of the criticism of the book was aimed at debunking the purported authenticity of that experience. Even foreign writers tumbled into the same critical trap. Charles Carrington, writing about *All Quiet*, is willing to admit that the depictions of the life of soldiers at the base were "true to life," nevertheless "the nearer the characters came to the front the more did critical readers doubt the author had ever been there."[58] In the politically charged atmosphere of late Weimar, subjectivity and multiplicity of experience were luxuries the nation couldn't afford. There could be only one "authentic" experience that embodied the national myth of the war, and that myth, increasingly, was the conservative one.

The importance of truth-telling in the war narratives emerges strikingly in a brochure prepared by Ullstein (Remarque's publisher) at the end of 1929, documenting the controversy over *All Quiet*. The material is arranged under the following six questions:

> Truth or not?
> Pacifistic?
> Indecent?
> A danger to youth?
> What was true heroism?
> A threat to religion and ethics?[59]

As a guide to national concerns in 1929, this list can scarcely be bettered, and the question of the novel's "truth" holds pride of place.

Before examining the implications of the Ullstein list, another aspect of the problem of authenticity demands comment. The complexities of the problem are exacerbated by the war writers' use of realistic prose. As I have already noted, realism is, almost without exception, the style of choice among war writers, and crosses the political spectrum from Köppen and Zweig on the left to Wehner and Zöberlein on the right. Consequently, realistic depiction of horrific carnage, which is characteristic of the German narratives as a whole, has nothing to do with whether any given narrative is perceived as true: that is rather a question of

---

[57]Gollbach, 44.

[58]Charles Carrington, *Soldier from the Wars Returning* (London: Hutchinson, 1965), 264.

[59]Quoted in Gollbach, 278 and Müller, 66.

Weltanschauung or even of morality. Zöberlein's suggestion that Remarque should be drowned by front soldiers in his own element, the latrine, is not, as it has usually been construed, an attack on the scatological realism of Remarque's depiction of war, but an attack on his falsification of the total experience of war.[60] In Zöberlein's view, Remarque's latrine mentality comes not from his depiction of latrines, but from his failure to find a higher (spiritual) dimension to the experience of war.

To return to Ullstein's questions, the coupling of truth and pacifism at the top of the list, and the inclusion of heroism further down signal the areas of greatest national and nationalist concern, and the grounds on which rightist critics attacked Remarque. The references to decency, religion and ethics raise the concern for traditional cultural and literary values. (The opening of *All Quiet* was considered by many to be scandalously indecent, as was the rendezvous with the young Frenchwomen.) Finally, the question of whether the book was a threat to youth again emphasizes that the war narratives were seen as an important examination of the German past and were expected to have an effect on the public view of the national past, and even more importantly, the national future. The next generation's comprehension of the meaning of the war would be the determining factor in their actions.

The obsession with authenticity of experience led, after the publication of *All Quiet*, to a rash of conservative novels that were written, the writers confidently asserted, to debunk Remarque's version of the truth. Liberal and leftist voices alike were drowned in a flood of conservative war experiences. Forewords and prefaces claimed to present a true picture of the war "as it really was." Bucher, always a reliable conservative source, proclaims that his book, dedicated to the dead of Germany, was published because of a book that held the German front soldier up to the ridicule of the world, so that there was a battle yet to be fought for those who had died. "I have written a sad and undistorted picture of what the war in the west really was ... to lay a wreath upon the graves of my comrades, those unhappy victims sacrificed for a yet more unhappy homeland."[61] One may infer that the insulting book was *All Quiet*, and Bucher's remark underlines the vital importance of "telling the truth" about the war. In characteristic conservative rhetoric, he invokes first the dead and then the pitiful state of the nation. Kröner, whose narrative was published in the same year as

---

[60]Quoted in Müller, 68–69.

[61]Georg Bucher, *Westfront 1914–1918: Das Buch vom Frontkameraden* (Vienna-Leipzig: Konegen, 1930). Tr. by Norman Gullick as *In the Line* (London: Cape, 1932), 13–14. " ... war doch alles so geschrieben, wie die unverzerrte, traurige Wirklichkeit im Westen einst war.... eins versucht der Soldat Bucher ... seinen toten Kameraden in Treue und Verehrung einen Grabschmuck zu pflanzen, diesen armen Opfern, die für eine noch ärmere Heimat gebracht wurden" (Foreword).

Bucher's (1931), names the offending author.[62] Kröner and Hitler (in his forward to Zöberlein's *Der Glaube an Deutschland*) dismiss the realities of war as insignificant in comparison to the authentic conservative experience of comradeship, from which comes the potential for national rejuvenation. The purpose of a war narrative was the creation of a "new belief in a better Germany."[63]

Both conservative authors and critics managed, in the last years of the Weimar Republic, to have the best of all worlds. They had begged the question. The only authentic, true war experience was one that was ideologically conservative, but because of its status as experience, it was automatically above question and debate. Political and ethical criteria had been substituted for aesthetic ones: the result was a critical legacy of "pro-war"or "anti-war" narratives.

Whatever the concerns and limitations of the contemporary critics, the modern critic cannot avoid the question of purpose, a question complicated by the historical intervention of National Socialism. Why did the war writers write their books? What did they hope to accomplish with their testimonies of friendship, suffering and loss? Are these books, particularly in the case of the conservative narratives, unadulterated proto-fascist propaganda? And finally, what effect did the war narratives have on German society?

The intentions of overtly liberal, leftist or pacifist writers are relatively easy to ascertain. Fundamentally communist texts such as Scharrer's *Vaterlandslose Gesellen* (Comrades without a Country, 1930) and Theodor Plievier's *Des Kaisers Kulis* (The Kaiser's Coolies, 1930) underscore the importance of communist revolutionary action against capitalist and imperialist society. Plievier's narrative, through its account of the Kiel mutiny, functions as a classic communist call to arms. Scharrer's novel directs its criticism against the "imperialist" war, and was thus favorably received by communist critics.[64] Leonhard Frank's *Der Mensch ist gut* is also a clearly pacifist plea for world peace and universal brotherhood, as is Latzko's *Men in Battle.*

Other texts are more difficult to pin down, as the preceding discussion on the reception of *All Quiet*—especially the split on the subject of its "pacifism" — shows. Renn's *War*, published just before *All Quiet* and often reviewed with it, is simultaneously so personal and so detached that it defies easy categorization, except perhaps as a realistic war narrative. Aside from the final sentence of *Afterwar*, where Renn speaks of finding his way to communism, it would be difficult to prove that he had any purpose other than recounting his personal experience. Köppen's *Higher Command*, on the other hand, one of the best and technically most innovative narratives to come out of the war, is clearly meant as an exposé of the madness of war, set in scenes that show the continu-

---

[62]See my discussion of Kröner in chapter 4.

[63]Hitler in Zöberlein, *Der Glaube an Deutschland*, 9.

[64]See Gollbach, 314–319 for the reception of Scharrer's work.

ing influence of expressionism. An earlier text in the same vein, Unruh's *Opfergang* is a potent "anti-war" text of expressionist fervor.

Conservative narratives present a different set of problems. Internal and external evidence suggests that most were written primarily to convince the reader of the authenticity of the conservative war experience — an experience based on the society of front comradeship. That is obviously the case in books that appeared after 1933, such as Beumelburg's quasi-history *From 1914 to 1939*. After 1933 the conservative war experience was institutionalized both in war narratives and in any criticism of them.

Criticism is remarkably indicative of the degree to which the conservative experience had been apotheosized into the only accepted version of the national experience of the war. Several lengthy studies of the war narratives that appeared in the mid-thirties reinforced the exclusivity of that conservative myth. Hermann Pongs's series of articles from 1934 to 1938 in *Dichtung und Volkstum* (formerly *Euphorion*) emphasized a *völkisch* analysis of the war narratives, concentrating on the war as a part of *Volksschicksal* (fate of the nation) and castigating individualist narratives such as those of Remarque and Köppen.[65] Günther Lutz, in turn, glorified the experience of comradeship and insisted on the primacy of the *Führer-Prinzip*, as did Till Kalkschmidt.[66]

For books that appeared before 1933, unraveling the strands of personal expression from political conviction is more complex. The question is rendered more difficult by the traditional belief— seriously held by many soldiers — in the subordination of the individual to the needs of the group of comrades, and by extension, to the needs of the nation.[67] However easily such feelings might be perverted to political ends, and were, the literary evidence suggests that in most cases the experience of comradeship produced a genuine and deeply-held conviction of its importance, both in itself and as the key to national renewal. To dismiss the possibility of an experience of war that emphasizes the warmth of comradeship and the use of that experience to a positive end is to fall into the trap of regarding the only valid war experience as a negative, even horrific one — a position as dangerous to the critic as its opposite.

[65] See Hermann Pongs's articles cited above.

[66] Lutz concentrates on the idea of comradeship and its relation to the principle of natural leadership. His "Europas Kriegserlebnis: Ein Überblick über das außerdeutsche Kriegsschriftum," *Dichtung und Volkstum* 39 (1938):133–168, provides an interesting National Socialist view of non-German war literature. For other examples of thirties criticism, see Till Kalkschmidt, "Kameradschaft und Führertum der Front," *Dichtung und Volkstum* 39 (1938):180–192, and Helmut Hoffmann, "Mensch und Volk im Kriegserlebnis," *Germanische Studien* 189 (Berlin: Evering, 1937) 1–81. For a review of criticism in the thirties, see Holgar Klein, "Weltkriegsroman und Germanistik, 1933–1938," *Journal of English and Germanic Philology* 4 (October 1985):467–484.

[67] See for example the characteristic letters included in Witkop's collection, numbers 16 and 108 (German 20 and 81–82).

The sanctification of comradeship as the enduring German experience of the war is entirely consistent with its philosophical and social antecedents — Romantic nationalism, *völkisch* ideology, the *Vereine, Bunde* and *Burschenschaften*, and above all the youth movement and the Wandervogel — which prepared the psychological and philosophical ground. The young bourgeois who fought for Germany in the First World War had been conditioned by education and experience for the emotional bonding of comradeship — a comradeship that in form and content seemed to them to be entirely different from anything to be found on the other side of the Rhine or the Channel. I have specified the bourgeois soldier, because soldiers from other backgrounds sometimes did not share the belief in comradeship. Adam Scharrer, the major communist writer, dismissed comradeship as "the greatest lie" of the war and as "a community of candidates for death."[68] On the other hand, Ernst Wiechert, who, as a dissenter, became a part of the "inner emigration" during the Third Reich, depicts comradeship as an enduring value. After carrying their friend Percy's body back across the Rhine and burying it on the German side, the two able-bodied comrades of *Jedermann* return home to find the fourth comrade, a double amputee. At the end of the book the three report to Johannes's mother as two and a half men.[69]

Thus the weight of the evidence implies that most of the German war writers, in depicting the war and their experience of comradeship, had as their purpose a desire to share what they believed to be the genuine individual and collective experience of the war. When the writers extrapolate from personal to national experience, they move into the political realm, although in most cases, philosophical musings about a society based on the pattern of comradeship remain vague and utopian, much like the fantasy novels of the period, with nothing of a practical political program about them.[70] At the same time it is worth recalling that early National Socialist rhetoric tended to be of the same ilk, and in common with other conservative groups drew from the same pool of conservative ideology.[71]

Two important questions remain to be answered. Did the flood of war narratives between 1928 and 1933 exert any influence on the readers of the Weimar Republic, and if so, in what direction? And secondly, did the conservative war narratives contribute to the rise of National Socialism, and if so, in what ways? It is notoriously difficult to establish generalized literary influence, but in the case of the war narratives there is some compelling evidence: the sheer quantity and range of criticism that the war books elicited argues for their cen-

[68]Quoted in Gollbach, 33.

[69]Wiechert, 3:499–510 and 533.

[70]See particularly Fisher's introduction and first chapter on the radical right.

[71]See Jost Hermand, *Der alte Traum vom neuen Reich: Völkische Utopien und Nationalsozialismus* (Frankfurt am Main: Athenäum, 1988), especially the chapters that follow "Ideen von 1914."

trality and influence in national thought. In a period of national self-examination, the war narratives provided explanations and interpretations of the seminal event of the period. As Colonel Hermann Foertsch of the general staff once remarked, "lost wars call more insistently for examination than those that have been won. They never let you rest, and they force you to reflect. . . ."[72] Much of that reflection was carried on in the war narratives and in the plethora of articles about them. The very existence of a large body of criticism — and highly fragmented criticism at that — suggests the extent to which questions about the impact of the war on the state of the German nation had permeated all segments of German society.

The Ullstein list cited above provides another indication of the influence of the war narratives. Amid concerns for truth, pacifism and heroism is the question "a danger to youth?" The existence of the topic indicates a significant critical interest in the effect of the war narratives on one segment of the readership: young people, specifically young men. Several critics conclude that whatever the pacifistic intentions of the authors, the effect has been just the opposite. In 1930, B. v. Brentano sadly concluded "I believe that the war novels, which have had so powerful an effect on us, even when they were meant to be anti-war novels, have had exactly the opposite effect."[73] In a similar vein, Selutus warned of the militarizing effect of the narratives: "The pacifists are mistaken to speak of the horrors of the trenches. . . . Danger doesn't frighten, danger excites. Path-finding boys will find *All Quiet on the Western Front* on the Christmas table. Then next year, if they don't join Stahlhelm, it will be Reichsbanner or the Red Front."[74] These passages suggest two important effects of the war narratives. First, they kept the experience of war and its aftermath at the forefront of national debate. The First World War did not recede quietly into the past and out of active memory; rather it was kept alive and at the center of virtually every assessment of the state of Germany. Secondly, the war narratives, even anti-war ones, kept the idea of war itself, and of war as a way of resolving problems, before a large readership. In my view, this subtext of war as resolution worked insidiously on a population trapped in a situation of such misery and daunting complexity that they believed only a total undoing of the results of the First World War could improve their situation, even if that necessitated another war.

The answer to the second question — whether the war narratives contributed to the rise of National Socialism — is only slightly less complex. It is very easy for non-German readers to dismiss the conservative war narratives as early Nazi propaganda, while conveniently ignoring the historical reality that the National Socialists were only one of many conservative movements that drew their ideology from common sources. Of the major conservative war writers, only

---

[72]Quoted in Barry Leach, *The German General Staff* (New York: Ballantine, 1973), 24.

[73]Quoted in Gollbach, 351.

[74]Quoted in Gollbach, 348.

Zöberlein was an early Nazi party member. Wehner, Binding and Beumelburg accepted important positions in the hierarchy of the writers' bureau after 1933. Ernst Jünger flirted briefly with Nazi ideology, but later withdrew from any association with the party. Dwinger was a Reich culture senator during the Third Reich.[75] One thing is certain: the books that they created glorified the spiritual unity and community of the front, and correspondingly denigrated its opposite — a postwar Germany that they could not comprehend and which they felt had betrayed them and their dead comrades.[76] In doing so, they created a literature that, if not itself National Socialist, was acceptable to the Nazis and could be easily appropriated by them after 1933.[77]

Toward a New Society

Whatever their individual political orientation, most of the German war veterans did share one conviction: the unshakable certainty that they had somehow been betrayed by the homeland, that Weimar Germany was not what they had fought and died for. There was something wrong with Germany. The identity of the problem depended upon individual political persuasion, but that something was amiss was incontrovertible among discontented veterans. Nationalist Theodor Bartram, in a 1919 speech to a newly-formed veterans' organization, stated categorically that "the entire organism, the entire body of the nation is sick."[78] As usual, the diction of German nationalism is notable for its organicism.[79]

The cure for this illness of the body politic depended, as everything in Weimar depended, on politics. Just as the repeated crises of the Republic had influenced the writers' interpretations of their war experience, so the unsettled atmosphere led to the positing of a variety of cures for Weimar, based always on the war experience, the root of everything for the war veterans, as well as the only valid credential for those wishing to effect national change. These visions

[75]For more details see the biographies in Ernst Loewy, *Literatur unterm Hakenkreuz: Das Dritte Reich und seine Dichtung* (Frankfurt am Main: Fischer, 1983), 301–329.

[76]Ritchie, *German Literature under National Socialism*, 3–20, especially 17–18.

[77]Karl Prümm, "Tendenzen des deutschen Kriegsromans nach 1918," in Klaus Vondung, ed., *Kriegserlebnis (Göttingen: Vandenhoeck, 1980), 215–218*. See also his *Die Literatur des soldatischen Nationalismus der 20er Jahre* (Kronberg: Scriptor, 1974).

[78]Theodor Bartram, *Der Frontsoldat: Ein deutsches Kultur- und Lebensideal* (Berlin: Verlag der Gegenseitigen Hilfe, 1934), 6. Reprint of speech delivered in 1919. " . . . der Gesamtorganismus is krank, unser ganzer Volkskörper" (6). The organization is not named, but is almost certainly Stahlhelm, founded at the end of 1918 with the membership requirement of at least six months' service at the front. See James M. Diehl, *Paramilitary Politics in Weimar Germany* (Bloomington: U of Indiana P, 1982), 96–97.

[79]See Klaus Theweleit, *Männerphantasien* (Frankfurt am Main: Roter Stern, 1978), 2:9–26 on the identification of filth and disease with the masses.

of the German future tended to be vaguely utopian, and to have little to do with the democratic party politics of the Weimar Republic.

For those veterans for whom the war had been an experience of unrelieved horror, pacifism was a logical retreat.[80] In Germany, pacifism was historically associated with left-wing politics, and both had come under attack during the war by the government and conservative majority on the grounds of being at the least unpatriotic, and at the worst treasonous. The movement survived, but in a weakened form.[81] Unlike Britain and France, where pacifist movements became well-established and widely influential, pacifism made little headway in Germany after the war, due primarily to the defeat. The bitterness of the defeat and the conditions of the Treaty of Versailles created a populace largely bent on revenge, or at least on correcting an injustice, and disinclined to the universal brotherhood espoused by organized pacifism. In that embittered atmosphere, pacifism was, for most, an unpalatable alternative.[82]

Communism found itself in much the same position as pacifism, and for similar reasons. Communism and socialism, as movements, were essentially international and based on rational philosophies. Outside their natural home in the urban proletariat, the leftist movements were regarded as alien and un-German. Despite the patriotic gesture of the 1914 *Burgfrieden* and the voting of war credits, even the relatively moderate Social Democrats were regarded with suspicion by the conservative *Mittelstand* (middle class). The defeat of the extreme-left November Revolution and later disastrous leftist riots and uprisings had weakened the position of the left in general, and international connections with former enemies did it no good in the mind of the average patriotic German. In an emotionally charged period, the rationalism and progressivism of leftist thought had little more appeal to average citizens than pacifism. Both pacifists and leftists rejected the possibility of the war meaning anything; for them it was meaningless slaughter, rendered even more meaningless for the radical left because it had failed, except in Russia, to trigger the expected wave of revolutions. But for the average German, the doctrine of meaninglessness was intolerable. The war had to be a *Bildungserlebnis* and had to point the way to future development.

It was left, therefore, to the conservatives to turn the experience of war into a foundation and model for a new society. The experience of comradeship was to provide the model for a new German community (*Gemeinschaft*) and that model came primarily from the conservative war narratives. The closest links between

---

[80]Among them were Tucholsky, Ossietzky, Toller, and Köppen. Otto Dix is sometimes included in this group, but his artistic reaction to the war is too complex for simple categorization. See D. Harth, D. Schubert, R.M. Schmidt, eds., *Pazifismus zwischen den Weltkriegen* (Heidelberg: Universitätsbibliothek, 1985).

[81]Karl Holl, *Pazifismus in Deutschland* (Frankfurt am Main: Suhrkamp, 1988) 103–138.

[82]Holl, 138–220; Harth et al., 17–22.

the ideology of the war narratives and that of National Socialism are discernible through the development of the *Frontgemeinschaft* paradigm. Comradeship in the context of the war experience and of its historical and cultural antecedents has already been examined in detail. Two components of the front experience had the greatest influence in the last years of the Weimar Republic. The first was the understanding of comradeship as a natural (read: organic) emotional bond between men belonging to the same *Volk*. The second is the *Führerprinzip*, or principle of the leader, one who emerges naturally from the group of comrades, and whose leadership is unquestioned because he is the first among equals — that is, he is still one of the comrades. These two components provided the conservatives, especially the National Socialists, with a social pattern based on the concept of an organic community of *Volk* directed by a natural leader espousing an organic, vitalist philosophy.

The experience of the front also provides the key to the political and military thinking of the "natural" leader of the National Socialists, Adolf Hitler. John Keegan has provided the most illuminating analysis of Hitler's First World War military experience and its impact on his thinking.[83] First, Hitler's flight from Vienna to Munich in 1913 was at least partly to avoid military service in the Hapsburg army, "which would have meant soldiering with the Czechs, Croats and Jews he shunned and despised" (237). Once in Munich he received an exemption from Hapsburg military service, but when war broke out, he immediately obtained permission from the King of Bavaria to enlist in the Bavarian army. Second, the regiment in which he enlisted, the 16th Bavarian Reserve Regiment, "was composed of exactly that class of young Germans to which Hitler had so long aspired but failed to be granted admission" (237). They were mostly high-school and university students and men training for the professions, precisely the sort of young men who eventually wrote war narratives about the comradeship of the trenches. Keegan compares Hitler's regiment to the British "Pals" battalions on the Somme. The 16th Bavarian Reserve was to be decimated in one battle, the October 1914 battle for Ypres, always called in Germany the *Kindermord bei Ypern* (Massacre of the Innocents at Ypres).[84] The deaths of so many promising young men brought the Germans face to face with the reality of a long, bloody war. The loss of his comrades may also, Keegan suggests, have shattered Hitler's sense of belonging to the "young Germany" of his dreams, and may have exacerbated his "loner" behavior.[85] His constant service with his regiment as a message runner, his decorations and wounds have

---

[83]John Keegan, *The Mask of Command* (New York: Penguin, 1987), 235–310.

[84]Keegan, *Mask*, 238–239. Note the use of sacrificial religious terminology. For a different analysis of the significance of Langemarck and the sacrifice of German students, see Bernd Hüppauf, "Langemarck, Verdun and the Myth of a 'New Man' in Germany after the First World War," *War and Society* 6:2 (Sept 1988): 70–103.

[85]Keegan, *Mask*, 239–240.

been noted earlier. He was indeed, with so many other men of his generation, what he ever after called himself: a *Frontkämpfer* (front fighter).

And it was as an old *Frontschwein* that Hitler presented himself. He wrote prefaces to the war books of Dreysse and Zöberlein, incorporating references to his own experience. *Mein Kampf* and his speeches are laced with allusions to his experience at the front. In his famous speech at the beginning of the Second World War, he stated first that he required no more of any German man than what he himself had been prepared to do during the First World War, and then declared, "I have put on the coat that was most sacred and dear to me."[86] Not only does he evoke his own service in the First World War, but also links himself to the national heritage with his echoes of Frederick the Great ("the first servant of the state") and the wearing of the "King's coat" — the colloquialism that described military service under Prussia and the Empire.[87]

J. P. Stern, in his excellent study of Hitler's rhetoric and philosophy, has identified the role played by the *Fronterlebnis*. Hitler, he maintains, transferred what had originally been a personal and private experience into the sphere of public life (as did the authors of war narratives), and proclaimed himself the representative of the nation by virtue of the genuineness of that experience.[88]

> In support of his views he [Hitler] cited, not facts or logic or justice, but the greatest of his assets, his "Fronterlebnis." . . . this violence [in speeches] too derives its sanction from the idea of authenticity, from the conveyed conviction that his every utterance is the expression of *this man's genuine feelings*. And are not feelings, unlike the complexities of economics or politics, something Everyman can understand and judge and share?"[89]

Stern recognizes that the *Fronterlebnis* can only become a model for a new society if it is a genuine experience, that is, if it stands in the irrational, organic tradition of *Erlebnis* and *Bildung*, rather than in the rational and contractual tradition of western democracy, since a rational model would have been unacceptable to the former *Frontkämpfer* and to the German people as a whole. Similarly, the only acceptable leader is a soldier among soldiers. The fact that the front experience was neither private nor limited, but very nearly universal for the male members of a generation, bestowed on that generation a sense of communal existence and common betrayal that was ripe for exploitation.

Of the many possible examples of the National Socialist exploitation of the war experience, none is more revealing than Alfred Hein's 1937 *Das kleine Buch*

[86]Quoted in Keegan, *Mask*, 235.

[87]On the influence of the Prussian past, see S. D. Stirk, *The Prussian Spirit, 1914–1940* (Port Washington: Kennikat, 1969). In the Weimar period, the seminal document on the idea of prussianism is Oswald Spengler's *Preußentum und Sozialismus* (München: Beck, 1920), which suggests the conflation of national and socialist ideas.

[88]J.P. Stern, *Hitler*, 23–24.

[89]J.P. Stern, *Hitler*, 26.

vom grossen Krieg (The Little Book about the Great War).[90] It was directed, as the title suggests, at young readers as an indoctrination into the cult of the *Kriegserlebnis*. The book is a virtual catalogue of Great War themes emphasized by the National Socialists, and as such merits a through analysis. The purpose of the text, Hein states in the foreword, is to arouse and inspire the German family, and to show "how the war is still with us."[91] As a narrative device, Hein creates a boy and a girl who are told about the war by their parents, assorted relatives, and their father's old comrade. Hein universalizes his characters by using only titles for the adults, for example the father, the teacher, the man in the brown shirt, and by giving the children the stereotypical names of Hans and Ilse.

The first chapter, "Of Field gray Death and Resurrection," opens with the children questioning their father about the war (he is, of course, a veteran). He begins with a patriotic statement couched in quasi-religious language: "'To fall in the field,' said the father, 'means: to rise again for the Fatherland, means: to lead the way for the Fatherland, means: to die so that Germany lives.'"[92] They had fought "a world of enemies" (7), he continues, in order to live at peace in the beauty of the homeland (6). When the war ended "unglücklich" (unhappily), the men only knew "how to be comrades" (7). Hans here interjects that he and his school fellows are "little field gray soldiers" (7), and the mother completes the cycle of comradeship by explaining that Hitler must be the *Führer* because he is "der einfache Soldat" (the simple soldier)(8). Sentimental patriotism surfaces again when Hans asks what his father's hand, which he has been holding, did in the war. The father replies that he has killed, bound wounds, and buried comrades, providing an effective, if maudlin, contrast with the current happy German family. The mother continues the narrative with the story of starvation on the home front, a tale to which Ilse, wide-eyed, demands "Not even potatoes?" (9), and the chapter concludes with the father's tale of how the soldiers suffered,

" . . . while against us were healthy, fresh, athletic Americans who wanted for nothing. Always ten against one — and still the front held. We had lost the

---

[90]Alfred Hein, *Das kleine Buch vom großen Krieg* (Langensalza: Beltz, 1937). Hein, pseudonym of Julius Beuthen, wrote extensively of his experiences in the First World War until the end of the Second. He died at the end of 1945. For a list of his works, see *Deutsches Literatur Lexikon* 7:686–687.

[91]Hein, *Das kleine Buch*, 3.

[92]Hein, *Das kleine Buch*, 5. Further brief references will be in the text. All translations from this text are mine. "Im Felde fallen' sprach der Vater, 'heißt: für sein Vaterland auferstehen, heißt: für sein Vaterland vorangehen, heißt: sterben, damit Deutschland lebt.'"

war. But the field gray fellow, who since that war is a part of every front German, was not defeated."[93]

The undefeated army appears frequently in Hein's conservative history for children. More interesting is the expansion of the community of comradeship from the family circle into the general population, effectively creating a nation of undefeated warriors. This large circle of comradeship strikingly echoes Beumelburg's circles in *Gruppe Bosemüller*, fulfilling his vision of a new society of comrades.

The second chapter, "The Reich Remains Ours," copes with the ethical problems of German militarism and nationalism by the simple expedient of declaring that the German Reich and God's Reich are one and the same, and that service to the community is equally service to God (12–13), reiterating along the way the standard apology (also found in Schauwecker) that Germany had only truly become a nation through the suffering of the war. The tone of this chapter is one of simple piety that attempts to echo the Prussian tradition. Appeals to the spirit of Frederick the Great and other great Prussians were a standard bromide in nationalist literature between the wars, and this is no exception.[94] The glorification of the Prussian spirit continues with "What East Prussia Suffered" and "Tannenberg," concluding with a paean to Hindenburg.

The significance of the war in family history is complemented by its importance in community history. In the next chapter, "Langemarck," the scene shifts to the school room. The teacher, who was a volunteer at Langemarck, tells the story of the battle, in which all the soldiers knew they had only one duty: "to stay in the front line and to be a true German comrade to the man at one's side."[95] The children, swept away by the teacher's story, conclude the lesson by singing "Deutschland" (28). The scene is ironically reminiscent of the famous schoolroom scene in the film of *All Quiet*.

The chapters that follow laud the "German spirit of organization" on the home-front and fallen family heroes: an uncle who died on the Russian front — the children visit his grave on *Totensonntag* (Remembrance Sunday) — and another who left a letter testifying that the experience of the war was the high point of his life (31, 33). The scene shifts back to the family with the father's story of his life as a message runner at Verdun, where he earned the Iron Cross (45). In fact, he discusses all the major battles of the war, concluding that "we

---

[93]Hein, *Das kleine Buch*, 9. " . . . während uns kerngesunde, keine Not leidende, frische sportkräftige Amerikaner gegenübergestellt wurden. Immer zehn gegen einen — Dennoch hielt die Front. Wir haben zwar den Krieg verloren. Aber der feldgraue Kerl, der seit jenem Krieg in jedem Frontdeutschen steckt, ist nie besiegt worden."

[94]See Stirk, *The Prussian Spirit*, 106–124 and 165–189.

[95]Hein, *Das kleine Buch*, 27. " . . . Vorn zu bleiben und dem Mann an der Seite ein treuer deutscher Kamerad zu sein."

were too few, we had too little,"[96] and "we Germans know that although we have lost the war, we do not feel conquered by the enemy armies."[97] The decisive factor in all of these accounts is the siren song of "feeling." Feeling is also the salient characteristic of the only thing that these "unglückselige Helden" (unhappy heroes) finally possess: "die Frontkameradschaft" (front comradeship) (75). The emotional, and therefore authentic experience of comradeship constitutes the keystone of National Socialist ideology.

The chapter called "Heroic Deeds of the Unknown Soldier" is largely narrated by the father's friend, an SA member who maintains that the anonymous German soldier has conquered in spite of defeat (76).

> "The Reich is ours," smiled the man in the brown shirt. "Because the Reich is not only the geographically limited German earth — the Reich is also the unlimited heaven above this beloved homeland, in which Reich live the greatest dead of all time, from the Teutons to Frederick the Great, from Goethe to the treacherously slain Hitler Youths."[98]

In this characteristic invocation, the Nazi's favorite historic heroes — the Teutons and Frederick the Great — combine with Goethe (a bow to culture), the anonymous soldier of the war, and finally the brown-shirt and the children to form the German Reich. Although the language is obviously different, the passage is oddly evocative of Lissauer's "Deutschland." It involves the same invocation of the dead "greats" of German history, who inhabit an ethereal Reich above the soil of Germany, and serve as its protectors.

Similar techniques appear in any number of wartime posters and postcards. One German poster on the theme of *Gott strafe England* depicts Germania in the garb of a medieval knight defending German shores from the encroachment of the British fleet. Another, *In Deo Gratia*, shows a medieval knight bearing Christian symbols closely patterned in image and style on the Dürer woodcut of St. George.[99] Such evocations of martial symbols remained standard fodder for the popular media throughout the First and Second World Wars.

[96]Hein, *Das kleine Buch*, 73. "Wir waren zu wenig. Wir besaßen zu wenig."

[97]Hein, *Das kleine Buch*, 57. "Und wir Deutschen wissen, daß wir zwar den Krieg verloren haben, daß wir uns aber von den feindlichen Heeren nicht besiegt fühlen."

[98]Hein, *Das kleine Buch*, 76. "'Das Reich ist unser,' lächelte der Mann im braunen Hemd. 'Denn das Reich ist nicht nur die geographisch umgrenzte deutsche Erde — das Reich ist auch der unbegrenzte Himmel über dieser geliebten Heimatscholle, in diesem Reich leben die großen Toten allzeit mit von den Teutonen an bis zum Fredericus Rex, von Goethe bis zum menschlings erschlagenen Hitlerjungen.'"

[99]The latter is shown in Jay Winter, *The Experience of World War I* (New York: Oxford UP, 1989), 184–185. See also Tonie and Valmai Holt, *Germany Awake!* (London: Longman, 1986), Maurice Rickards, *Posters of the First World War* (New York: Walker, 1968), and Anthony R. Crawford, ed., *Posters in the G.C. Marshall Research Foundation* (Charlottesville: U of Virginia P, 1979) for more examples. See Weigel et al., *Jeder Schuß ein Russ* for examples of postcards.

The appeal to mystical nationalism in the forms of *Frontkameradschaft* and *Gemeinschaft* continues through the last chapters of the book. Although the war was militarily lost, the "unzerbrechliche Kameradenmauer der Front" (unbreakable wall of front comrades) endured, and "Leid macht stark" (suffering makes you stronger) (91) — the latter a proverb. In the end, the children see themselves as a part of the spiritual nation, in which their actions, however small, mirror the actions of the front soldiers and are the result of the true comradeship of self-sacrifice. Hans and Ilse embody their union with the *Gemeinschaft* by joining the Hitler Youth and asking for uniforms for Christmas.

The pervasiveness and centrality of the First World War experience is also mirrored in its importance for the Hitler Youth. Alfons Heck, who has written and lectured widely on his experience as a Hitler Youth leader, has told me that the First World War was presented to the Hitler Youth as the main source of German strength. Ernst Jünger's war books were mandatory reading. The boys' vocabulary was replete with the aggressive terminology drawn from the assault tactics of the latter part of the war. *Sturm-* and *Stoßtruppe* figure prominently in the glossary (Hitler's first guards were called *Stoßtruppe*). Predictably, the stab-in-the-back legend and the exploits and character of Frederick the Great also loomed large in the curriculum.[100]

To the modern reader, Hein's *Das kleine Buch* may seem an outrageous piece of National Socialist propaganda, made even more odious by its targeting of children. Propaganda it indubitably is, but it is through examining such texts that one can see the links between the war narratives and the sublimation of that ideology into National Socialist rhetoric. The homey, familial tone of Hein's book gives way to genuinely militaristic diction in the Hitler Youth, but the bedrock of a specifically military comradeship underlies both. The real legacy of the war narratives to National Socialism was the conviction that the only redemptive model for German society was at once male, affective and military.

---

[100]Alfons Heck, Interview by author, Grand Forks, ND, 9 November, 1989.

Elk Eber, Der Meldegänger *(The Message Runner, 1942).*
Courtesy of Hoover Institute.

A German cemetery in territory retaken by the French.
L'Illustration, *9 October 1918 (262–263).*
Bibliothèque National Française.

Conclusion

Each November, English people of all ages join in the national commemoration of a war that was over long before most of them were born. They buy and wear artificial poppies, attend special services on Remembrance Sunday, and watch the official wreath-laying ceremony at the Cenotaph on television. Since the end of the Second World War, Remembrance Sunday has officially included the dead of that war in its commemoration, and has been expanded to include the dead of subsequent wars. But the symbolism of the poppy — blood, sacrifice and irrevocable loss — embodies the nation's quintessential myth of the First World War.

Finding a suitable way to commemorate the dead, and with them, the experience of the Great War, presented governments, veterans and the public with one of the most vexatious problems of the immediate postwar years. Political squabbles surrounded initiatives to create monuments and memorial days in Britain and France.[1] But those disputes were minor compared to the political brawl that erupted in Germany over the establishment of a memorial day and a national war monument. The bitterness of the conflicts ensured that Germany had no national war monument until 1931 (the Neue Wache in Berlin) and no national memorial day until 1934 (the National Socialists' *Heldengedenktag*, Heroes' Memorial Day).[2] Similar differences of opinion marked the creation of local war memorials. But paradoxically, the local monuments, expressing regional attitudes and sentiments, are better indicators of cultural attitudes. Village memorials in Britain tend to be simple columns or crosses; French monuments usually include sculpted symbolic figures, most frequently of Victory or the Republic, or alternatively, of an abstract, representative *poilu*. In contrast to the traditional simplicity of the British memorials, and the abstract aestheticizing of the French, German memorials often bear the two most important German symbols of the war: the *Stahlhelm* and a branch of oak leaves. The iconography of the *Stahlhelm* links it, via Dürer, to the medieval warrior tradition, while the oak leaves (often with acorns) evoke the Teutonic past and

---

[1] On Britain see Samuel Hynes, *A War Imagined: The First World War and English Culture* (New York: Athenaum, 1991), 270–283. On the conflicts surrounding the creation of the Tomb of the Unknown Soldier in France, see Antoine Prost, *Les Anciens combattants et la société française 1914–1939* (Paris: Fondation nationale des sciences politiques, 1977), 3:35–37; on other monuments to the dead, 3:40–51; and on ceremonies on November eleventh, 3:52–76.

[2] Whalen, *Bitter Wounds*, 183–185 and Mosse, *Fallen Soldiers*, especially 159–189.

simultaneously draw the viewer forward into the promise of regeneration.[3] This double perspective — backward to the warrior tradition, forward to rebirth — shapes the commemorative efforts of Weimar Germany.

National and even local monuments and ceremonies naturally brought forth partisan dispute because such commemorative acts were perceived as national or at least as official. But in Germany the same passions were stirred by what would usually be regarded as personal statements: the combat narratives. It is precisely because they were not personal statements, however ingenuous the author may have attempted to appear, that the combat narratives occupied the center of the debate about the meaning of the war, which was, perforce, a debate about remembrance and commemoration of the war. In the general dearth of official commemoration, of any effort to "lay the ghosts" of the war at a time when the economic and political situation demanded a reassessment of the recent past, the combat narratives assumed a disproportionately large share of that reassessment.

Several factors are significant in the elevation of the combat narratives to the status of privileged transmitters of the war myth. The first is their claim to be commemorative works. Almost all of the narratives are dedicated to dead comrades. A few, such as *All Quiet*, are dedicated to the survivors. In some cases, the language is distinctly funerary, as in Bucher's equation of his book to a funeral wreath for the graves of his comrades. In virtually all cases, the combat narratives insist that they are honoring the dead by telling — and this brings us to the second factor — a true story of authentic war experience. As I have argued above, the "authentic" war experience, *qua* experience, is unquestionable and undebatable. As Cru, a combatant himself, maintains in *Du témoinage*, "What we live, *exists*; whatever contradicts our experience *does not exist* . . . ."[4] That very exclusivity of the war experience, its limitation to initiates, contributes to the tendency to develop one national myth of the war consistent with the cultural traditions of the nation. Any doubts about the hegemony of veterans over the definition of authentic experience, and thus over the creation of war myth should have been laid to rest by the activities commemorating the fiftieth anniversary of the D-Day landings, or the battle over the Smithsonian exhibit on the Enola Gay. The mythologizing of the Second World War is still in progress, and still very much in the hands of its aging veterans.

But the German First World War narratives are not simple "war stories," untouched recollections of the past, any more than the speeches of the D-Day veterans. If accounts written shortly after an event are nonetheless shaped by intervening events, how much more is that the case with accounts written ten or more years after the event? In the case of the German *Kreigserlebnis*, that experience is altered not only by the passing of time, but by the nature of the inter-

---

[3]For a detailed analysis of these symbols, see my "Landscape and Symbol," 364–366.

[4]Jean Norton Cru, *Du témoinage*, 1930, (n.p.: Pauvert, 1967), 37.

vening events. If victory promotes smug certainty, military defeat, political revolution and economic and cultural chaos loose the devils of betrayal and bitterness. For the fundamentally nationalist German veterans, only one question was worth asking and answering: was the German state worthy of their suffering? The answer from most quarters, the left as well as the right, was a resounding "no." Beyond the war experience itself, the single most important factor in the shape of the German myth of the war was the almost universal discontent of the veterans with the nation they believed they had suffered and died for. The war narratives, especially the rightist ones, are acts of political and cultural rebellion against the Weimar Republic. Kurt Sontheimer goes so far as to say that the war narratives were created less from the war experience itself than from a hatred of Weimar.[5]

The injuries, real and imagined, suffered by the men of the war generation crystallized in their hatred of Weimar. Basing his thought on Freud's analysis of melancholia, Whalen has argued that those he calls "war victims" manifested two apparently contradictory forms of behavior: a tendency to withdrawal ending in suicide, and an equally strong impetus toward manic activity, which he equates with Jünger's "total mobilization."[6] Of the latter group many became involved with veterans' organizations and other political groups of paramilitary character. Some, overwhelmingly belonging to the middle class, wrote accounts of their war experience. The war generation may have been "lost" in Britain and France, but in Germany a significant proportion of that generation mobilized for action against the Weimar Republic.

The war narratives were a remarkably effective part of that mobilization. The narratives, along with published criticism and discussion of them, reached a surprisingly large audience. The popular military history series *Schlachten des Weltkriegs* (Battles of the World War), began publication in 1921 under the aegis of the Reichsarchiv and produced its thirty-sixth volume in 1930. By 1928 there were 40,000 to 50,000 copies of each volume in circulation.[7] Although few narratives were produced in the early twenties, the histories kept the experience of the war alive for a wide popular audience. When the combat narratives began to appear in the late twenties, a large audience was ready for them. No other author can compete with the sales figures for Remarque's *All Quiet* — one and a half million by the end of 1929, three million by mid-1930 — but many of the narratives reached a large readership. Beumelburg's quasi-history

[5]Kurt Sontheimer, *Antidemokratisches Denken in der Weimarer Republik* (Munich: Nyphenburg, 1962), 137.

[6]Whalen 189–191.

[7]Reinhard Brühl, *Militärgeschichte und Kriegspolitik: Zur Militärgeschichtsschreibung des preußisch-deutschen Generalstabes 1816–1945* (Berlin: Militärverlag der DDR, 1973), 278–279. A number of the volumes were written by Werner Beumelburg. Brühl provides a full list of titles and authors on 276–277.

Sperrfeuer reached a circulation of 120,000 by 1930. Thirty thousand copies of Schauwecker's *The Furnace* were in circulation in early 1930. Wehner's *Sieben vor Verdun* had reached 60,000 copies by 1935.[8] The figures for conservative stalwarts such as Beumelburg, Zöberlein and Wehner, who were National Socialists and in effect the "official" war writers, rose precipitously after 1933. *Gruppe Bosemüller* reached 250,000 by 1942, Wehner's *Verdun* 130,000 in 1940, and Zöberlein's *Der Glaube an Deutschland* an astonishing 470,000 copies by 1939.

All of these figures suggest an obsessive public interest in the war — an interest that was served even by the liberal narratives, as I have already remarked. That public interest was clearly centered in the middle class. Most of the narrative authors were from the middle class and their books, traditional in style, form and content, are obviously aimed at middle-class readers. Battered by inflation and depression, convinced that Germany was tumbling into chaos, many a traditional, angst-ridden bourgeois shunned paramilitary organizations as violent and lower-class, even while agreeing with the organization's political position. But while he might not join the Stahlhelm or the National Socialists, he would read the war narratives. Like the narrator's cultured mother in Gläser's *Class of 1902*, they "believed in the war as in a new writer."[9]

In the end, the cultural gloss of the conservative war narratives probably lulled the comfortable, conventional bourgeois in his armchair into acquiescence with the conservative interpretation of the war far more persuasively than the crude ravings of the *Völkische Beobachter* could have done. If the National Socialist view of the war was correct, did not everything else follow from that? The tragedy of modern Germany was that it did.

---

[8]Publication figures are difficult to establish. I have employed those enumerated by Gollbach in his notes, as they seem the most reliable.

[9]Ernst Gläser, *Jahrgang 1902* (Berlin: Kiepenheuer, 1929). Tr. by Willa and Edwin Muir as *Class of 1902* (New York: Viking, 1929), 173.

Works Consulted

Alverdez, Paul. *Reinhold oder die Verwandelten*. Munich: Müller, 1932. Tr. by Basil Creighton as *Changed Men*. London: Secker, 1933.

———. *Grimbarts Haus*. Konstanz: Südverlag, 1949.

———. *Die Pfeiferstube*. Munich: Ehrenwirth, 1962.

Amberger, Waltraud. *Männer, Krieger, Abenteuer: Der Entwurf des 'soldatischen Mannes' in Kriegsromanen über den Ersten und Zweiten Weltkrieg*. Frankfurter Beiträge zur neueren deutschen Literaturgeschichte 2. Frankfurt am Main: Fischer, 1984.

Anderson, Benedict. *Imagined Communities: Reflections on the Origin and Spread of Nationalism*. London: Verso, 1983.

Anz, Thomas and Joseph Vogl, eds. *Die Dichter und der Krieg: Deutsche Lyrik 1914–1918*. Munich: Hanser, 1982.

Armin, Albrecht. *Die Welt in Flammen*. Leipzig: Verlag "Die Welt in Flammen," 1914. Vol. 1 of *Illustrierte Kriegschronik*, number of volumes unknown, 1914–1918.

Ashworth, A. E. "The Sociology of Trench Warfare, 1914–1918." *British Journal of Sociology* 19 (1968): 407–423.

Ashworth, Tony. *Trench Warfare 1914–1918: The Live and Let Live System*. New York: Holmes and Meier, 1980.

Audoin-Rouzeau, Stéphane. *14–18: Les Combattants des tranchées*. Paris: Colin, 1986.

Baeumer, Max L. "Imperial Germany as Reflected in its Mass Festivals." In *Imperial Germany*. Volker Dürr, Kathy Harms and Peter Hays, eds., 62–74. Madison: U of Wisconsin P, 1985.

Bartels, Adolf. *Die deutsche Dichtung der Gegenwart*. Leipzig: Haessel, 1921.

Bartram, Theodor. *Der Frontsoldat: Ein deutscher Kultur- und Lebensideal*. Berlin: Verlag der Gegenseitigen Hilfe, 1934. (Speech, 1919).

Baumgarten, Otto. *Geistige und sittliche Wirkungen des Krieges in Deutschland*. Wirtschafts- und Sozialgeschichte des Weltkrieges. Deutsche Serie. (Carnegie Institute). Stuttgart: Deutsche Verlags-Anstalt, 1927.

Beck, Ranier, ed. *Otto Dix, 1891–1969*. Exhibition catalogue from Museum Villa Stuck, Munich, 23 August to 27 October, 1985.

Becker, Jean-Jacques. *1914: Comment les Français sont entrés dans la guerre*. Paris: Presses de la Fondation nationale des sciences politiques, 1977.

———. *The Great War and the French People*. Leamington Spa: Berg, 1985.

Beddow, Michael. *The Fiction of Humanity: Studies in the Bildungsroman from Wieland to Thomas Mann*. Cambridge: Cambridge UP, 1982.

Berghahn, Volker R. *Der Stahlhelm: Bund der Frontsoldaten*. Düsseldorf: Droste, 1966.

Bergmann, Karl. *Wie der Feldgraue spricht: Scherz und Ernst in der neusten Soldatensprache*. Giessen: Töpelmann, 1916.

Bergonzi, Bernard. *Heroes' Twilight: A Study of the Literature of the Great War*. 1965. London: Macmillan, 1980.

Beumelburg, Werner. *Die Gruppe Bosemüller. Der große Roman des Frontsoldaten*. Oldenburg i.O./Berlin: Stalling, 1930.

———. *Sperrfeuer um Deutschland*. Oldenburg i.O.: Stalling, 1929.

———. *Von 1914 bis 1939. Sinn und Erfüllung des Weltkrieges*. Leipzig: Reclam, 1940.

Binding, Rudolf G. *Dies war das Maß. Die gesammelten Kriegsdichtungen und Tagebücher*. Potsdam: Rutten, 1940.

———. *Aus dem Kriege*. Translated by Ian F. D. Morrow as *A Fatalist at War*. London: Unwin, 1929.

Blackbourn, David and Geoff Eley. *The Peculiarities of German History: Bourgeois Society and Politics in Nineteenth-Century Germany*. Oxford: Oxford UP, 1984.

Bohrer, Karl Heinz. *Die Ästhetik des Schreckens. Die pessimistische Romantik und Ernst Jüngers Frühwerk*. Munich: Hanser, 1978.

Bostock, J. Knight. *Some Well-known German War-Novels, 1914–1930*. Oxford: Blackwell, 1931.

Bracher, D., et al. *Deutscher Sonderweg — Mythos oder Realität?* Kolloquien des Instituts für Zeitgeschichte. Munich: Oldenbourg, 1982.

Bridgewater, Patrick. *The German Poets of the First World War*. London: Croom Helm, 1985.

Bröger, Karl. *Bunker 17*. Jena: n.p., 1929. Translated by Oakley Williams as *Pillbox 17*. London: Butterworth, 1930.

Brophy, John. Introduction to *The Fiery Way* by Hans Schauwecker. London: Dent, 1929. v.-vii.

Brown, Marshall. *The Shape of German Romanticism*. Ithaca: Cornell UP, 1979.

Bruford, W. H. *The German Tradition of Self-cultivation. "Bildung" from Humbolt to Thomas Mann*. Cambridge: Cambridge UP, 1975.

Brühl, Reinhard. *Militärgeschichte und Kriegspolitik: Zur Militärgeschichtsschreibung des preußisch-deutschen Generalstabes 1816–1945*. Berlin: Militärverlag der Deutschen Demokratischen Republik, 1973.

Bucher, Georg. *Westfront 1914–1918. Das Buch vom Frontkameraden*. Vienna-Leipzig: Konegen, 1930. Translated by Norman Gullick as *In the Line: 1914–1918*. London: Cape, 1932.

Bullevant, Keith. "The Conservative Revolution." In *The Weimar Dilemma: Intellectuals in the Weimar Republic.* Anthony Phelan, ed., 47–70. Manchester: Manchester UP, 1985.

Burke, Kenneth. *The Philosophy of Literary Form.* 1941. Berkeley: U California P, 1973.

Cadogan, Mary and Patricia Craig. *Women and Children First: The Fiction of Two World Wars.* London: Gollancz, 1978.

Carossa, Hans. *Rumänisches Tagebuch.* Leipzig: n.p., 1924. Translated by Agnes Neil Scott as *A Romanian Diary.* New York: Knopf, 1930.

Carrington, Charles. *Soldier from the Wars Returning.* London: Hutchinson, 1965.

Chickering, Roger. *We Men Who Feel Most German.* Boston: Allen and Unwin, 1984.

Christadler, Marieluise. *Kriegserziehung im Jugendbuch. Literarische Mobilmachung in Deutschland und Frankreich vor 1914.* Frankfurt am Main: Haag und Herchen, 1978.

Cobley, Evelyn. *Representing War: Form and Ideology in First World War Narratives.* Toronto: Toronto UP, 1993.

Conzelmann, Otto. *Der andere Dix: Sein Bild vom Menschen und vom Krieg.* Stuttgart: Klett, 1983.

Craig, Gordon. *The Germans.* New York: Putnam, 1982.

Crawford, Anthony R. *Posters in the G.C. Marshall Research Foundation.* Charlottesville: U of Virginia P, 1979.

Crawford, Fred D. *British Poets of the Great War.* Selingsgrove: Susquehanna UP, 1988.

Cru, Jean Norton. *Du témoinage.* 1930. Reprint, n.p.: Pauvert, 1967.

———. *Témoins.* Paris: Les Étincelles, 1929.

Cysarz, Herbert. *Zur Geistesgeschichte des Weltkriegs.* 1931. Bern: Lang, 1973.

Dahlin, Ebba. *French and German Public Opinion on Declared War Aims.* Stanford: Stanford UP, 1933.

Dahrendorf, Rolf. *Society and Democracy in Germany.* London: Weidenfeld and Nicholson, 1968.

Dehio, Ludwig. *Germany and World Politics in the Twentieth Century.* London: Chatto, 1959.

Denham, Scott D. *Visions of War: Ideologies and Images of War Before and After the Great War.* Bern: Lang, 1992.

Diehl, James M. *Paramilitary Politics in Weimar Germany.* Bloomington: U of Indiana P, 1982.

Digeon, Claude. *La Crise allemande de la pensée française, 1970-1914.* Paris: Presses universitaires de France, 1959.

Dreysse, Wilhelm. *Langemarck 1914*. Minden i.W.: Kohler, 1934?

Dundes, Alan. *Life is Like a Chicken Coop Ladder: A Portrait of German Culture through Folklore*. New York: Columbia UP, 1984.

Dupuy, T. N. *A Genius for War: The German Army and General Staff, 1807–1945*. London: Macdonald, 1977.

Durkheim, Émile. *L'Allemagne au-dessus de tout: la mentalité allemande et la guerre*. Paris: Colin, 1915.

Dwinger, Edwin Erich. *Die Armee hinter Stacheldraht*. Jena: Diederichs, 1929. Tr. by Ian F. D. Morrow as *Army behind Barbed Wire*. London: Unwin, 1930.

———. *Wir rufen Deutschland*. Jena: Diederichs, 1932.

———. *Zwischen Weiß und Rot*. Jena: Diederichs, 1930. Tr. by Marion Saunders as *Between White and Red*. New York: Scribner's, 1932.

Eberle, Matthias. *World War I and the Weimar Artists*. New Haven: Yale UP, 1985.

Eksteins, Modris. *The Limits of Reason: The German Democratic Press and the Collapse of Weimar Democracy*. Oxford: Oxford UP, 1975.

———. *Rites of Spring: The Great War and the Birth of the Modern Age*. New York: Anchor/Doubleday, 1989.

Esselborn-Krumbiegel, Helga. *Der 'Held' im Roman: Formen des deutschen Entwicklungsromans im frühen 20. Jahrhundert*. Impulse der Forschung 39. Darmstadt: Wissenschaftliche Buchgesellschaft, 1983.

Evera, Stephen Van. "The Cult of the Offensive and the Origins of the First World War." In *Military Strategy and the Origins of the First World War*. Steven E. Miller, ed. Princeton: Princeton UP, 1985.

Falk, Walter. *Der kollektive Traum vom Krieg*. Heidelberg: Winter, 1977.

Fichte, Johann Gottlieb. *Reden an die Deutsche Nation*. In *Die Deutschen Romantiker*. 2 vols. Gerhard Stenzel, ed. Salzburg: Bergland, n.d., 2:389–426.

Fischer, Fritz. *Bündnis der Eliten: Zur Kontinuität der Machtstrukturen in Deutschland 1871–1945*. Düsseldorf: Droste, 1979.

———. *Germany's Aims in the First World War*. London: Chatto, 1967.

———. *War of Illusions: German Politics from 1911–1914*. Tr. Marian Jackson. New York: Norton, 1975.

Fisher, Peter S. *Fantasy and Politics: Visions of the Future in the Weimar Republic*. Madison: U of Wisconsin P, 1991.

Flex, Walter. *Der Wanderer zwischen Beiden Welten. Ein Kriegserlebnis*. 1915. Reprint, Heusenstamm: Orion-Heimreiter, 1979.

Flitner, Wilhelm. *Der Krieg und die Jugend*. Wirtschafts-und Sozialgeschichte des Weltkrieges, Deutsche Serie. Stuttgart: Deutsche Verlags-Anstalt, 1927.

Ford, Ford Madox. *Parade's End*. 1924–1928. Reprint, New York: Knopf, 1966.

Frank, Leonhard. *Der Mensch ist Gut*. 1918. Reprint, Munich: Nymphenburg, 1953.

Francke, Kuno. *German After-war Problems*. Cambridge: Harvard UP, 1927.

Fraser, Lindley. *Germany between Two Wars: A Study of Propaganda and War-Guilt*. Oxford: Oxford UP, 1944.

Fried, Hans Ernest. *The Guilt of the German Army*. New York: Macmillan, 1942.

Friedel, V. H. *Pédagogie de guerre allemande*. Paris: Fischbacher, 1918.

Frye, Northrop. *Anatomy of Criticism*. Princeton: Princeton UP, 1957.

Fussell, Paul. *The Great War and Modern Memory*. New York: Oxford UP, 1975.

———. *Wartime*. New York: Oxford UP, 1989.

Gay, Peter. *Freud, Jews and other Germans*. Oxford: Oxford UP, 1978.

———. *Weimar Culture*. London: Secker, 1968.

Geibel, Emanuel. *Werke*. 2 vols. Wolfgang Stammler, ed. Leipzig: Bibliographisches Institut, 1918.

Genno, Charles N. and Heinz Wetzel, eds. *The First World War in German Narrative Prose*. Toronto: U of Toronto P, 1980.

Gerhard, Melitta. *Der deutsche Entwicklungsroman bis zu Goethes* Wilhelm Meister. Halle/Saale: Niemeyer, 1926.

Gerschenkron, Alexander. *Economic Backwardness in Historical Perspective*. Cambridge: Belknap, 1962.

Gilbert, Sandra M. and Susan Gubar. "Soldier's Heart: Literary Men, Literary Women, and the Great War." In vol. 2 of *No Man's Land: The Place of the Woman Writer in the Twentieth Century*. New Haven: Yale UP, 1989.

Gläser, Ernst. *Jahrgang 1902*. Berlin: Kiepenheuer, 1929. Tr. by Willa and Edwin Muir as *Class of 1902*. New York: Viking, 1929.

Glaser, Hermann. *The Cultural Roots of National Socialism*. Tr. Ernest A. Manze. Austin: U of Texas P, 1978.

———. *Literatur des 20. Jahrhunderts in Motiven*. 2 vols. Munich: Beck, 1979.

Goerlitz, Walter. *History of the German General Staff, 1657–1945*. Tr. Brian Battershaw. Westport: Greenwood, 1975.

Gohlman, Susan Ashley. *Starting Over: The Task of the Protagonist in the Contemporary Bildungsroman*. New York: Garland, 1990.

Gollbach, Michael. *Die Wiederkehr des Weltkrieges in der Literatur*. Kronberg/Taunus: Scriptor, 1978.

Goltz, Joachim von der. *Der Baum von Cléry*. Berlin: Gutenberg, 1934.

Goote, Thor. *Wir fahren den Tod*. Gütersloh: Bertelsmann, 1930.

Grand-Carteret, John. *La Kultur et ses hauts faits*. Paris: Chapelot, 1916.

Graves, Robert. *Goodbye to All That*. New York: Blue Ribbon, 1930.

Grebing, Helga, ed. *Der "deutsche Sonderweg" in Europa 1806–1945: Eine Kritik.* Stuttgart: Kohlhammer, 1986.

Hagbolt, Peter. "Ethical and Social Problems in the German War Novel." *Journal of English and Germanic Philology* 32 (1933): 21–32.

Hafkesbrink, Hanna. *Unknown Germany: An Inner Chronicle of the First World War Based on Letters and Diaries.* New Haven: Yale UP, 1948.

Harth, D., D. Schubert and R. M. Schmidt, eds. *Pazifismus zwischen den Weltkriegen.* Heidelberg: Universitätsbibliothek, 1985.

Hartmann, Nicolai. *Die Philosophie des deutschen Idealismus.* 1923. Reprint, Berlin: de Gruyter, 1960.

Heck, Alfons. Interview by author. Grand Forks, ND. 9 November 1989.

Hein, Alfred. *Das kleine Buch vom großen Krieg.* Langensalza: Beltz, 1937.

———. *Eine Kompagnie Soldaten in der Hölle von Verdun.* Minden i.W.: Kohler, 1930. Tr. by F. H. Lyon as *In the Hell of Verdun.* London: Cassell, 1930.

Herf, Jeffrey. *Reactionary Modernism: Technology, Culture and Politics in Weimar and the Third Reich.* Cambridge: Cambridge UP, 1984.

Hermand, Jost. *Der alte Traum vom neuen Reich: Völkische Utopien und Nationalsozialismus.* Frankfurt am Main: Athenäum, 1988.

Hermand, Jost, and Frank Trommler. *Die Kultur der Weimarer Republik.* Munich: Nymphenburg, 1978.

Hermann, Carl Hans. *Deutsche Militärgeschichte.* Frankfurt am Main: Bernard, 1966.

Hermann, Gerhard. *Der Weltkriegsroman.* Hamburg: n.p., 1931.

Higonnet, Margaret R., ed. *Behind the Lines: Gender and the Two World Wars.* New Haven: Yale UP, 1987.

Hitler, Adolf. Forward to *Der Glaube an Deutschland* by Hans Zöberlein. Munich: Nachfolger, 1931.

Hobsbawm, Eric and Terence Ranger, eds. *The Invention of Tradition.* Cambridge: Cambridge UP, 1983.

Hobsbawm, Eric. *Nations and Nationalism since 1780.* Cambridge: Cambridge UP, 1990.

Hof, Walter. *Der Weg zum heroischen Idealismus.* Bebenhausen: Rotsch, 1974.

Hoffmann, Helmut. *Mensch und Volk im Kriegserlebnis.* Germanische Studien 189, 1–81. Berlin: Ebering, 1937.

Hoffmann, Richard. *Frontsoldaten.* Hamburg: Fackelreiter, 1928.

Holborn, Hajo. *Germany and Europe.* Garden City: Doubleday, 1970.

Holl, Karl. *Pazifismus in Deutschland.* Frankfurt am Main: Suhrkamp, 1988.

Holt, Tonie and Valmai. *Germany Awake!* London: Longman, 1986.

Howard, Michael. "Men against Fire: Expectations of War in 1914." In *Military Strategy and the Origins of the First World War*, Steven E. Miller, ed. Princeton: Princeton UP, 1985.

Hughes, Glyn Tegai. *Romantic German Literature*. New York: Holmes, 1979.

Hüppauf, Bernd, ed. *Ansichten vom Krieg*. Königstein/Taunus.: Forum Academicum, 1984.

———. "Langemarck, Verdun and the Myth of a 'New Man' in Germany after the First World War." *War and Society* 6 (Sept 1988): 70–103.

———. "Räume der Destruktion und Konstruktion von Raum: Landschaft, Sehen, Raum und der Erste Weltkrieg," *Krieg und Literatur* 3: 5/6 (1991): 105–123.

Hynes, Samuel. *A War Imagined: The First World War and English Culture*. New York: Athenaum, 1991.

Iggers, Georg C. *The German Conception of History*. Middletown: Wesleyan UP, 1968.

Ille, Gerhard and Günther Köhler. *Der Wandervogel: Es begann in Steglitz*. Berlin: Stapp, 1987.

Johannsen, Ernst. *Vier von der Infanterie: Ihre letzten Tage an der Westfront 1918*. Hamburg: Fackelreiter, 1929. Tr. by A.W. Wheen as *Four Infantrymen on the Western Front, 1918*. London: Methuen, 1930.

Jones, Nigel H. *Hitler's Heralds: The Story of the Freikorps, 1918-1923*. London: Murray, 1987.

Jünger, Ernst. *In Stahlgewittern: Aus dem Tagebuch eines Stoßtruppführers*. Berlin: Mittler, 1922. Tr. by Basil Creighton as *The Storm of Steel*. New York: Fertig, 1929.

———. *Das Wäldchen 125*. Berlin: Mittler, 1929. Tr. by Basil Creighton as *Copse 125*. London: Chatto, 1930.

———. *Werke*. 10 vols. Stuttgart: Klett, 1960–1965.

Jungnickel, Max. *Brennende Sense*. Bad Pyrmont: Schelle, 1928.

Kaes, Anton, ed. *Weimarer Republik: Manifeste und Dokumente zur deutscher Literatur 1918–1933*. Stuttgart: Metzler, 1983.

Kalkschmidt, Till. "Kameradschaft und Führertum der Front." *Dichtung und Volkstum* 39 (1938): 180–192.

Keegan, John. *The Face of Battle*. New York: Viking, 1976.

———. *A History of Warfare*. New York: Knopf, 1993.

———. *The Mask of Command*. New York: Penguin, 1987.

Keller, Ernst. *Nationalismus und Literatur: Langemarck, Weimar, Stalingrad*. Bern: Francke, 1970.

Ketelsen, Uwe-Karsten. *Völkisch-nationale und nationalsozialistische Literatur in Deutschland 1890–1945*. Stuttgart: Metzler, 1976.

Kitchen, Martin. *The German Officer Corps, 1890–1914*. Oxford: Clarendon, 1968.

Klein, Holgar, ed. *The First World War in Fiction.* London: Macmillan, 1978.

———. "Weltkriegsroman und Germanistik 1933–1938." *Journal of English and Germanic Philology* 4 (1985): 467–484.

Kniesche, Thomas W. and Stephen Brockmann, eds. *Dancing on the Volcano: Essays on the Culture of the Weimar Republic.* Columbia: Camden House, 1994.

Koester, Eckart. *Literatur und Weltkriegsideologie.* Kronberg: Scriptor, 1977.

Kohn, Hans. *The Mind of Germany.* London: Macmillan, 1961.

Kontje, Todd. *Private Lives in the Public Sphere: The German Bildungsroman as Metafiction.* University Park: Pennsylvania State UP, 1992.

Köppen, Edlef. *Heeresbericht.* Berlin-Grunewald: Horen, 1930. Tr. as *Higher Command,* no translator listed. London: Faber, 1931.

Kracauer, Siegfried. *From Caligari to Hitler.* Princeton: Princeton UP, 1947.

Der Krieg: Illustrierte Chronik des Krieges, 1914. Stuttgart: Franckh'sche Verlagshandlung, 1914.

Krieger, Leonard. *The German Idea of Freedom.* Boston: Beacon, 1957.

Kröner, Richard. *Landser: Im Westen viel Neues. Das Buch des Frontsoldaten in vier Jahren Krieg.* Chemnitz: Pickenhahn, 1931.

Kronprinz Wilhelm. *Meine Erinnerungen aus Deutschlands Heldenkampf.* Berlin: Mittler, 1923. Tr. as *My War Experiences,* no translator. New York: McBride, 1923.

Laffin, John. *World War I in Postcards.* Gloucester: Sutton, 1988.

Lamprecht, Helmut, ed. *Deutschland, Deutschland: Politische Gedichte.* Bremen: Schünemann, 1969.

Laqueur, Walter. *Weimar: A Cultural History, 1918–1933.* New York: Putnam, 1974.

———. *Young Germany: A History of the German Youth Movement.* London: Routledge, 1962.

Latzko, Andreas. *Menschen im Krieg.* Zurich: Rascher, 1918. Tr. by Adele N. Seltzer as *Men in Battle.* London: Cassell, 1918.

Leach, Barry. *The German General Staff.* New York: Ballantine, 1973.

Lebovics, Herman. *Social Conservatism and the Middle Classes in Germany, 1914–1933.* Princeton: Princeton UP, 1969.

Leed, Eric J. *No Man's Land: Combat and Identity in World War I.* Cambridge: Cambridge UP, 1979.

Linder, Ann P. "Landscape and Symbol in the British and German Literature of World War I." *Comparative Literature Studies* 31:4 (1994): 351-369.

———. Review of *Representing War: Form and Ideology in First World War Narratives* by Evelyn Cobley. *SubStance* 78 (1995): 126-130.

Loewy, Ernst. *Literatur unterm Hakenkreuz: Das Dritte Reich und seine Dichtung.* Frankfurt am Main: Fischer, 1983.

Lowie, Robert H. *The German People: A Social Portrait to 1914*. New York: Farrar, 1945.

Lutz, Günther. "Europas Kreigserlebnis: Ein Überblick über das außerdeutsche Kriegsschriftum." *Dichtung und Volkstum* 39 (1938): 133–168.

———. *Das Gemeinschaftserlebnis in der Kriegsliteratur*. Greifswald: Adler, 1936.

McMillan, James F. *Dreyfus to De Gaulle*. London: Arnold, 1985.

Mahrholz, Werner. *Deutsche Literatur der Gegenwart*. Berlin: Sieben-Stäke, 1931.

Mann, Thomas. *Betrachtungen eines Unpolitischen*. Berlin: Fischer, 1918.

———. *Briefe I*. Frankfurt am Main: Fischer, 1961.

———. "Gedanken im Kriege." *Friedrich und die große Koalition*. Berlin: Fischer, 1916. Tr. H. T. Lowe-Porter, *Three Essays*. New York: Knopf, 1929.

———. *Von Deutscher Republik*. Berlin: Fischer, 1923.

Marchandiau, Jean-Noël. *L'Illustration 1843–1944: Vie et mort d'un journal*. Toulouse: Privat, 1987.

Marsland, Elizabeth A. *The Nation's Cause: French, English and German Poetry of the First World War*. London: Routledge, 1991.

Mausser, Otto. *Deutsche Soldatensprache: Ihr Aufbau und ihre Probleme*. Strassburg: Trübner, 1917.

Merker, Paul and Wolfgang Stammler, eds. 5 vols. *Reallexikon der Deutschen Literaturgeschichte*. Berlin: de Gruyter, 1925- 1926.

Merkl, Peter H. *The Making of a Stormtrooper*. Princeton: Princeton UP, 1980.

Meyer, Jacques. *La Vie quotidienne des soldats pendant la Grande Guerre*. Paris: Hachette, 1966.

Monaco, Paul. *Cinema and Society*. New York: Elsevier, 1976.

Moretti, Franco. *The Way of the World: The Bildungsroman in European Culture*. London: Verso, 1987.

Mosse, George L. *The Crisis of German Ideology*. New York: Grosset, 1964.

———. *Fallen Soldiers: Reshaping the Memory of the World Wars*. Oxford: Oxford UP, 1990.

———. *Masses and Man*. New York: Fertig, 1980.

———. *The Nationalization of the Masses*. New York: New American Library, 1975.

Müller, Hans-Harald. *Der Krieg und die Schriftsteller: Der Kriegsroman der Weimarer Republik*. Stuttgart: Metzler, 1986.

Pachter, Henry M. *Modern Germany*. Boulder: Westview, 1978.

Pankau, Johannes G. "History as Myth: Historical Processes in Early German Film." In *Fact and Fiction: German History and Literature, 1848–1924*, Gisela Brude-Firnau and Karin J. MacHardy, eds. Tübingen: Francke, 1990.

Pascal, Roy. *The German Novel*. Manchester: Manchester UP, 1956.

Paulsen, Friederich. *German Education: Past and Present*. Tr. T. Lorenz. London: Unwin, 1908.

Petzold, Joachim. *Wegbereiter des deutschen Faschismus: Die Jungkonservativen in der Weimarer Republik*. Cologne: Pahl-Rugenstein, 1978.

Peukert, Detlev. *Der Weimarer Republik*. Frankfurt am Main: Suhrkamp, 1987.

Pfeiler, William K. *War and the German Mind: The Testimony of Men of Fiction who Fought at the Front*. New York: Columbia UP, 1941.

Phelan, Anthony. *The Weimar Dilemma: Intellectuals in the Weimar Republic*. Manchester: Manchester UP, 1985.

Picht, Werner. *Der Frontsoldat*. Berlin: Herbig, 1937.

———. *Das Schicksal der Volksbildung in Deutschland*. Braunschweig: Westermann, 1950.

Pingaud, Albert. *La Guerre vue par les combattants allemands*. Paris: Perrin, 1918.

Pinson, Koppel S. *Modern Germany*. New York: Macmillan, 1954.

Plessner, Helmuth. *Die verspätete Nation*. Stuttgart: Kohlhammer, 1959.

Plievier, Theodor. *Des Kaisers Kulis*. 1929. Reprint, Munich: DTV, 1984.

Pongs, Hermann. "Krieg als Volkschicksal im deutschen Schriftum." *Dichtung und Volkstum* 35 (1934): 40–86; 182–219.

———. "Neue Kriegs-und Nachkriegsbücher." *Dichtung und Volkstum* 37 (1936): 219–235.

———. "Weltkrieg und Dichtung." *Dichtung und Volkstum* 39 (1938): 193–212.

Prost, Antoine. *Les Anciens combattants et la société française 1914–1939*. 3 vols. Paris: Presses de la Fondation nationale des sciences politiques, 1977.

Prümm, Karl. *Die Literatur des soldatischen Nationalismus der 20er Jahre*. Kronberg: Scriptor, 1974.

———. "Tendenzen des deutschen Kriegsromans nach 1918." In *Kriegserlebnis*, Klaus Vondung, ed., 215-218. Göttingen: Vandenhoeck, 1980.

Raulet, Gérard, ed. *Weimar ou l'explosion de la modernité*. Paris: Anthropos, 1984.

Remarque, Erich Maria. *Im Westen nichts Neues*. Berlin: Propyläen, 1929. Tr. by A.W. Wheen as *All Quiet on the Western Front*. London: Putnam, 1929.

———. *Der Weg Zurück*. Berlin: Propyläen, 1931. Tr. by A.W. Wheen as *The Road Back*. Boston: Little, 1931.

Renn, Ludwig. *Krieg*. Frankfurt: Frankfurter Societäts-Druckerei, 1929. Tr. by Edwin and Willa Muir as *War*. London: Secker, 1929.

———. *Nachkrieg*. Berlin: Agie, 1930. Tr. by Edwin and Willa Muir as *After War*. London: Secker, 1931.

————. *Krieg* und *Nachkrieg*. Berlin: Aufbau, 1985. (Ed. cited).

Rickards, Maurice. *Posters of the First World War*. New York: Walker, 1968.

Riegel, Léon. *Guerre et littérature*. Nancy: Klincksieck, 1978.

Riefenstahl, Leni. *Der Triumph des Willens*. Film. 1934.

Rieuneau, Maurice. *Guerre et révolution dans le roman français de 1919–1939*. Nancy: Klincksieck, 1974.

Ritchie, J. M. *German Literature under National Socialism*. London: Helm, 1983.

————. "Johst's 'Schlageter' and the End of the Weimar Republic." In *Weimar Germany: Writers and Politics*. Alan Bance, ed., 153–167. Edinburgh: Scottish Academic Press, 1982.

Ritter, Gerhard. *The Sword and the Scepter*. Vol. 3. Coral Gables: U of Miami P, 1972.

Rohkrämer, Thomas. *Der Militarismus der "kleinen Leute": Die Kriegervereine im Deutschen Kaiserreich, 1871–1914*. Munich: Oldenbourg, 1990.

Rose, William and J. Isaacs, eds. *Contemporary Movements in European Literature*. London: Routledge, 1928.

Rose, William. *Men, Myths, and Movements in German Literature*. London: Unwin, 1931.

Sassoon, Siegfried. *Complete Memoirs of George Sherston*. London: Faber, 1937.

Saunders, Thomas J. "History in the Making: Weimar Cinema and National Identity." In *Framing the Past: The Historiography of German Cinema and Television*, Bruce A. Murray and Christopher J. Wickham, eds. Carbondale: Southern Illinois UP, 1992.

Schaffner, Randolph. *The Apprenticeship Novel*. New York: Lang, 1984.

Scharrer, Adam. *Vaterlandslose Gesellen*. 1930. Reprinted in *Gesammelte Werke*. Berlin: Aufbau-Verlag, 1974.

Schauwecker, Franz. *Aufbruch der Nation*. Berlin: Frundsberg, 1930. Tr. by R. T. Clark as *The Furnace*. London: Methuen, 1930.

————. *Der feurige Weg*. 1926. Reprint, Berlin: Frundsberg, 1929. Tr. by Thonald Holland as *The Fiery Way*. London: Dent, 1929.

Schenda, Rudolf. *Die Lesestoffe der kleinen Leute: Studien zur populären Literatur im 19. und 20. Jahrhundert*. Munich: Beck, 1976.

Schlawe, Fritz. *Literarische Zeitschriften, 1910–1933*. Stuttgart: Metzler, 1962.

Schlump: Geschichten und Abenteuer aus dem Leben des Unbekannten Musketiers. Munich: Wolf, 1928. Tr. by Maurice Samuel as *Schlump: The Story of a German Soldier. Told by Himself*. New York: Harcourt, 1929.

Schröter, Klaus. *Literatur und Zeitgeschichte: Fünf Aufsätze zur deutschen Literatur im 20. Jahrhundert*. Mainz: Hase und Koehler, 1970.

————. "Chauvinism and its Tradition: German Writers and the Outbreak of the First World War." *Germanic Review* 43 (March 1968): 120–135. (A shorter English version of the previous entry.)

Selbmann, Rolf. *Der deutsche Bildungsroman.* Stuttgart: Metzler, 1984.

Shapiro, Theda. *Painters and Politics: The European Avant-Garde and Society, 1900–1925.* New York: Elsevier, 1976.

Sharp, Alan. *The Versailles Settlement: Peacemaking in Paris, 1919.* New York: St. Martin's, 1991.

Snyder, Louis L. *The Roots of German Nationalism.* Bloomington: Indiana UP, 1978.

Soergel, Albert. *Dichter aus deutschem Volkstum.* Leipzig: Voigtländers, 1935.

Soergel, Albert and Curt Hohhoff. *Dichtung und Dichter der Zeit.* 2 vols. Düsseldorf: Bagel, 1964.

Sokel, Walter H. *The Writer in Extremis: Expressionism in Twentieth-Century German Literature.* Stanford: Stanford UP, 1959.

Sombart, Werner. *Händler und Helden: Patriotische Besinnungen.* Munich: Duncker, 1915.

Sontheimer, Kurt. *Antidemokratisches Denken in der Weimarer Republik.* Munich: Nymphenburg, 1962.

————. "Der Tatkreis." *Vierteljahrshefte für Zeitgeschichte* 7:3 (1959): 229–260.

Spengler, Oswald. *Preußentum und Sozialismus.* Munich: Beck, 1920.

Stackelberg, Roderick. *Idealism Debased: From Völkisch Ideology to National Socialism.* Kent, OH: Kent State UP, 1981.

Stern, Fritz. *The Failure of Illiberalism: Essays on the Political Culture of Modern Germany.* New York: Knopf, 1972.

————. *The Politics of Cultural Despair: A Study in the Rise of the Germanic Ideology.* Berkeley: U of California P, 1961.

Stern, J. P. *The Heart of Europe: Essays on Literature and Ideology.* Oxford: Blackwell, 1992.

————. *Hitler: The Führer and the People.* Berkeley: U of California P, 1975.

Stirk, S. D. *The Prussian Spirit, 1914–1940.* Port Washington, N.Y.: Kennikat, 1969.

Stith Thompson. *Motif-Index of Folk Literature.* 5 vols. Bloomington: Indiana UP, 1975.

Stromberg, Roland N. *Redemption by War: The Intellectuals and 1914.* Lawrence: Regents Press of Kansas, 1982.

Sulzbach, Herbert. *Zwei lebende Mauern: 50 Monate Westfront.* Berlin: Bernard und Graefe, 1935. Tr. by Richard Thonger as *With the German Guns.* Hamden: Archeon, 1981.

Swales, Martin. "In Defence of Weimar: Thomas Mann and the Politics of Republicanism." In *Weimar Germany*. Alan Bance, ed., 1–13. Edinburgh: Scottish Academic Press, 1982.

———. *The German Bildungsroman from Wieland to Hesse*. Princeton: Princeton UP, 1978.

Taylor, A. J. P. *War by Timetable*. London: McDonald, 1969.

Taylor, Richard. *Film Propaganda: Soviet Russia and Nazi Germany*. London: Croom Helm, 1979.

Taylor, Ronald. *Literature and Society in Germany, 1918–1945*. New York: Barnes, 1980.

Taylor, Tom. "Images of Youth and the Family in Wilhelmine Germany: Toward a Reconsideration of the German *Sonderweg*." *German Studies Review* (winter 1992): 55–73.

Theweleit, Klaus. *Männerphantasien*. 2 vols. Frankfurt am Main: Roter Stern, 1978.

Tombs, Robert, ed. *Nationhood and Nationalism in France: From Boulangism to the Great War, 1889–1918*. London: Harper Collins, 1991.

Troeltsch, Ernst. *Deutscher Geist und Westeuropa*. Tübingen: Mohr, 1925. Reprint, Aalen: Scientia, 1966.

Unruh, Fritz von. *Opfergang*. Berlin: Eriss, 1919.

Veblen, Thorstein. *Imperial Germany and the Industrial Revolution*. 1915. Reprint, Ann Arbor: U of Michigan P, 1966.

Viereck, Peter Robert. *Metapolitics*. New York: Knopf, 1941.

Vincent, Paul. *Cartes postales d'un soldat de 1914–1918*. Paris: Gisserot, 1988.

Volkmann, Ernst. *Deutsche Dichtung im Weltkrieg, 1914–1918*. Leipzig: Reclam, 1934.

Vondung, Klaus, ed. *Kriegserlebnis*. Göttingen: Vandenhoeck, 1980.

Vring, Georg von der. *Der Goldhelm*. Oldenburg i.O.: Stalling, 1938.

———. *Soldat Suhren*. Berlin: Spaeth, 1928. Tr. by Fred Hall as *Private Suhren*. London: Methuen, 1929.

Wall, Richard, and Jay Winter, eds. *The Upheaval of War: Family, Work and Welfare in Europe, 1914–1918*. Cambridge: Cambridge UP, 1988.

Wehner, Josef Magnus. *Sieben vor Verdun*. Munich: Langen/Muller, 1930. Reprint, Hamburg: Deutsche Hausbücherei, 1932.

Weigel, Hans, Walter Lukan and Max D. Peyfuss: *Jeder Schuß ein Russ, jeder Stoß ein Franzos*. Wien: Brandstätter, 1983.

Whalen, Robert Weldon. *Bitter Wounds: German Victims of the Great War, 1914–1939*. Ithaca: Cornell UP, 1984.

Wheeler-Bennett, John W. *The Nemesis of Power: The German Army in Politics, 1918–1945*. London: Macmillan, 1964.

Wiechert, Ernst. *Jedermann: Geschichte eines Namenlosen.* Munich: n.p., 1931.

———. *Sämtliche Werke.* Vol. 3. Vienna: Desch, 1957.

Willett, John. *The New Sobriety, 1917–1933.* London: Thames, 1978.

———. *The Weimar Years: A Culture Cut Short.* London: Thames, 1984.

Williams, C. E. *Writers and Politics in Modern Germany.* London: Hodder, 1977.

Williams, John. *The Other Battleground: The Home Fronts.* Chicago: Regnery, 1972.

Winter, J. M. *The Experience of World War I.* New York: Oxford UP, 1989.

Witkop, Philipp, ed. *Kriegsbriefe gefallener Studenten.* 1916. Reprint, Munich: Muller, 1928. Tr. by A. F. Wedd as *German Students' War Letters.* London: Methuen, 1929.

Wohl, Robert. *The Generation of 1914.* Cambridge: Harvard UP, 1979.

Zöberlein, Hans. *Der Glaube an Deutschland.* Munich: Nachfolger, 1931.

Zweig, Arnold. *Einsetzung eines Königs.* Amsterdam: Querido, 1937. Tr. by Eric Sutton as *The Crowning of a King.* New York: Viking, 1938.

———. *Erziehung vor Verdun.* Amsterdam: Querido, 1935. Tr. by Eric Sutton as *Education before Verdun.* New York: Viking, 1936.

———. *Junge Frau von 1914.* Berlin: Kiepenheuer, 1931. Tr. by Eric Sutton as *Young Woman of 1914.* New York: Viking, 1932.

———. *Der Streit um den Sergeanten Grischa.* Potsdam: Kiepenheuer, 1928. Tr. by Eric Sutton as *The Case of Sergeant Grischa.* New York: Viking, 1928.

Index

Alverdez, Paul
  *Reinhold oder die Verwandelten
    (Changed Men)* 101–102
Arndt, Ernst Moritz 32
artists, First World War 128, 148, 157
  See also images, visual
Aufbruch der Nation (The Furnace) see
  Schauwecker, Franz, works by
Aus dem Kriege See Binding, Rudolf

Bartels, Adolf 159–160, 162
Bartram, Theodor 171
Baumgarten, Otto 100, 110
Der Baum von Cléry See Goltz, Joachim
  von der
Beumelburg, Werner 171
  Works by:
  Gruppe Bosemüller (Group Bosemüller)
    54, 57, 60, 63, 76, 77, 82, 98, 103,
    104, 108, 143, 146–147, 149, 176
  Sperrfeuer um Deutschland 183–184
  Von 1914 bis 1939 168
Bildung 36, 95, 96, 101, 131, 172 See also
  war experience
  as educational ideal 36
  experience in 45–47, 50
Bildungsroman 50, 119–120, 131
  perceived as German form 120–122
  and war narratives 119–127
Binding, Rudolf 171
  Aus dem Kriege (A Fatalist at War) 68–
    69
Bröger, Karl
  Works by:
  "Bekenntnis eines Arbeiters" 13
  Bunker 17 (Pillbox 17) 135
  "Die Gärten des Todes" 139
Brooke, Rupert 101
Bruck, Möller van den 24
Bucher, Georg 49

Westfront 1914–1918 (In the Line) 49,
  69, 73–74, 93–94, 97, 102, 111,
  130, 143, 166, 182

Carossa, Hans 130
  *Rumänisches Tagebuch (Rumanian Di-
    ary)* 130, 143
Carrington, Charles
  Soldier from the Wars Returning 165
cinema, German 161
communism 172 See also marxism
comradeship 74–85, 168, 178
  as community 76–77, 78–79, 80, 83–
    84, 97, 108, 147, 175–176
  definition of 74–77
  influence of 53, 74–75, 81–82, 168–
    169
  the leader and 82–85
  loss of 95–96
  as male experience 75, 80–81
  as social model 77–78, 84–85, 108–
    109, 110–112, 166–167, 168, 172–
    174
  in the Wandervogel 42–43, 77–78

Dante
  Inferno 129, 141–142
Dehmel, Richard 13
Doktor Faustus See Mann, Thomas,
  works by
Dolchstoßlegende (stab-in-the-back legend)
  29, 60, 151, 155
  and undefeated army 71–74, 151,
    153, 177
Dreysse, Wilhelm
  Langemarck 1914 99, 174
Dürer, Albrecht 144, 177, 181
Dwinger, Edwin Erich 123, 171

Ebert, Friederich 151
education, British 37, 39
education, French 39
education, German 35–40

authoritarianism of 38–39
and bourgeoisie 35
militarism of 38–40, 42
   in youth literature 39–40
modernization of 36–37
and nationalism 30, 35–36, 37, 42–43
public 35–36
Erziehung vor Verdun See Zweig, Arnold,
   Works by
Etappenschwein (headquarters pig) 55–57,
   83–84, 111, 152 See also trench warfare, alienation from rear in
expressionism 86–91, 159, 160
and pacifism 86–87, 90
and war narratives 87–90, 144, 167–
   168

Falkenhayn, Erich von 149
Feuer und Blut (Fire and Blood) See
   Jünger, Ernst, works by
Der feurige Weg (The fiery Way) See
   Schauwecker, Franz, works by
Fichte, Johann Gottlieb 37, 85, 158
   Reden an die deutsche Nation
      (Addresses to the German Nation)
      28–29, 109
Flex, Walter
   Works by:
   "Deutsche Schicksalstunde" 13
   Der Wanderer zwischen beiden Welten
      (The Wanderer between Two
      Worlds) 42, 163
folklore 50, 130
   journey to otherworld 50–51, 119,
      130
Ford, Ford Madox 63
Frank, Leonhard
   Der Mensch ist Gut (Man is Good)
      88–90, 167
Frederick the Great 174, 176, 177
Freikorps (Free Corps) 78, 155
Frontgeist (front spirit) 108, 111, 112
Frontgemeinschaft (front community) See
   Frontgeist; comradeship as community
Frontschwein (front pig) 55, 56–57, 68,
   83, 133, 174
Frontsoldaten See Hoffmann, Richard

"Gedanken im Kriege" See Mann, Tho-
   mas, Works by
Geibel, Emanuel 9–10
General Staff, German 9
generation of 1914 19–21, 183
   centrality of war experience for 14–16,
      174
   members of 19–20
   patriotism of 20–21
   and revolt 41, 49
Germany, history 13–14, 36–37
   November Revolution (1918) 151,
      157, 172
   Second Empire (Imperial Germany)
      3, 30, 31–32, 35, 37
   Thirty Years' War 42, 65
   War of 1870 (Franco-Prussian War)
      39–40, 42
   Wars of Liberation 27–28, 29, 32, 36,
      39–40, 42, 74, 75
Gläser, Ernst 6–7
   Jahrgang 1902 (Class of 1902) 7–11,
      14–15, 23, 38–39
Der Glaube an Deutschland See Zöberlein,
   Hans
Goethe, Johann Wolfgang von 129
   Faust 129, 141, 142–143
Der Goldhelm See Vring, Georg von der,
   Works by
Goltz, Joachim von der
   Der Baum von Cléry (The Tree of
      Cléry) 54, 58, 68, 69, 70, 82, 104–
      106, 129
Goote, Thor
   Wir fahren den Tod (We Drive Death)
      51–52, 82–83, 137–138
Gruppe Bosemüller See Beumelburg,
   Werner, Works by

Heck, Alfons 178
Hein, Alfred
   Works by:
   Der kleine Buch vom großen Krieg (The
      little Book about the Great War)
      84–85, 112, 174–178
   Eine Kompagnie Soldaten in der Hölle
      von Verdun (In the Hell of Verdun)
      56–57, 82, 111–112, 138, 140,
      141–142, 146

Herder, Johann Gottfried 27
Heeresbericht See Köppen, Edlef
Hindenburg, Paul von 71, 73, 151–153
Hitler, Adolf 37, 40, 47, 84–85, 111, 167
  Mein Kampf 174
  use of war experience 84–85, 111,
    173–174
Hitlerjungend (Hitler Youth) 178
Hoffmann, Richard
  Frontsoldaten (Frontsoldiers) 62, 94,
    102

idealism, German 5–6, 10, 23–27, 101
  See also *Kultur*; organicism; national-
    ism; spirituality
  anti-materialism of 26
  influence of 23–24, 101
  irrationalism of 23–24, 75–80
images, visual
  in First World War 128–129
  posters 177

Jahrgang 1902 (Class of 1902) See Gläser,
  Ernst
Jedermann See Wiechert, Ernst
Johannsen, Ernst
  *Vier von der Infanterie (Four Infantry-
    men on the Western Front)* 76, 79–
    81
Johst, Hans 162
Jünger, Ernst 2, 139–140, 163, 171, 178,
  183
  Works by:
  Feuer und Blut (Fire and Blood) 163
  "Der Krieg als inneres Erlebnis" 47–
    48, 101, 143, 163
  In Stahlgewittern (Storm of Steel) 16,
    130, 136–137, 163
  Das Wäldchen 125 (Copse 125) 99,
    106–107, 138, 139–140, 163
Jungnickel, Max
  Brennende Sense (Burning Scythe)
    131, 136, 143–145, 149

Des Kaisers Kulis See Plievier, Theodor
Kindermord bei Ypern (Massacre of the In-
  nocents at Ypres) 173
Das kleine Buch vom großen Krieg See
  Hein, Alfred, Works by

Eine Kompagnie Soldaten See Hein, Al-
  fred, Works by
"Der Krieg als inneres Erlebnis" See
  Jünger, Ernst, Works by
Kriegsbriefe gefallener Studenten See Wit-
  kop, Phillip
Köppen, Edlef 55, 75, 99, 165
  Heeresbericht (Higher Command) 88,
    146, 148, 167–168
Krieg See Renn, Ludwig, Works by
Kröner, Richard
  Landser (Lancer) 50–51, 116–117,
    166–167
Kultur See also war narratives, image and
  symbol, and war narratives, structure
  of
  reverence for 24–26, 34
  and *Zivilisation* 28, 34
Kunstmärchen
  battlefield landscapes and 137–140
  narrative structure of 50, 120

Lagarde, Paul de 28, 30, 41
Langbehn, Julius 24, 28, 30, 41
Langemarck, Battle of 64, 68, 176
Langemarck 1914 See Dreysse, Wilhelm
Latzko, Andreas 148
  Menschen im Krieg (Men in Battle) 90,
    143, 148, 149, 167
Lissauer, Ernst
  Works by:
  "Führer" 11–12
  "Haßgesang" 11
Ludendorff, Erich 71, 151–153

Mann, Thomas 6–7, 34, 90
  Works by:
  Doktor Faustus 6
  "Gedanken im Kriege" (Thoughts in
    War) 6–7, 9–10
  Der Zauberberg (The Magic Mountain)
    45
marxism 78
materialism
  German dislike of 10, 98, 124–125
  anti-techological bias 54, 124–125
Materialschlacht (war of material) 33, 61–
  74, 74–75, 121, 123, 124, 129–130,
  132, 141

centrality of 61
human defenselessness in 66–68
survival of 68–71, 99, 100–101
as triumph of material 61, 64–66
Der Mensch is Gut See Frank, Leonhard
Menschen im Krieg See Latzko, Andreas
middle class, German 7, 183–184
Milestone, Lewis
    All Quiet on the Western Front (film)
        92
militarism, German 12–13, 15
    in education 37–40
Mobilization 50
    rhymes from 15, 51
Moltke, Helmut von (the younger) 9
monuments, national 31–32
    and public ceremonies 32
    to war dead 181–182
myth of the war, British 46, 74–75, 85–
    86, 97, 106, 115, 130, 135–138
myth of the war, German 97, 156–157,
    163–165, 181
    as conservative experience 2, 74–75,
        115, 156–157
    as liberal experience 91
    as representative experience 46–47,
        117–118, 119, 126–127, 165
    and war narratives 182–184
mythology, Germanic 10
    Odin 144
    Siegfried 10, 161

Nachkrieg See Renn, Ludwig, Works by
Napoleon 27
nation
    rebirth of through war 106–113, 160–
        161, 166–167
    veterans as creators of 110–113
nationalism, German 5–6, 178
    irrationalism and 28–29, 38
    origins of 27–30
    pervasiveness of 19–20, 30, 35, 40,
        154–155, 156, 169 See also educa-
        tion, German
    rhetoric of 109–110, 157–158, 171
    social-darwinism and 10, 41
    values of 6, 10, 11–13, 28, 33, 39–40
nationalism, other countries 35

National Socialism 24, 48, 155, 156,
    158–159, 161–162, 167, 181, 184
    Führerprinzip (principle of the leader)
        27–28, 168, 173–174
    ideology 40, 73, 111–112, 170–171,
        174–178
    rhetoric of 109–110, 157–158, 169
Die Niebelungen (film) See cinema, Ger-
    man
Nietzsche, Friederich 8, 70, 129–130
    *Also sprach Zarathustra (Thus spake
        Zarathustra)* 129–130, 141, 143
Novalis 24, 31

Opfergang See Unruh, Fritz von
organicism 10, 27, 28–29, 30–31, 67,
    140, 171
    as model of cyclical development 27,
        97–98, 105–106, 119–121, 126–
        127
    as positive influence 27, 101

Pabst, G. W. 79
pacifism
    and the expressionists See expression-
        ism
    in Germany 90–91, 172
    in other countries 172
    in war narratives 91, 164, 165–166,
        170
Pan-German movement 30
Pfembert, Fritz 87
Picht, Werner 48, 61, 70
Plievier, Theodor
    Des Kaisers Kulis (The Kaiser's Coo-
        lies) 167
poetry, First World War 129
    British 51–52
    German 168
    patriotic 11–13
Prussia 35, 87, 176

Reden an die deutsche Nation See Fichte,
    Johann Gottlieb
Reinhold oder die Verwandelten See Alver-
    dez, Paul
Remarque, Erich Maria
    Works by:
        *Im Westen nichts Neues (All Quiet on the
            Western Front)* 24, 48–49, 54, 57,

59, 60, 62–63, 66–67, 86–87, 91–
92, 94, 116–117, 124, 135, 140,
145, 163, 166–167, 170, 176, 182,
183
reception of 164–166, 168
Der Weg zurück (The Road Back) 91,
92–93, 94–96, 98–99, 102, 119
Renn, Ludwig 76, 99, 123, 126
Works by:
Krieg (War) 51, 55–56, 59, 91, 163,
167
Nachkrieg (After War) 38, 78, 91, 93,
95, 96
Romanticism 77–78
in German nationalism 10–11, 13, 78

scatology 145–147
Scharrer, Adam, 167
Vaterlandslose Gesellen (Comrades
without a Country) 167
Schauwecker, Franz 95, 106–108, 109–
110, 164
Works by:
Aufbruch der Nation (The Furnace) 13,
55, 65–67, 71, 77, 81–82, 91–92,
99, 105, 112–113, 135, 139–140,
141, 142–143, 184
Der feurige Weg (The fiery Way) 52,
58–59, 60, 65–66, 76, 79, 106–109,
110–111, 140, 141, 142, 148
Schlachten des Weltkrieges (Battles of the
World War) 163, 183
Schröder, Rudolf 13
Schutzvereine 37–38
Seeger, Alan 106
Seldte, Hans 81, 84
Sieben vor Verdun See Wehner, Joseph
Magnus
Siegfried See mythology, Germanic
Soldat Suhren See Vring, Georg von der,
Works by
Sombart, Werner 159, 161, 162
Händler und Helden 9, 12–13, 22, 26–
27, 66
Somme, Battle of 64–65
Sonderweg 21–23
Sorley Charles 106
Speerfeuer um Deutschland See Beumel-
burg, Werner, Works by

Spengler, Oswald 161
spirit of August (*der Geist des Augusts*) 5,
6–7, 125
patriotic ideas 7, 8–9, 11, 39
unity of 5, 13–14, 28
universality of 5–6
spirituality, German 5–6
obsession with 6–7, 34, 100–101
superiority of 6, 8–10, 28, 34
uniqueness of 6, 28
as victory 98, 100–101
In Stahlgewittern (Storm of Steel) See
Jünger, Ernst, works by
Stahlhelm 81, 94, 155, 184 See also
Weimar Republic, paramilitary organizations in
Stramm, August 187
Die Streit um den Sergeanten Grisha See
Zweig, Arnold, Works by
Sulzbach, Herbert 72–73
*Zwei lebende Mauern (With the Ger-
man Guns)* 72–73, 136

Thomas, Edward 106
Treitschke, Heinrich von 36
trench warfare 52–53, 134–135
effects of 53–60
alienation from civilians 58–60
alienation from rear echelons 55–
58
disillusionment 54–55
rejection of education 53–54
rations 57, 61–63
weapons 63–66
Troeltsch, Ernst 6, 9, 29, 158
Turnvater Jahn 37
Turnvereine 37–38, 78

Uhland, Ludwig 74–75
Unruh, Fritz von 75
Opfergang (Way of Sacrifice) 60, 87–
88, 89, 90, 131–132, 163, 168

Vaterlandslose Gesellen See Scharrer, Adam
Verdun 61, 64, 66, 67–68, 141–142, 147,
149
Versailles, Treaty of 73, 152, 153–154,
172
Volk 29, 46, 83–84, 173
unity of 29, 31, 77–78

and the Wandervogel 41–42
völkisch ideology 8–9, 10, 30–34, 82, 155
  beliefs of 30–31
  industrialization and 33–34
  influence of 30, 77–78, 168
  landscape and 31–32, 33
  the leader in 82–83
Von 1914 bis 1939 See Beumelburg,
  Werner, Works by
Vring, Georg von der 129
  Works by:
    Der Goldhelm (The Gold Helmet)
      137
    Soldat Suhren (Private Suhren) 78, 137

Das Wäldchen 125 See Jünger, Ernst,
  works by
Der Wanderer zwischen beiden Welten See
  Flex, Walter, Works by
Wandervogel 10, 15, 25–26, 40–43, 120,
  125, 131
  ideals of 40–41
  influence of 42–43, 77–78, 169
  origins and membership of 40–41
  Romanticism of 40–41, 42, 75
  and *völkisch* ideology 40, 41, 42–43
war experience
  authenticity of 48, 55–56, 56–57, 101,
    105, 117–118, 165–167, 168, 182
  betrayal of 156–157, 161, 171, 182
  defeat (loss of war) 70–74, 153–155,
    171–172
  disillusionment of 93–94, 154
  importance of 45–47, 105–106, 117,
    166, 172–173, 174, 176, 178
  as journey 49–52 See also war narra-
    tives, imagery and symbolism, way
    of the cross
  meaning of 47–48, 85–113, 117–118,
    163
  as representative 28–29, 45–46, 117–
    118, 126, 166–167, 168, 182
  as transformation 49, 101–106
war narratives, German 1, 115, 162–171,
  182
  audience for 115–117
  authenticity of 47–49, 116–119, 165–
    167, 168, 182
  and the grotesque 133–134, 145, 150
  imagery and symbolism 4, 39–40, 52
    battlefield landscapes 133–140
    birds 136–137
    front as grotesque garden 138–140
    front as labyrinth See western front
      as labyrinth
    front as otherworld 133–134
    Golgotha 107–108, 141–142
    hell 140–142
    latrines 145–147
    machines 147–150
    oak leaves 52, 181–182
    poppies 52, 137–138, 181
    sources of 129–130
    Stahlhelm 52, 181–182
    storms 140
    sythe of death 143–145
    Totentanz 143, 145
    Walpurgisnacht 142–143
    way of the cross 107–108, 131–
      133
  influence of 163, 166, 167, 169–171,
    183–184
  and minority views 85–96, 97–98
  narrative structure 4, 49–50, 115,
    118–119
  as product of middle class 19–20,
    173–174, 183–184
  as proto-fascist works 2, 49, 167
  reception and criticism of 3, 49, 99,
    115–117, 163–167, 168, 169–170
  relationship to National Socialism 1,
    40, 161–162, 169–171, 172–178
  as representative experience 19–20,
    28–29, 118–119, 127–128
  role in conservative movement 4,
    172–173
  women in 80–81
Der Weg zurück (The Road Back) See Remarque, Erich Maria, Works by
Wehner, Joseph Magnus 94, 95, 106,
  165, 171
  Sieben vor Verdun (Seven before Ver-
    dun) 102, 110, 133–134, 149, 184
Weimar Republic 1, 2–4, 112, 151–162,
  162–163, 171, 182–183
  anti-democratic forces in 154–158,
    182–183

conservative culture in 158–162
   opposition to avant-garde 159–
      160, 161–162
culture wars in 2–3, 117, 157–162,
   162–163, 165
fantasy literature in 160–161
paramilitary organizations in 155–
   157, 184
perodicals in 164
Im Westen nichts Neues See Remarque,
   Erich Maria, Works by
western front 3, 75, 115
   as center of myth making 3, 141
   journey to 50–52
   as labyrinth 50, 134–135
Wessel, Horst 13
Westfront 1918 (film) See Pabst, G. W.
Wiechert, Ernst
   Jederman (Everyman) 78–79. 102,
      103–104, 119, 125–126, 132–133,
      143, 148, 169
Wilhelm II 6, 14, 36–37, 38
Wilhelm, Crown Prince 71–72
Wir fahren den Tod See Goote, Thor
Witkop, Phillip
   Kriegsbriefe gefallener Studenten
      (German Students' War Letters) 24–
      26, 69–70

youth movement See Wandervogel

Der Zauberberg See Mann, Thomas,
   Works by
Zöberlein, Hans 95, 106, 111, 165–166,
   170–171
   Der Glaube an Deutschland (Belief in
      Germany) 111, 132, 167, 174, 184
Zwei lebende Mauern See Sulzbach, Her-
   bert
Zweig, Arnold 75, 81, 91, 95, 117, 123,
   124, 165
   Works by:
   Erziehung vor Verdun (Education before
      Verdun) 79, 95, 124, 138–139, 149
   Die Streit um den Sergeanten Grisha
      (The Case of Sergeant Grisha) 79